BISHOP AUXENTIOS OF PHOTIKI

THE PASCHAL FIRE
IN JERUSALEM

—

A Study of the Rite of the Holy Fire in the Church of the Holy Sepulchre

Second Edition

D1607969

With a Foreword by
Archbishop Chrysostomos of Etna
and the Saint Gregory Palamas Monastery

SAINT JOHN CHRYSOSTOM PRESS

Berkeley, California 1995

LIBRARY OF CONGRESS CATALOG CARD NO. 93–83497

Copyright 1993 by
SAINT JOHN CHRYSOSTOM PRESS
Post Office Box 40176
Berkeley, California 94704–4176

ISBN 0–9634692–0–7

Acknowledgements

A debt of gratitude for helpful advice in my study of the rite of the Holy Fire I owe especially to the Reverend Dr. John F. Baldovin and the Reverend Dr. Eugene M. Ludwig, both of the Graduate Theological Union, Berkeley, and to the Most Reverend Dr. Chrysostomos, Archbishop of Etna and the Saint Gregory Palamas Monastery and Academic Director of the Center for Traditionalist Orthodox Studies. I would also like to express my gratitude to His Beatitude, Diodoros I, Greek Orthodox Patriarch of Jerusalem; the Most Reverend Cyprian, Metropolitan of Oropos and Fili and President of the Synod of Bishops of the True (Old Calendar) Orthodox Church of Greece; Archimandrite Cyprian of the Holy Monastery of Saints Cyprian and Justina in Fili, Greece; and the Reverend Dr. Gregory Telepneff and Reader Gregory Klaassen of the Saint John Chrysostomos Old Calendar Greek Orthodox Church in Colma, California, for their kind aid in collecting various materials for my research. Finally, I would like to acknowledge an enduring debt to one of my mentors, the late Protopresbyter Georges Florovsky, a man of scholarly eminence and of great devotion to his Faith.

Cover

The cover photograph of *The Miracle of the Holy Fire, Church of the Holy Sepulchre at Jerusalem* (1893–1899), an oil on canvas by the British artist William Holman Hunt (1827–1910) given to the Fogg Art Museum at Harvard University by Grenville L. Winthrop, was reproduced with the permission of the President and Fellows of Harvard College and the Harvard University Art Museums, Cambridge, Massachusetts. I am especially indebted to Mr. Andrei Charles Kovacs of Bates College for providing me with the photograph.

Dedication

For Metropolitan Cyprian of Oropos and Fili, "...εἰς ἔργον διακονίας, εἰς οἰκοδομὴν τοῦ σώματος τοῦ Χριστοῦ..." (Ephesians 4:12).

FOREWORD

The Christian East and the Christian West are separated by centuries of mutual distrust and honest disagreements over some very basic matters of theological, ecclesiological, and spiritual moment. In this age of ecumenism, manifold efforts have been made to dismiss as inconsequential this tragic estrangement, which has nonetheless marked all of the free and uncoerced historical exchanges between the Orthodox Church and Roman Catholicism, especially, in the past centuries. Too often these efforts have fostered polite exchange for the sake of superficial and premature proclamations of unity and at the cost of leaving unresolved and unacknowledged the profound issues that separate the Orthodox East from the Western Christian confessions. It has long been the argument of more circumspect Orthodox Churchmen, at least, that reconciliation between the Orthodox Church and the Latin Catholic West and its Protestant scions can best be accomplished by a return to the pre–Schism commonality of Christian experience which the Orthodox Church believes that it embodies: to a commonality of belief and practice which entails not the statements of compromise put forth by the failed union councils of the thirteenth and fifteenth centuries and Orthodox–Protestant dialogues over the past two centuries or so, but which demands careful study of the past and a frank acknowledgement of persistent areas of disagreement and debate. Only then will dialogue reflect the truth, as it must, and not the rubrics of diplomatic interchange.

Bishop Auxentios, in his excellent and comprehensive study of the rite of the Holy Fire in the Church of Jerusalem, paves the way for this kind of mutual understanding. In the phenomenon of the Holy Fire we have a remarkable artifact that dates back to the undivided Church of the Roman (Byzantine) Empire, the one Church of Old and New Rome. The history of the rite provides us with glimpses into the sad effects of the Great

Schism, which drew the Christian West away from a pious commemoration of the Resurrection of Christ that is today an Orthodox rite *par excellence,* but which is also very much a legacy of the Orthodox roots of the Christian West. This common heritage is lost in the polemical attitude that now leads most Latin Catholics and Protestants to disregard the fascinating ceremony as a hoax or a fraud and which, ironically enough, has also led even some Eastern Christians to shun it as "pious legerdemain" because of its supposed "Latin origins."

Bishop Auxentios' account of the rite of the Holy Fire thus reveals both the tragedy of the Great Schism and the complexity of its consequences, a complexity which once more tells us that, in order to achieve Christian unity in the future, we must address the past with care, acumen, and the humility to submit to the majesty of that undivided Christian witness which shines forth in the Orthodox Faith with the same quiet but illuminating Fire of the Resurrection that descends yearly on the Tomb of Christ in Jerusalem. His Grace's book is a pivotal contribution to the kind of studies that will ultimately accommodate such a future, a future so longed for by all sincere Christians and so ill-served by the relativistic superficiality of the contemporary ecumenical movement.

Archbishop Chrysostomos of Etna and
the Saint Gregory Palamas Monastery
Center for Traditionalist Orthodox Studies
Etna, California

TABLE OF CONTENTS

The Holy *Kouvouklion,*
Site of the Rite of the Holy Fire

CHAPTER I

AN HISTORICAL OVERVIEW OF THE
PHENOMENON OF THE HOLY FIRE

Every year on Holy and Great Saturday in the Church of the
Resurrection, or the *Anastasis* (Ναὸς τῆς Ἀναστάσεως), in Jerusalem, the Greek Orthodox Patriarch of that city, multitudes of
Patriarchate clergy, and thousands of faithful pilgrims from the
Holy Land and many other parts of the world celebrate a remarkable ritual with a long and complex history. Historical accounts of this ritual, the rite of τὸ Ἅγιον Φῶς, the Holy Fire (or
literally and more accurately, "the Holy Light"[1]), and its celebration have varied over time, and the ritual itself may well have
evolved with time. But for those unfamiliar with the phenomenon—an unfamiliarity widely found among Orthodox and non–
Orthodox Christians alike—, some initial observations can be
made about the present–day ceremony which will both help
shed some light on the historical data and enable the reader to
identify those common elements which link the historical witness with contemporary practice.

There are two basic components of the ceremony of the Holy Fire, which we will describe in greater detail in a subsequent
section, as it is celebrated in Jerusalem today. First, there are the
preparatory acts performed by all of the clergy and participants
in the ceremony. The vigil lamps in the Cave of the Holy Sepulchre, which is situated in a large shrine (τὸ Ἅγιον Κουβούκλιον,
the Holy *Kouvouklion*) inside the Church of the Resurrection,
and those in the surrounding Church are extinguished and prepared for relighting. The expectant Faithful gather around the

---

[1] As Peter Dörfler observes, when referring to the Holy Fire in Greek,
one "...redet immer von φῶς, nicht von πῦρ [...speaks always of light, not of
fire]" (Peter Dörfler, "Das Heilige Ostefeuer in Jerusalem," *Hochland*, Vol. 24
[1927], p. 4).

Sepulchre, each holding a candle to receive the Holy Fire. The Patriarch and his clergy then enter the Church and approach the Holy Sepulchre, which has remained dark and closed and sealed until this moment. The Patriarch enters the Holy Sepulchre, first having been searched to verify that he carries no implements for igniting a flame. After he enters, the Holy Sepulchre is again closed.

Second, after these preparatory acts and following supplications inside the Tomb by the Patriarch and outside by the Faithful, the Patriarch emerges holding a bundle of candles lit from a lamp—earlier placed on the marble slab in the Tomb—that is believed to ignite spontaneously each year at the prayers of the Patriarch and Faithful.[2] The Faithful then light their candles from those held by the Patriarch, passing from believer to believer the miraculous light of the Resurrection, the Holy Fire. It is this second component of the ceremony of the Holy Fire, the spontaneous ignition of a lamp in the Holy Sepulchre, which accounts for the persistent interest in the ritual and the controversy surrounding it. The peculiar sights, sounds, and sensations associated with the Holy Fire (claps of thunder, flashes of lightning, *etc.*), the purportedly supernatural qualities of the flame (a peculiar color, a mildly warm temperature, and a temporary unconsuming character), and the remarkable effects of the ceremony on the participants themselves (from profound contrition and jubilation among the believers to expressions of outrage from the skeptical)—all of these things have fascinated religious and non–religious investigators for centuries.[3]

For the Eastern Orthodox Christian, the miracle of the Resurrection goes beyond the splendor of the Paschal liturgical cycle

---

[2] See an excellent photograph of the Patriarch emerging from the Tomb in Joseph Judge, "This Year in Jerusalem," *National Geographic*, Vol. 63 (April 1983), p. 505.

[3] The ceremony as it is celebrated today is aptly described in a brochure distributed by the Jordanian Tourism Authority, excerpts from which appear in Betty Hartman Wolf, *Journey through the Holy Land* (Garden City, NY: Doubleday & Co., 1967), pp. 36–37.

and the inspiring imagery of the hymnographic *corpus* of Great
(Holy) Week and the Paschaltide. The festal greeting "Χριστὸς ɩ
'Ανέστη!"—"Christ is Risen!"—inevitably takes the Faithful back
to the Cave of the Holy Sepulchre and the phenomenon of the
Holy Fire. The yearly manifestation of light or "fire" from the
Tomb of Christ is, for the Orthodox world, the central focus of
the commemoration of Christ's victory over death. As the oldest
"custodians" of the Holy Fire and the chief celebrants in the service which surrounds its manifestation, Orthodox Christians of
Greek origin, especially, count this event as one of the greatest
miracles of Christianity. The Latin churches have variously re-
acted to the Holy Fire. Among the few Reformed Christians
who know of it, the phenomenon is usually considered religious
legerdemain, the piety surrounding it preposterous.

Contemporary reactions to and assessments of the phenomenon of the Holy Fire are varied, as we shall subsequently see.
This variation attaches to the complex history of the phenomenon—one not always easy to decipher. The controversy surrounding the Holy Fire and the fiery polemics of those who have
written about it over the centuries have not yet yielded to a comprehensive or objective survey of the historical data or a careful
analysis of the phenomenon.[4] Indeed, a careful review of materials about the Holy Fire essentially yields nothing more than
the kind of crude categorization that one would associate with a
fairly new piece of historical evidence, not something as old as
this phenomenon. It is not our goal, in this historical overview
of the yearly miracle in the Cave of the Holy Sepulchre, to correct this historiographical deficit. Rather, we wish to look at the
historical sources in order to find those common elements which
lend themselves to a clearer understanding of the evolution and
theological significance of the rite of the Holy Fire as it is celebrated today and as it is reflected in the Paschal ceremonies of

---

[4] See Protopresbyter Georges Florovsky's remarks about such objective
histories in his essay, "The Predicament of the Christian Historian," chap. in
Christianity and Culture, Vol. 2 of *Collected Works* (Belmont, MA: Nordland
Publishing Co., 1974), pp. 31–65.

the contemporary Greek Churches outside Jerusalem.

THE SITE WHERE THE CEREMONY OF THE HOLY FIRE IS CELEBRATED. Let us begin our historical investigation with some comments about the Holy Sepulchre itself. Though the Holy Fire has several times appeared outside the confines of the Cave of the Holy Sepulchre, it has always been associated with this shrine. The Cave is actually now an ornate Edicule or covering (κουβούκλιον), a sort of Church within the Church of the Resurrection,[5] that covers the carved stone on which, according to tradition, Christ's Body was placed after the Crucifixion. A memorandum on the *status quo* in the Holy Places issued by the government of Palestine in 1929,[6] briefly describes the Holy *Kouvouklion* as follows:

> The Edicule which encloses the Chapel of the Angel and the Tomb that was erected in the place of the Crusaders [*sic*] shrine after the fire of 1808; the architect was a certain Commenus of Mitylene, whose name is inscribed just inside the inner doorway. ...The Tomb chamber itself is covered by a marble slab, and over it hang forty–three lamps that are always kept burning.[7]

A contemporary Orthodox source portrays the modern–day Edicule in greater detail, describing it as being covered with

> ...precious marble and lavish ornamentation. Its façade is most magnificent. It is 8 meters in length, 5.55 meters wide, and 5.50 meters high. It is divided into two parts, the antechamber, which is called the Holy Stone, and the All–Holy Sepulchre.[8]

---

[5] We should note that the Holy *Kouvouklion* is often called the "Church of the Holy Sepulchre," a name also sometimes applied to the Church of the Resurrection. It is the curious existence of the Holy Sepulchre as what we have called "a Church within a Church" that accounts for this confusing nomenclature.

[6] Lionel George Archer Cust, *An Account of the Practices Concerning the Status Quo in the Holy Places* (Government of Palestine, 1929).

[7] This excerpt is taken from "Appendix 6" in Walter Zander, *Israel and the Holy Places of Christendom* (London: Weidenfeld & Nicolson, 1971), pp. 204–205.

[8] These two divisions are also commonly known as the "Chapel of the

The Holy Stone is a square area 3.23 by 3.23 in dimension. At its sides, there are two apertures through which, at the rite of the Holy Fire, the Patriarch distributes the flame to the Orthodox and Armenians.... In the center of the Holy Stone there is a [short] pillar with a hollow indentation on top, upon which lies a fragment of the stone which the Angel rolled away from the Tomb of the Lord and from which the antechamber takes its name. The Holy *Kouvouklion* has only one outside door, facing east, from which one enters into the Holy Stone.

Across from the door to the Holy *Kouvouklion* and to the west of the Holy Stone there is a small inside door, 1.33 meters high and 0.95 meters wide, which leads to the All–Holy Sepulchre. Since this door is low, whenever one enters the All–Holy Sepulchre, one is obliged to bow before it. The All–Holy Sepulchre is a nearly square chamber, 2.20 meters by 1.85 meters in dimension, carved in rock. At the right of this chamber is the All–Holy Crypt, the Life–Giving Tomb, where the Lord was buried and arose....

Over the Holy *Kouvouklion* there is a 2.10 meter dome. There are Icons of the Resurrection, inscriptions, and sayings on the façade and interior of the Holy Sepulchre. And the whole of the structure of the Holy *Kouvouklion* is encircled with [a carved inscription] of the following *troparion.*[9] 'Let the nations and the people praise Christ our God, Who willingly suffered the Cross for us and abode for three days in Hell, and let them worship His Resurrection from the dead, which sheds light unto all corners of the world.'[10]

Writing of the Holy Sepulchre as he saw it in his day, the

Angel" and the "Tomb" or "Tomb Chamber"; see Zander, *Israel,* p. 204.

[9] This hymn is taken from the Στιχηρὰ Ἀνατολικὰ of Lauds for Sunday Matins in the Second Tone; see Παρακλητική, ἤτοι Ὀκτώηχος ἡ Μεγάλη (Athens: Apostolike Diakonia tes Ekklesias tes Hellados, 1976), p. 67.

[10] Ioanna P. Tsekoura, Τὸ Ἅγιον Φῶς στὰ Ἱεροσόλυμα, 3rd ed. (Lamia, Greece: 1991), pp. 32–35. Photographs of the *Kouvouklion* and its interior, along with an excellent historical commentary, can be found in Sven Hedin, *Jerusalem* (Leipzig: F. U. Brockhaus, 1918), pp. 184–189; though dated, this is an excellent resource book and the structures described have not substantially changed from the time of Hedin's publication.

sometimes irreverent, nineteenth–century writer Mark Twain (Samuel Clemens, 1835–1910) described the Church of the Holy Sepulchre and the Tomb of Christ, which he visited during his world travels, in uncharacteristically pious words:

> The Church of the Holy Sepulchre—the most sacred locality on earth to millions and millions of God's creatures. In its history from the first, and in its tremendous associations, it is the most illustrious edifice in Christendom. With all its clap–trap side–shows and unseemly humbuggery of every kind, it is still grand, reverend, venerable—a God died there; for fifteen hundred years its shrines have met with the tears of Pilgrims from the earth's most remote confines.... History is full of this old Church of the Holy Sepulchre—full of blood that was shed because of the respect and veneration in which men held the last resting–place of the meek and lowly, the mild and gentle, Prince of Peace![11]

Twain's contemporary, the novelist Herman Melville (1819–1891), has less reverent things to say about the Sepulchre in his *Journals*. Describing the Church of the Resurrection as a place of "plague–stricken splendor," he notes that

> ...in the midst of all stands the Sepulchre; a church in a church. It is of marbles, richly sculpted in parts and bearing the faded aspect of age. From its porch, issue a garish stream of light, upon the faces of the pilgrims who crowd for admittance into a space which will hold but four or five at a time. First passing a wee vestibule where is shown the stone on which the angel sat, you enter the tomb. It is like entering a lighted lanthorn. Wedged and half–dazzled, you stare for a moment on the ineloquence of the bedizened slab, and glad to come out, wipe your brow glad to escape from the heat & jam of a show–box. All is glitter & nothing is gold. A sickening cheat.[12]

Yet in a poetic tribute to Jerusalem, he writes the following nos-

---

[11] Mark Twain, *Traveling with the Innocents Abroad,* ed. Daniel M. McKeithan (Norman, OK: University of Oklahoma Press, 1958), pp. 280–281.

[12] Herman Melville, *Journals,* ed. Harrison Hayford, Vol. 15 of *The Writings of Herman Melville* (Evanston and Chicago: Northwestern University Press, 1989), p. 88.

talgic lines about the Burial Place of Christ in his poem "The Sepulcher," as though the negative impressions of his visit there were but the displeasures of the moment:

> For dust thereon will settle down,
> And gather, too, upon the Tomb
> And places of the Passion's moan.
> Tradition, not device and fraud
> Here rules—tradition old and broad.[13]

The original transformation of the Holy Sepulchre from a Cave to something not unlike the modern Edicule which we have described was part of a building project initiated by Saint Constantine the Great (†337) in the fourth century.[14] The Edicule erected at that time, along with the other magnificent Churches surrounding the Holy Sepulchre, was demolished by the tragic order of the Caliph al–Hakim in 1009. Rebuilt by the Emperor Constantine IX Monomachos in 1048 and periodically restored in the ensuing centuries, the present reconstruction of the Edicule was occasioned by the effects of a devastating fire in 1808.[15] In its various reconstructions, the Edicule has long pre-

---

[13] *Idem, Clarel: A Poem and Pilgrimage in the Holy Land* (New York: Hendricks House, 1960), p. 14.

[14] For a brief description of the complex of buildings built by Saint Constantine, see John Baldovin, s.j., *The Urban Character of Christian Worship: The Origins, Development, and Meaning of Stational Liturgy* (Rome: Pontificale Institutum Studiorum Orientalium, 1987), pp. 47–48. Pointing to the significance of the site of Christ's Burial and Resurrection for Christian salvation history, Father Baldovin notes that, "...this complex later tradition considered...to be the center of the world. Other traditions associated it with the burial place of Adam, and with Mount Moriah where Abraham was to have sacrificed Isaac" (p. 48). In his *Liturgy in Ancient Jerusalem* (Bramcote, Nottingham: Grove Books, Ltd., 1989), Baldovin also reproduces a helpful sketch of the Holy Sepulchre complex as it was in the fourth and fifth centuries (p. 10).

[15] Zander, *Israel,* p. 204. As Alistair Duncan describes it, this fire "...which started in an Armenian chapel, swept through the Church, bringing down the Dome of the Anastasis and doing immense damage throughout the building, especially to the aedicule about the Tomb" (Alistair Duncan, *The Noble Heritage: Jerusalem and Christianity: A Portrait of the Church of the Resur-*

sented historians with a difficult question: that of its fidelity to the original structure built by Saint Constantine. Such fidelity has more often than not been called into question. John Wilkinson's impressive and full survey of the extant historical data, however, leads him to what now seems to be a widely accepted and well established view among contemporary scholars. He concludes that, "...closer study of the documents and representations only serves to accentuate that the Edicule of modern times is in a far closer continuity with the earliest Cave than has usually been imagined."[16] One can fairly safely presume, therefore, that the manifestation of the Holy Fire occurs in a place long associated with Christ's Resurrection and in a chamber dating at the very least to the fourth century.

HISTORICAL SOURCES FOR THE PHENOMENON OF THE HOLY FIRE. The bulk of the historical testimony regarding the Holy Fire is found in two sources: first, references to the Holy Fire in the *typica* (τυπικά), or liturgical documents recording the order (and, usually, significant rubrics) for services on various days of the liturgical year; and second, the accounts of the phenomenon recorded by visitors and pilgrims to the Holy Land, many of whom travelled to the Christian Sacred Places to attend services during the Paschal season. Some auxiliary sources, though not extensive, also contain references to or provide data about the Holy Fire: the lives of Saints, historical chronicles, and various religious treatises.[17] We will divide the available testimony into two periods: the somewhat moot and ambiguous material from

---

rection [London: Longman Group, Ltd., 1974], p. 58).

[16] *Egeria's Travels to the Holy Land,* trans. John Wilkinson, (Warminster, England: 1981), p. 252. For a current survey of the complex archæological data about the the Church of the Holy Sepulchre and other historical sites in Jerusalem, see Klaus Wessel and Marcell Restle, eds., *Reallexicon zur Byzantischen Kunst* (Stuttgart: Anton Hiersemann, 1978), Vol. 3, *s.v.* "Jerusalem," by Yoram Tsafrir, esp. cols. 588–600.

[17] A good, though not complete, survey of these auxiliary sources is Gustav Klameth's *Das Karsamstagsfeuerwunder der heiligen Grabeskirche* (Vienna: Mayer & Co., 1913), esp. pp. 24–42.

pre–ninth–century sources and accounts from the ninth and following centuries. These latter materials offer clear descriptions and vivid accounts of the phenomenon of the Holy Fire and the rites attached to it—descriptions and accounts that very much correspond to the phenomenon and rites as they can be observed in Jerusalem today.

THE PRE–NINTH–CENTURY WITNESS. As we have noted, pre–ninth–century references to the rite of the Holy Fire are problematic. There are only limited sources from this period that offer details of Great Week services and the Paschal Vigil in the complex of the Holy Sepulchre. Moreover, only one of these identifies the Holy Fire by name. Those, then, who would find some form of the rite in these first Christian centuries have but a handful of ambiguous or at least problematic allusions with which to work. Nonetheless, when viewed in the light of later sources, these early references take on greater significance and appear to suggest a link between the pre–ninth–century reports of a ceremony of light in Jerusalem and later descriptions of the rite of the Holy Fire.

Saint Eusebios of Cæsarea. In his ecclesiastical history, Saint Eusebios (†340) makes reference to a miracle attributed to the revered Saint Narkissos (†211), who was Bishop of Jerusalem in the late second century and the early third century. The miracle tells us nothing about the ceremony of the Holy Fire itself, but it does involve the miraculous lighting of Paschal lamps, which may have some connection with subsequent development of the ceremony. Saint Eusebios tells us that:

> Many stories of miracles wrought by Narcissus, handed down by generations of Christians, are told by members of the community. Among these they narrate the following tale of wonder. Once during the great all–night–long vigil of Easter, the deacons ran out of oil. The whole congregation was deeply distressed, so Narcissus told those responsible for the lights to draw water and bring it to him, and they obeyed him instantly. Then he said a prayer over the water, and instructed them to pour it into the lamps with absolute faith in the Lord. They again obeyed him, and, in defi-

ance of natural law, by the miraculous power of God the substance of the liquid was physically changed from water into oil. All the years from that day to our own a large body of Christians there have preserved a little of it, as proof of that wonderful event.[18]

Saint Cyril of Jerusalem. The celebrated Baptismal instructions of Saint Cyril of Jerusalem (†386) are rich in language related to light. In the time of Saint Cyril, Baptism was associated with the Feast of Pascha, and the catechumens were, in fact, Baptized on Great Saturday. Carl–Martin Edsman suggests that Baptism itself, therefore, was connected or occurred in conjunction with some ceremony of light, and that this is implied in the instructions given to the catechumens. Characteristically, for example, Saint Cyril writes:

> May God show you that night that shines as day, of which he says: 'Yea, the darkness hideth not from Thee; the darkness and the light are both alike to Thee.'[19] Then the Gate of Paradise shall be opened to each one, man or woman.[20]

On the basis of this and similar passages, Edsman observes that

> ...Cyril in his baptismal instructions uses many of the Scriptural readings which are appointed for the Paschal vigil. The material is thusly in and of itself somewhat ambiguous; but in light of the later liturgical books, these materials take on greater significance. Cyril was obviously aware of a ceremony of light of some kind in relationship to the Paschal vigil.[21]

It is indeed problematic as to whether Saint Cyril's Baptismal instructions use the image of light in order to initiate the newly Baptized into the ceremony of the Holy Fire or a similar

---

[18] [Saint] Eusebius, *The History of the Church*, trans. G. A. Williamson (New York: Penguin Books, 1965), Bk. VI, Chap. 9, pp. 248–249.

[19] Psalm 139:12 (*Septuaginta*).

[20] Jacques–Paul Migne, ed., *Patrologia Græca: Cursus Completus* (Paris: 1857–1866), Vol. 33, col. 357A.

[21] Carl–Martin Edsman, "Påskaftonens nya eld i Jerusalem, II," *Svenska Jerusalemsföreningens Tidskrift*, Vol. 54 (1955), pp. 9–10.

ceremony. Since the Mystery, or Sacrament, of Baptism is also associated with φωτισμός, or enlightenment, in the writings of ⌐ the early Greek Fathers,[22] the imagery of light is not inconsis- • tent with the Mystery itself.[23] The lack of any clear reference to a ceremony of light as such in Saint Cyril's Baptismal catecheses makes Edsman's speculation interesting but essentially inconsequential.

Egeria. The earliest clear testimony about a light ceremony in Jerusalem comes from fragments of a diary that most scholars attribute to a nun named Egeria (sometimes called Eucheria, Ætheria, or Sylvia), a pilgrim "from either Galicia (Northern Spain) or Aquitaine (now Western France)."[24] Her accounts, the so-called *Peregrinatio Egeriæ,* have limited historical value, but nonetheless provide some insight into Paschal worship in Jerusalem. Father John Baldovin observes that

> ...though Egeria's account is informative it makes no pretense at being a treatise. Her use of language is often inconsistent. Furthermore, she describes services as though the reader were already familiar with them..., so there must already have been many usages common to both Northern Spain or Western France and Jerusalem at this period, among them the Paschal Vigil, and the Sunday eucharist. However, she is admittedly smitten with curiosity and pays close attention to detail. Hence the *Peregrinatio Egeriae,* while not a technical liturgical source, provides invaluable information....[25]

---

[22] See, for example, Saint Justin Martyr, "The First Apology," in Cyril C. Richardson, *Early Christian Fathers* (New York: Macmillan Publishing Co., 1979), p. 283. Saint Justin Martyr writes: "This washing [Baptism] is called illumination [φωτισμός], since those who learn these things are illumined within."

[23] Father Baldovin does, however, suggest that physical light may have played a role in the Baptismal services in Jerusalem at the time of Saint Cyril. With the catechumens standing in the dark vestibule of the Baptistry, he tells us, "...the doors of the baptistry proper were most probably opened at this point creating a sharp contrast to the darkened vestibule" (*Liturgy,* pp. 16–17).

[24] Baldovin, *Urban Worship,* p. 57.

[25] *Ibid.*

Egeria witnessed and recorded the events of Great Week in Jerusalem in 384.[26] About the Paschal Vigil itself she finds only one thing noteworthy:

> There is no service, however, at the ninth hour on [Great] Saturday, for preparation is being made for the Easter vigil in the major church, the Martyrium. The Easter vigil is observed here exactly as we observe it at home. Only one thing is done more elaborately here. After the neophytes have been baptized and dressed as soon as they came forth from the baptismal font, they are led first of all to the Anastasis [the Rotunda Church enclosing the Holy Sepulchre, the Church of the Resurrection] with the Bishop. The Bishop goes within the railings of the Anastasis [that is, within the Edicule], a hymn is sung, and he prays for them. Then he returns with them to the major church, where all the people are holding the vigil as is customary.[27]

As G. Bertonière points out in his study of the Paschal Vigil in the Greek Church, Egeria's silence about an actual *ceremony* of light in her description of services on Holy Saturday need not be so uninformative:

> While Egeria does not speak explicitly of the *Lucernarium* on Holy Saturday, her remark that the Paschal Vigil was celebrated '*quemadmodum ad nos*' suggests that in Jerusalem, as in all the Western rites of which we have evidence, there were *Lucernarium* elements present at the beginning of the service. Even apart from her remark on this occasion, the importance of the *Lucernarium* and the special connection which it had in Jerusalem with the theme of the Resurrection (the taking of the light used in the service from the tomb) lead us to believe that it would hardly have been omitted on Holy Saturday evening.[28]

---

[26] On the problem of naming and dating this source, see Wilkinson, *Egeria's Travels,* pp. 235–239, 329–331.

[27] *Egeria: Diary of a Pilgrimage,* trans. G. E. Gingras (New York: Newman Press, 1970), p. 114.

[28] G. Bertonière, *The Historical Development of the Easter Vigil and Related Services in the Greek Church* (Rome: Pontificale Institutum Studiorum Orientalium, 1972), p. 22. This is an excellent study of various services in the

Let us see what Egeria herself says of the *Lucernarium:*

> At the tenth hour, which is here called Licinicon, or, as we say,
> vespers, a great multitude assembled at the Anastasis. All the tor-
> ches and candles are lighted, and this makes a tremendous light.
> The light, however, is not brought in from outside, but is taken
> from inside the grotto [the Holy Sepulchre], that is, from within
> the railings where night and day a lamp always burns.[29]

We will comment at length on this material after we have considered several pertinent sources of a liturgical kind. Suffice it to
say at this point that Egeria is describing, in her account of the
Licinicon, a service which contains some of the elements which
are found in the rite of the Holy Fire. This service must have
been, as Bertonière contends, part of the Great Saturday service,
a service which she reports as having been done in a manner familiar to her, a manner that, in her native Europe, doubtlessly
involved a ceremony of light.[30]

The Armenian Lectionary (AL). This lectionary, containing
information on readings (Old Testament and New Testament
[*Apostolos* and Gospel]), processional Psalms and their refrains,
verses sung for the "Alleluia," and occasional rubrics, reflects liturgical practices in the Church of the Resurrection in Jerusalem
between the years 417 and 439. *AL* is not, as Father Baldovin tells
us,

> ...a real lectionary with the full text of the lessons for Sundays and
> feasts. Rather it indicates the proper readings and psalms by means

Greek Church; however, the apparatuses are at times faulty and there are frequent *lacuna* in the transcription of original sources.

[29] Gingras, *Egeria,* p. 90.

[30] If Egeria was a Spanish religious, as evidence strongly suggests, she
may be identifying with the Great Saturday service in Jerusalem a ceremony in
the Spanish Church which, as we shall observe below, was in fact very similar to
the rite of the Holy Fire: a rite in which the clergy, sequestered in the sacristy,
kindle a fire with flint and tinder, light a lamp, and from it light a Paschal
candle from which the Faithful, gathered in the Church, then light their tapers.
If this is so, one can assume that what she saw in Jerusalem was at least a prototype of the ceremony of the Holy Fire.

of *incipit* and conclusion, as well as the stations for major celebrations in Jerusalem during the year. ...It should be considered an embryonic form of the later typikon.[31]

As a description of worship in Jerusalem, nonetheless, *AL* is a valuable source of information about what may be a primitive form of the rite of the Holy Fire. Since it is not a subject pivotal to our investigation, we will pass over the complexities of the manuscript tradition[32] and simply note that there are three principal manuscripts, reflecting different stages in the development of the *Lectionary*. Bertonière labels these manuscripts *J, P,* and *Er*.[33] *J* dates to the ninth or tenth century, while *P* was written in 1192. Both manuscripts represent *AL* in its earliest form, which dates from the fifth century and "describes a liturgy of specifically Jerusalem type."[34] *Er* dates to the ninth or tenth century, but is thought to be taken from Armenian translations of the *typikon* of the Church of the Resurrection at a later period than *J* and *P*.[35] *J* and *P,* then, seem to best represent Jerusalem worship in the fifth century.[36]

All three manuscripts of *AL* indicate that the Paschal Vigil

---

[31] Baldovin, *Urban Worship,* p. 64.

[32] The complexities of the various manuscripts are discussed by Bertonière, *Easter Vigil,* pp. 8–10.

[33] The manuscripts of *AL* by code are found as follows: *J*—(Codex Jerusalem Armenian [selections and rubrics]), A. Renoux, "Un manuscrit du Lectionnaire Arménien de Jérusalem (Cod. Jerus. Arm. 121)," *Le Muséon,* Vol. 74 (1961), pp. 361–385; *idem,* "Un manuscrit du Lectionnaire Arménien de Jérusalem (Cod. Jerus. Arm. 121), Addenda et Corrigenda," *Le Muséon,* Vol. 75 (1962), pp. 385–398; *P*—(Bibliothèque National Arménien 44), F. C. Conybeare, *Rituale Armenorum* (Oxford: 1905); *Er*—(Erévan 985), Dom A. Renoux, "Le Codex Erévan 985: Une Adaptation Arméniennes du Lectionnaire Hiérosolymitain," chap. in *Armeniaca: Mélanges d'Études Arméniennes* (Venice: 1969).

[34] Bertonière, *Easter Vigil,* pp. 8–9.

[35] *Ibid.,* p. 8.

[36] Father Baldovin identifies *J* and *P* as the major manuscripts in *AL* and uses the latter as the primary source for his investigation of the Jerusalem stational Liturgy (*Urban Worship,* p. 65). *J* and *P* also provide us with more specific evidence about a lighting ceremony at the Paschal Vigil.

service in Jerusalem begins in the *Anastasis* with a light ceremony, after which the clergy begin the Paschal Vigil. There is
appointed a reading or chanting of Psalm 112 (*Septuaginta*) at the
beginning of the ceremony, presumably as a processional. *P*
notes that "three candles are lit" after this,[37] while *J* and *Er* as-
sign the candle lighting to another point in the service. All three
manuscripts then indicate that the believers should go to the
Martyrion, or the basilica adjacent to the *Anastasis. J* notes at this
point that the Bishop lights a candle, while *Er* simply indicates
that "...l'évêque fait d'abord le lucernaire [...the Bishop first does
the light service]."[38] Bertonière summarizes the witness of the
three manuscripts with regard to this preparatory ceremony of
light:

> The lucernary character of the preparation is clear from the light-
> ing of the lamps. Two significant items are different in *J, Er,* and
> *P*. First of all, in the case of the first two codices, after a brief gath-
> ering in the Anastasis where the Bishop chants Psalm 112, the
> lighting of the candles takes place in the martyrium, whereas in *P*
> this is done in the Anastasis itself. Secondly, in *J* only a single lamp
> is explicitly referred to as being lit, whereas *P* calls for three. *Er*
> does not enter into the question of how many are lit.[39]

Whereas in Egeria's account, the light for the *Lucernarium* was
brought out of the Tomb and with it all of the "torches" and
"candles" of those gathered in the *Anastasis* were lighted, *AL*
does not specifically refer to the Sepulchre as playing any rôle in
the ceremony. Nonetheless, it does give us clear evidence of a
ceremony of light associated with the celebration of the Paschal
Vigil—indeed, of a separate and distinct service like that of the
rite of the Holy Fire in modern times.

The Georgian Lectionary (GEORG). This lectionary—or, as
Baldovin notes, "...not strictly speaking a lectionary..., but a typikon pieced together from a series of gap–filled manu-

---

37 Edsman, "Påskaftonens II," p. 11.

38 Bertonière, *Easter Vigil*, p. 30.

39 *Ibid.*

scripts"⁴⁰—offers somewhat more detail about the Jerusalem Paschal Vigil than the *Armenian Lectionary.* Its manuscript tradition is also complex, and there is no firm opinion on its dates. Edsman dates it between 640 and 720.⁴¹ Bertonière contends that it "...represents a later stage of development in the Jerusalem liturgy," containing *strata,* perhaps, from the fifth century, but in its entirety dating only from the eighth century or later.⁴² He identifies four principal manuscripts: *P* (tenth century), *S* (copied in 982), which provides a parallel account of the Paschal Vigil at the Monastery of Saint Sabbas, *L* (tenth century), and *Ka* (tenth century),⁴³ and outlines the *Lucernarium* material as follows (to various degrees the manuscripts represent adaptations to local usage in Georgia and lack the stational information from Jerusalem, which information we have supplied in brackets):

a) gathering in the church [of the *Anastasis*] (lighting of a single candle in *L*)

b) 3 processions [around the inside of the Church and thus around the Edicule] with at least one psalm and *kverexi et oratio* (the *kverexi et oratio* after the procession in *L*)

c) kiss of peace

d) blessing of candle[s]⁴⁴

---

⁴⁰ Baldovin, *Urban Worship,* p. 72.

⁴¹ Edsman, "Påskaftonens II," p. 11.

⁴² Bertonière, *Easter Vigil,* pp. 10–12.

⁴³ The manuscripts of *GEORG* (*P*—Bibliothèque Nationale Géorgien 3; *S*—Sinai 37; *L*—Mestia 635 of Lathal; and *Ka*—Kala) are found as follows: M. Tarchnischvili, ed, *Le Grand Lectionnaire de L'Eglise de Jérusalem* (Louvain: 1959). An early manuscript, taken from what Baldovin calls "the two *lacuna*–ridden manuscripts of Kala and Lathal" (*Urban Worship,* p. 72, n. 139) was published in 1912 by K. Kekelidze in his *Jerusalimskij Kanonar XII veka* (Tiflis, Georgia: 1912). These two manuscripts are the least informative with regard to worship in Jerusalem, since they often refer to local Georgian usage.

⁴⁴ For a detailed discussion of the varying number of candles cited in each manuscript, see Edsman, "Påskaftonens II," pp. 11–12; Edsman also notes the similarities between this ceremony and the lighting of the "new fire" and the Paschal candle in the Mozarabic and Gallican rites, an issue, again, which we shall address subsequently.

　e)　lighting of other candles
　f)　opening of doors [of the *Martyrium*].[45]

The *kverexi et oratio,* notes Bertonière, "...seems to have been a prayer preceded by some sort of diaconal petitions or at least by an invitation to prayer."[46] Baldovin succinctly summarizes this material as follows:

> On Holy Saturday the Martyrium is the setting for a morning service together with an additional stational service. Vespers is the beginning of the great vigil for which the typikon reads: 'When the sun has set, they assemble in the holy Anastasis, close the doors, prepare three thuribles and make intercession and prayer.'
>
> There follows a three–fold perambulation and censing of the church, a blessing of the new candle, of the candles held by the faithful, the opening of the doors and procession to the Martyrium.[47]

In *GEORG,* we see an expansion of the lighting ceremony in *AL.* According to Bertonière,

> ...the elaboration of GEORG, with its three processions, the lighting of the 'new candle' presumably from the lamp in the taphos, and the procession to the basilica all seem to point to a symbolic celebration of the risen Christ coming forth from the tomb. ...All of this is in line with the relationship between τάφος and φῶς implied in the daily practice described by Egeria.[48]

Edsman believes that, the relationship which Bertonière sees between Egeria's account of the daily lighting service and *GEORG* aside, "...it appears more difficult to understand the Georgian

---

[45] Bertonière, *Easter Vigil,* p. 33; see Tarchnischvili, *Grand Lectionnaire,* pp. 107ff.

[46] *Ibid.,* p. 35. Bertonière argues that *kverexi,* "...a difficult term for which no precise translation has been found," as Baldovin observes (*Urban Worship,* p. 74, n. 149), can be traced to the Greek word "κήρυξις," *i.e.,* "proclamation" or "announcement"; thus he speaks of *kverexi et oratio* as a combination of intercessions and a prayer.

[47] Baldovin, *Urban Worship,* p. 78.

[48] Bertonière, *Easter Vigil,* p. 36.

lectionary [*kanonariet*] from the ancient Armenian lectionary" than from the next source which we will consider, a twelfth–century codex of the Jerusalem *typikon*.[49]

   Codex Jerusalem Patriarchate Hagios Stauros 43 (HS 43).[50] In Egeria and in the liturgical documents which we have thus far examined, we have disjointed data about a lighting service associated with or preceding the Paschal Vigil, about the Vigil itself, and, of course the Paschal Eucharistic service. The present manuscript, however, contains a fairly detailed *typicon* and complete texts of the prayers and liturgical poetry used in Great and Bright Weeks at the Jerusalem Patriarchate. Copied and adapted from an earlier document by the scribe Basil in 1122,[51] the manuscript seems to be composed of two *strata* of material, evidencing some of the customs of the Great Church in Constantinople as well as those in Jerusalem. Anton Baumstark argues that the earlier *stratum* of the manuscript reflects late ninth–century liturgical practice in Jerusalem, while the later *stratum* belongs to the time of the Latin Kingdom in Jerusalem.[52] If this dating is correct, it would be stretching our parameters for the pre–ninth–century witness to consider the *typicon* here. However, we would emphasize that there is great uncertainty about the dating of *HS 43*. In fact, Baumstark, in his initial investigation of the document—an argument which he admittedly later retracted—, con-

---

[49] Edsman, "Påskaftonens ii," p. 13.

[50] *HS 43* was discovered in 1894 in the library of the Patriarchate of Jerusalem and published as follows: A. Papadopoulos–Kerameus, "Τυπικὸν τῆς ἐν Ἱεροσολύμοις Ἐκκλησίας," Ἀνάλεκτα Ἱεροσολυμητικῆς Σταχυολογίας (St. Petersburg), Vol. 2 (1894), pp. 1–254. A corrected text with an extensive and useful introduction was published in the Ukraine by A. Dmitriesvkii a little more than a decade later: *Drevneishie Patriarshie Tipikoni: Sviatogrobskii Ierusalimii i Velikoi Konstantinopolskoi Tserkvi* (Kiev: 1907).

[51] So a postscript in the *typicon* itself tells us; see Papadopoulos–Kerameus, "Τυπικόν," pp. 252ff.

[52] Anton Baumstark, "Denkmäler der Entstehungsgeschichte des byzantinischen Ritus," *Oriens Christianus,* Vol. 2 (1927), pp. 19ff.; *cf.* Bertonière, *Easter Vigil,* p. 14; Papadopoulos–Kerameus, "Τυπικόν," p. 78.

tends that its first *stratum* reflects early eighth–century usage.[53]
More importantly, the close parallels between *HS 43* and the
Georgian Lectionary facilitate a clearer understanding of the latter
document and provide, if the later date for *HS 43* is indeed accurate, an excellent nexus between the two chronological periods
into which we have divided historical accounts of the Paschal
service in Jerusalem. Of the Paschal Vigil we read the following
in this *typicon:*

> And when the Myrrh–bearers have finished filling and preparing
> the lamps, the Patriarch seals the Holy Sepulchre and takes the
> keys with him, and then all the lamps in the church are extin-
> guished. The Patriarch goes with the clergy, all in white vestments,
> into the Church of the Holy Resurrection, without igniting the
> lamps and, without a censer, quietly begins Vespers behind the
> Holy Sepulchre.... Immediately after the end of the readings of the
> prophecies the Patriarch ascends the steps of the sacred altar and
> entrusts the censing to the metropolitan, the bishops and the pres-
> byters, and they begin to cense—he himself, the hierarchs, and the
> priests with him, censing the church outside the Holy Sepulchre
> and going around it three times. The Sepulchre is then closed.
> Then they go out and, after censing the lower level, go up to Holy
> Golgotha also to cense it and the Holy Garden, and the Church of
> St. Constantine, and the Holy Prison until they come to the doors
> of (the Church of) the Holy Resurrection, to the so–called 'Door
> of the Myrrh–bearers.' Then the sub–deacons take the censers
> from the hierarchs and the priests and all of them go up the sacred
> steps. The Patriarch begins to say slowly and without ceasing,
> 'Lord, have mercy.' When the Patriarch comes down the steps, the
> archdeacon and protodeacon support his arms on both sides; be-
> fore them goes the *sakkelarios,* while the *paramonarios* and *kastrin-
> cios* follow after. Then the Patriarch falls with his face to the
> ground opposite the steps of the altar and tearfully prays for the
> ignorances of the people and extends his hand aloft. This he does
> three times, and those with him also do likewise. The people with-
> out interruption exclaim: 'Lord, have mercy.' When the Patriarch

53 See his "Die Heiligtümer des byzantinischen Jerusalem nach einer
übersehenden Urkunde," *Oriens Christianus,* Vol. 5 (1905), pp. 282ff.

and those with him go into the Holy Sepulchre, they prostrate themselves three times and pray for themselves and for the people, and the Patriarch then takes a light from the Holy Fire and gives it to the archdeacon, and the archdeacon to the people; thereafter the Patriarch goes out and those with him, singing the verse 'Shine, shine, O new Jerusalem....'[54]

Baldovin provides a brief summary of the witness of *HS 43* with regard to the lighting ceremony and the changes in practice from the *Georgian Lectionary* (which he refers to as *GL*):

> On Holy Saturday morning orthros is held in the Anastasis and at the ninth hour *Lucernare* begins. In contrast to the order in the GL, this typikon has a three-fold incensation of the entire complex of buildings. The holy fire is then retrieved from the edicule of the Resurrection within the Anastasis and all process to the Martyrium.[55]

There is no specific evidence as such in *HS 43* of the miraculous nature of the Holy Fire from the Sepulchre, but for the first time it is called "τὸ Ἅγιον Φῶς," an appellation apparently distinguishing it from a normal light.[56] Moreover, as Baldovin notes, the Holy Fire is clearly and indisputably retrieved from the Tomb itself. Gustav Klameth, admitting to the unambiguous witness of *HS 43* with regard to the retrieval of light from the Tomb, argues that the light is taken from a lamp which is left

---

[54] Quoted in Archimandrite Callistos, "The Holy Fire," trans. Timothy Fisher, *Orthodox Life*, Vol. 34, No. 2 (1984), pp. 9–10; this text is from the Russian translation of the original Greek text. The pertinent historical materials, for which we have consulted the Greek, are found in Archimandrite Kallistos, "Τὸ Ἅγιον Φῶς· Α΄," *Νέα Σιών*, Vol. 28, Nos. 4 & 5 (1933), pp. 232–247, 280–293.

[55] Baldovin, *Urban Worship*, p. 81; *cf.* Dörfler, "Heilige Ostefeuer," who also provides a useful summary of this material (pp. 3–4). Dörfler generally follows Klameth in his consideration of the Holy Fire, though his study is in places more objective.

[56] Edsman believes that there is in *HS 43* an intimation of the miraculous nature of the Holy Fire both because of the name applied to the light taken from the Sepulchre and because of the elaborate way in which the Patriarch prepares to receive it ("Påskaftonens II," p. 13).

lighted by the Myrrh–bearers when they earlier prepare the lamps, just before the Patriarch seals the Tomb.[57] Nonetheless, *HS 43* affords us data about a pre–ninth–century lighting ceremony in the Holy Sepulchre on Great Saturday which is in many details similar to later accounts of what is clearly the rite of the Holy Fire as it has survived in Jerusalem to this day.

A Review of the Pre–Ninth–Century Sources. In all of the foregoing descriptions of the Paschal services in pre–ninth–century Jerusalem, it is true that we find references to the ceremony of the Holy Fire which are not as clear or as complete as accounts from later centuries and which do not make specific reference to the miraculous nature of the Holy Fire. Saints Eusebios and Cyril, for example, provide us with what is at best circumstantial evidence for the phenomenon. Nonetheless, in the account of the nun Egeria—despite the fact that she makes no general distinction between the Paschal Vigil in Jerusalem and what she was accustomed to observing at home—, it is not unreasonable, as Bertonière writes, to find special significance in her reference to the *Lucernarium* (the term by which she refers both to the Vespers service and the candle– or lamp–lighting ceremony itself). She found the light of the *Lucernarium* as she saw it in Jerusalem worthy of particular note, in fact identifying the rite with the Tomb itself: "The light, however, is not brought in from outside, but is taken from inside the grotto."[58] Though there is no specific mention of the miraculous nature of this light, Egeria's reference to the light being "brought in" from the Sepulchre may well be an allusion to an important element of the ritual of the Holy Fire as we see it emerge from post–ninth–century sources: its distribution to the Faithful. Moreover, her allusions to the extinguishing of the lights and to Psalms and antiphons, in the context of the *Lucernarium,*[59] bring us immediately to other elements of the ritual as we clearly see it in later sources. Taken together, her observations strongly suggest that we are dealing with

---

57 Klameth, *Das Karsamstagsfeuerwunder,* p. 22.

58 Gingras, *Egeria,* p. 90.

59 *Ibid.*

the rite of the Holy Fire as it is described more completely in these later sources. As Klameth remarks:

> We already come across in Ætheria [Egeria] a complete sequence of elements which later appear to be assimilated into the [ceremony of the] Paschal Fire [*Osterfeuer*] in Jerusalem.... Also, one should not overlook the noteworthy fact that the time of the celebration of the light ceremony according to Ætheria and that of the rite of the Holy Fire [*Feuerritus*] in later accounts is [*sic*, "*ist*"] the same.[60]

The prayer of fervent supplication, an essential part of the ritual as we know it in subsequent sources, is the only remaining element that is absent from Egeria's narrative of the Paschal services which she observed in Jerusalem.

Two of the pre–ninth–century liturgical documents which we have examined, the Armenian and Georgian lectionaries, also contain no extensive references to the rite of the Holy Fire as such during the Paschal services in Jerusalem. But this is something not entirely unusual, since economy of expression is the rule in such documents. Moreover, these documents present no evidence inconsistent with the assumption that the rites being described correspond to the ritual of the Holy Fire. In the *Armenian Lectionary* we find explicit references to the lighting of one or three candles, which, Bertonière presumes, takes place in the Tomb, even in *J*,[61] where the rubrics have already assigned the Faithful to the *Martyrium*. This lectionary also testifies to the hymnody (in this case, Psalm 112) that constitutes one of the elements of the ceremony. In the *Georgian Lectionary* we find these same elements and, significantly enough, a rubric for the fervent prayer that makes up another element of the ceremony: the *kverexi et oratio*. Three processions also now supplement the hymnody, as they do in many later witnesses and in the modern–day rite. These two lectionaries attest to the special nature of the *Lucernarium* in the Jerusalem Paschal rite and strongly suggest that

---

[60] Klameth, *Das Karsamstagsfeuerwunder,* p. 18.

[61] Bertonière, *Easter Vigil,* p. 31.

what is being described is the ritual of the Holy Fire. Bertonière supports this observation in his reflections on *GEORG* and the other documents to which we have made reference:

> In this entire series of rites, there seems to be more involved than a simple Lucernarium in the Anastasis followed by a Vigil in the basilica. The elaboration of GEORG with its three processions, the lighting of the 'new candle,' presumably from the lamp in the taphos, and the procession to the basilica all seem to point to a symbolic celebration of the risen Christ coming forth from the tomb. It is even possible that the three processions (which precede the blessing of the 'new candle') are intended to signify the three days in the tomb, especially in *L* and *S* where there is no mention of the lighting of a candle before the processions. All of this is in line with the relationship between τάφος and φῶς implied in the daily practice described by Egeria...of taking the light from the lamps in the *'spelunca'* for use in the Lucernarium.[62]

In *HS 43*, the final liturgical document which we have cited, we find two significant developments. The candle–lighting ritual is moved to a later point in the Paschal Vigil, now following the readings.[63] It thus assumes a certain independence and takes on the character of a separate and distinct ritual. As well, the light taken from the Tomb is called, in this document, "the Holy Light" (or "Fire"): τὸ Ἅγιον Φῶς. It is clear from this expression that the light is something more than a simple or common flame. Citing Scriptural examples of forgoing the declension of words to emphasize a certain sacredness in their usage (*e.g.*, Revelation 1:4, "Χάρις ὑμῖν καὶ εἰρήνη ἀπὸ ὁὤν..." [emphasis ours]), Bertonière argues that the special nature of "the Holy Fire" in *HS 43* is established by the fact that, when used in the document with the preposition "ἐκ," τὸ Φῶς is not rendered in the genitive, as one would expect (*i.e.*, "ἐκ τοῦ Φωτός"). He discounts an error on the part of the scribe—justifiably so, we think, if only because such a grammatical error is so obvious and since the manuscript

---

[62] *Ibid.*, p. 36.

[63] *Ibid.*, p. 39.

is not seriously flawed by a general weakness of this kind.[64] He also observes that the character of the lighting ceremony in *HS 43*

> ...is one of extreme solemnity: triple incensation of the tomb, the entire church, and the other holy places in the vicinity...; solemn entry of the patriarch into the tomb accompanied by the clergy; the triple prostrations.... Also noteworthy is the penitential note found in the fact that the patriarch prays for his own sins and those of the people.[65]

Given the disputed date for *HS 43*, we cannot unequivocally say that it constitutes clear and unambiguous evidence of a pre–ninth–century reference to the Holy Fire as the phenomenon is later understood. But taken together with evidence that can be confidently assigned to the ancient Christian centuries, it certainly points us to a position of maintaining that there is consistent evidence from the earliest Christian times of a ceremony in the Paschal services at the Holy Sepulchre that corresponds to that of the Holy Fire. If nothing else, this document says without obfuscation what can be logically inferred from other documents.

THE POST–NINTH–CENTURY WITNESS. Most historians agree that the first unambiguous reference[66] to the ceremony of the Holy Fire as an event involving the miraculous appearance of light in the Holy Sepulchre in the non–Arabic sources[67] is an

---

[64] *Ibid.*, n. 86.

[65] *Ibid.*, pp. 40–41.

[66] John Wilkinson cites a reference to the miracle of the Holy Fire in the eighth–century "Life of St. Theodore the Sabaite," in his *Jerusalem Pilgrims Before the Crusades* (Warminster, England: Aris & Phillips, Ltd., 1977), p. 142; this reference is, however, uninformative. Edmond Martène also dates to 800 an unclear liturgical reference to the Paschal Vigil: "...in sepulcro Domini lampas ab angelo illuminator." There is a clear allusion here to a miraculous event, but it is the very same claim made by the monk Bernard and is probably a misdated reference to his account; see Edmond Martène, *De Antiquis Ecclesiæ Ritibus Libri* (Hildesheim, Germany: Georg Olms Verlagsbuchhandlung, 1967), Vol. 3, p. 414.

itinerary by the Western monk Bernard, who witnessed the phenomenon in 870.[68] We will include this reference, one so close to the end of the ninth century, among our post–ninth–century data, if only because it and similar Moslem accounts clearly belong among these materials and not to the earlier references which we have cited.[69] Bernard, in his *Itinerary*,[70] describes with reasonable detail the miracle of the Holy Fire:

> Amongst the Churches inside the city there are four of special importance, and their walls adjoin each other. One is on the east, and inside it are Mount Calvary and the place where the Lord's Cross was found; this one is called the 'Basilica of Constantine.' There is another one on the south and a third on the west; this one [on the west] has the Lord's Sepulchre in the middle of it. Round the

---

[67] Although we will here look only at an anonymous late ninth–century Arabic source and the witness of al–Biruni in the early eleventh century, F. E. Peters, in his *Jerusalem: The Holy City in the Eyes of Chroniclers, Visitors, Pilgrims, and Prophets from the Days of Abraham to the Beginning of Modern Times* (Princeton, NJ: Princeton University Press, 1985), argues that a number of Moslem authors bear witness to the rite of the Holy Fire as early as the ninth century (p. 262).

[68] Bernard, according to Klameth, is the first witness to attribute to the light from the Paschal ceremonies a supernatural origin; see Klameth, *Das Karsamstagsfeuerwunder*, p. 24.

[69] It should be noted that Bernard's *Itinerary* is dated within the manuscript at 970. This error has been discussed by Thomas Wright, ed., *Early Travels in Palestine, Comprising the Narratives of Arculf, Willibald, Bernard, Sæwulf, Sigurd, Benjamin of Tudela, Sir John Maundeville, de la Brocquière, and Maundrell* (London: Henry G. Bohn, 1848), who argues that an early manuscript in the British Museum, no longer extant, places Bernard's travels in the year 870 (p. *xvi*). References to Pope Nicholas I, who died in 867, have led scholars to agree that this earlier date for the document is correct and that the extant manuscripts contain an error by an unknown scribe.

[70] A Latin text of his *Itinerary* can be found in Titus Tobler and Augustus Molinier, eds., *Itinera Hierosolymitana et Descriptiones Terræ Sanctæ* (Osnabrück, Germany: Otto Zeller, 1966). An excellent English text is Wilkinson, *Jerusalem Pilgrims*, pp. 141–145; according to Wilkinson, the oldest text of Bernard's *Itinerary*, preserved at Lincoln College, Oxford University, calls the author "Bernard the Wise" (*ibid.*, p. 141, n. 1).

sepulchre are nine columns, and the walls between them are made of excellent stone. Four of the nine columns are in front of the actual tomb, and these [with the railing behind them] surround the stone, placed by the tomb, which the angel rolled back, and on which he sat after the Lord had risen. It is unnecessary to write a great deal about this sepulchre because Bede says quite enough about it in his history.[71] But it is worth saying what happens on Holy Saturday, the Vigil of Easter. In the morning the office begins in this Church. Then, when it is over they go in singing *Kyrie eleison* till an angel comes and kindles light in the lamps which hang above the sepulchre [...veniente angelo, lumen in lampadibus accendatur, que pendent super predictum sepulcrum[72]]. The patriarch passes some of this light to the bishops and the rest of the people, and each one has light where he is standing.[73]

Though this account is shorter than many subsequent accounts, the details which it contains are significant. Bernard reports that the Holy Fire descends on the day of the Paschal Vigil, Great Saturday, after the completion of the morning office. More importantly, he is the "first commentator," according to Klameth, to observe that the fire is *miraculously kindled* (by an Angel) in the vigil lamps of the Sepulchre, "...which would become the characteristic element *par excellence* of the entire fire celebration."[74] Bernard also notes that the descent of the Holy Fire occurs during what appears to be a special penitential or supplicatory service specifically focused on the reception of the light. The Holy Fire is then distributed to the other clergy and to the Faithful by the Patriarch.

In an account by an anonymous Moslem source dated by I. Krachkovskii to the late ninth century, we also read of the mirac-

---

[71] See [Saint] Bede, *A History of the English Church and People*, trans. Leo Sherley–Price, rev. R. E. Latham (London: Penguin Books, 1968), pp. 300–302.

[72] *Cf.* Martène, n. 66 *supra;* the Latin says literally, "An angel having come, light is lit in the lamps, which hang on the aforementioned Sepulchre."

[73] Wilkinson, *Jerusalem Pilgrims,* pp. 142, 144; Tobler and Molinier, *Itinera,* p. 315.

[74] Klameth, *Das Karsamstagsfeuerwunder,* p. 24.

ulous nature of the Holy Fire:

> When the Pascha begins among the Christians, on the day of
> Great Saturday, the people come out from the place of the tomb to
> the place of the stone, around which is a gallery. From there they
> look on the place of the tomb, and all pray and bow down before
> the Most High God, from the time of the morning prayers until
> the setting of the sun. The Emir and Imam of the mosque are
> present. A guard locks the door to the tomb and sits before it.
> They all remain thus, until they see a light, similar to a white fire,
> coming forth from within the tomb. The guard then opens the
> door to the tomb and enters within. In his hands is a candle, which
> he lights from the fire and then carries outside. The candle, howev-
> er, though it is lit, does not burn.[75] He gives it to the Imam, who
> takes the candle and lights the lamps of the mosque. When this
> candle is passed on to a third person, it begins to burn and changes
> into fire.[76] They [the Christians] write to the capital [presumably
> the capital of the Caliphs, as we read in al–Biruni, *infra*] concern-
> ing the descent, relating that the fire came down at a certain time
> on a certain day. If it comes down on this day during the time of
> the morning prayer, this serves as an indication that the year, while
> not fertile, will nonetheless not have a drought; if, however, it
> comes around mid–day, then this indicates a year without har-
> vest.[77]

The liturgical details supplied by this writer are perhaps faulty.
He seems to place the Faithful in the antechamber of the Edicule
of the Holy Sepulchre ("the place of the stone, around which
there is a gallery"), looking in on the Tomb from the Chapel of

[75] This is one of the first clear references to the miraculous properties of
the Holy Fire.

[76] The idea that the Holy Fire loses its unconsuming quality shortly after
its appearance is found in contemporary accounts of the phenomenon, too.

[77] I. Krachkovskii, "Blagodatnyi ogon' po razskazu al–Biruni i drugikh
musulmanskikh pisatelei x–xiii vv," *Khrisitianskii Vostok,* Vol. 3, No. 2 (1914), p.
232; the association in this passage of the descent of the Holy Fire with good
fortune is, as the witness of al–Biruni and Matthew of Edessa aver (*infra*), an
important characteristic of the rite.

the Angel. However, there is a clear understanding that the ceremony of the Holy Fire involves the descent of a miraculous light.[78]

Another brief account of the fire can be found in a letter from Arethas, Metropolitan of Cæsarea, in Cappadocia, to the Emir of Damascus. This document dates to the beginning of the tenth century:[79]

> ...[Every year] until now His holy and precious tomb on the day of the Resurrection works miracles.... [All lights in Jerusalem having been extinguished] and...a lamp with emblems and (unintelligible ⊁ word) [κανδήλα μετὰ ἀκτρίου καὶ τουρίου[80]] having been prepared by the Christians, the Amir of Jerusalem standing near the Holy Sepulchre, the doors of which the Amir seals,[81] and the Christians standing outside in the nave of the Anastasis, crying *Kyrie eleison,* with a sudden flash the lamp lights, and again from it all

[78] Bertonière quotes another Arabic source, Ma'sûdi, who, writing in 926, denies that the Holy Fire is of supernatural origin. Writing of the Great Saturday celebrations, Ma'sûdi says: "The Christians assemble for the festival from out [sic] all lands. For on it the fire of heaven doth descend among them, and they kindle therefrom the candles.... The Christians hold many legends there anent; but the fire is produced by a clever artifice, which is kept a great secret" (*Paschal Vigil,* p. 41). The importance of this witness is that, while the writer denies that the Holy Fire is supernatural, he nonetheless attributes this belief to the Christians of his time.

[79] So contends A. Papadopoulos–Kerameus; see Bertonière, *Easter Vigil,* pp. 40–41, n. 90.

[80] Papadopoulos–Kerameus (*ibid.,* p. 41, n. 91) finds the words "ἀκτρίου" and "τουρίου" unintelligible. With regard to the first word, we tend to agree; however, it is not unreasonable to assume that the Metropolitan is describing an emblem and some other decoration on the lamp. To this day, vigil lamps in Orthodox Churches are often decorated with ribbons and emblems on festive occasions. The word "τουρίου," therefore, may be derived from "τουρᾶς," an insigne or emblem (usually employed, in fact, in reference to the Sultan's various insignia or seals).

[81] *Cf.* the foregoing anonymous Moslem narrative and the "ruler" at the Tomb. Later accounts confirm this detail, that in the days of Moslem rule over Jerusalem a Moslem official sealed and guarded the Tomb. As we shall see, it is to the secular officials of Jerusalem that the sealing of the Tomb prior to the celebration of the rite of the Holy Fire is left even today.

the inhabitants [of] Jerusalem take, lighting [their] flame.[82]

It is important to note that the author of this account emphasizes that the manifestation of the Holy Fire has a continuous history, taking place "μέχρι τοῦ νῦν," literally "up to now," or "every year." The sealing of the Tomb and the brilliant flash that accompanies the kindling of the light are also details that we should note with care.

In the year 947, a cleric of the imperial court of Constantine VII Porphyrigenitos, a certain Niketas, sent a letter to the Emperor recounting the attempt of an enraged Emir to put an end to the rite of the Holy Fire.[83] This letter provides rich data about the fire. The Emir had demanded the outright termination of all future celebrations on Great Saturday, "...since," as Niketas reports the Emir's demand to the Patriarch of Jerusalem, "in performing your celebrated miracle with magic artifices, you have filled all of Syria with the religion of the Christians and you have all but destroyed all of our customs; you have made of it a 'Romania.'"[84] Thwarted in his first attempt to stop the celebration by the clever response of the Patriarch's supporters—that a cessation of Paschal celebrations in Jerusalem would jeopardize the hefty revenues collected from Christian pilgrims during the event by the Islamic authorities—, the Emir concocted another scheme to end the ritual. Niketas continues his report to the Emperor:

---

[82] *Ibid.,* p. 41; the translation here is from Bertonière's Greek text.

[83] There are lingering accusations against this document as a forgery. However, Papadopoulos–Kerameus has argued persuasively for the authenticity of the letter in his edition of the Greek text; see his "Poslanie k Imperatorou Konstantinou Porfirorodnomou," *Pravoslavnii Palestinskii Sbornik* (St. Petersburg), Vol. 38 (1894), pp. 1–6. English texts of the letter can be found in Peters, *Jerusalem,* pp. 261–262 (selected excerpts), and Callistos, "Holy Fire," pp. 11–13 (the entire extant document).

[84] Peters, *Jerusalem,* p. 261. By "Romania," the Emir means "a Christian land," since Christianity was associated with the Roman Empire, or Byzantium, accounting for the fact that Greek Orthodox Christians were known as "Romans" by their Moslem rulers. The appellation is still used by Orthodox Greeks (*e.g.,* "Ρωμαῖος").

[He]...demanded of the Patriarch, under the threat of prohibiting the popular feast of the Resurrection of Christ, a payment of 7,000 gold pieces. This payment would not have been made except for an immediate disbursement by the secretaries of 2,000 gold pieces with a guarantee of the remaining 5,000. While the patriarch was being held in custody in the Pretorium, the God of miracles filled two of the lamps of the triple lamp suspended at the place where they said the body of Christ was taken down from the cross to be washed. When the news of the wonder came to the Pretorium, Christians and Muslims ran pell–mell to the church. But the Muslims came filled with bloody thoughts and murderous designs, armed and ready to slay every Christian carrying a lighted lamp. The Patriarch arrived, followed by the clergy, and having determined that the illumination of the sacred fire had not yet taken place, with the help of the Muslims had the Holy Sepulcher closed and began to pray with the Christians. Toward the sixth hour, fixing his gaze on the Holy Sepulcher, he saw the supernatural appearance of the light. He entered the Holy Sepulcher whose entrance was shown to him by an angel. At the moment when he took a taper to give of the divine fire to all of those in the church who had torches, scarcely had he come out of the tomb, when he saw the church suddenly filled with a divine light. The faithful were standing on the right and the left, some near the door, some by Calvary, others near the cruciform chain suspended from the ceiling and all around which they had hung their lamps, the chain, that is, which passes for representing the center of the world and which is there as a sign, so that all men might be astonished at the apparition of the divine fire. The Muslims themselves were filled with astonishment since up to that point the apparition of the light annually occurred only at one of the lamps inside the Holy Sepulcher, while on this day the entire church was filled with light. The amir, who was looking on from above on one of the tribunes, was witness to an even greater miracle. The largest of the lamps [which exceeded in size a *kratir* (ὑπερ κρατῆρος μέγεθος)[85]] suspended in

---

[85] So reads Callistos, "Holy Fire," p. 13; the Greek is in Papadopoulos–Kerameus, "Poslanie k Imperatorou Konstantinou," p. 5. The word "κρατήρ" apparently escaped the translator of Callistos' text; Greek for "crater," it also means a "jug" or large container, especially such as were used in past times for

front of him let escape the oil and water which it contained and was suddenly filled with a divine fire even though it had no wick at all.[86]

The Tomb sealed with Moslem collaboration, the Holy Fire apparently appeared around noon, according to this source, the Church having become filled with a Divine light in anticipation of the Patriarch's distribution of the fire from within the Tomb. We learn that "...the apparition of this light annually occurred at only one of the lamps inside the Holy Sepulcher," as reported in other sources. And finally, Niketas asserts that the light that manifested throughout the Church exhibited the same miraculous properties attributed to the light within the Tomb, sustaining itself, before the Emir, without benefit of oil or wicks.

Eleventh Century. A Moslem source, al–Biruni, writing in the early eleventh century[87] and drawing on a tenth–century source, offers further testimony about attempted interventions of the Islamic rulers in the ritual and to their frustration at the supernatural qualities of the Holy Fire. He also contends that the particular time of the descent of the Holy Fire—which was unpredictable—presaged, according to popular lore, events during the following year. His testimony, coming as it does from an unsympathetic if not hostile witness, affords definite corroboration of Niketas' claim, in the foregoing passage, that the annual miracle in the Tomb enjoyed widespread popularity even within the Moslem community. More importantly, it represents an objective report of the phenomenon from a non–Christian source with little or no reason to believe in such a phenomenon. The passage is from al–Biruni's work on the festivals of the various religious populations in the Islamic world:

> A story is told in connection with the Saturday of the Resurrection that astonishes the investigator of the physical sciences and whose

storing wine.

[86] Peters, *Jerusalem*, p. 262.

[87] Krachkovskii presents the text in Russian and dates it at 1000 ("Blagodatnyi ogon' po razskazu al–Biruni," pp. 228–229).

basis is impossible to uncover. If it were not for the agreement on the phenomenon of persons with differing views who report that it is based on eyewitness testimony and has been perpetuated by excellent scholars and other people in their books, one would give it no credence. I have learned of it in books and heard of it from al–Faraj ibn Salih of Baghdad.... A report is made on the subject which is sent to the capital of the caliphs as soon as the fire has descended. They say that if the fire comes down quickly and at a • time close to midday, that presages a fertile year and that, on the contrary, if the occurrence is delayed until the evening or afterwards, that that presages a year of famine. The one who told me of this said that some of the [Moslem] authorities had the wick of the lamp replaced by a copper wire to the end that it would not take light and the ceremony thus be disrupted. But when the fire descended it was lit nonetheless.[88]

We should draw attention, here, to the fact that it was also in the early eleventh century (probably in 1009[89]) that al–Hakim ordered the destruction of the entire complex of the Church of the Resurrection,[90] one of the most devastating attacks on the Christian monuments in Jerusalem. The complex was thoroughly razed, as were other Christian Churches. At least for the Syrian historian ibn al–Qalanisi, who in the mid–twelfth century wrote the most detailed account of al–Hakim's actions, this destruction was indeed the direct result of the Caliph's reaction to reports of the miraculous manifestation of the Holy Fire in Jerusalem.[91] Though al–Hakim's destructive rampage is at odds with earlier reports of the sympathetic attitude taken towards the rite by the Moslem rulers, Gregory Abûl Faraj,[92] in his *Chrono-*

[88] Peters, *Jerusalem,* p. 263.

[89] Various sources date the destruction of the Church to 1007 (Bar Hebræus, *History* [*infra*], p. 184), 1008, 1009 (Peters, *Jerusalem,* p. 7; Tsafrir, "Jerusalem," p. 598), and even 1010 (Duckworth, *Holy Sepulchre* [*infra*], p. 194).

[90] Which, according to Peters (*Jerusalem,* p. 258), the Moslems popularly called "Kanisat al–Qumâma," or "the Church of the Dungheap."

[91] *Ibid.,* pp. 258–261.

[92] Also known as Bar Hebræus (d. 1286), or Bar 'Ebhrâyâ ("son of the

graphy, supports ibn al–Qalanisi's contention that al–Hakim was outraged at the Christian miracle of the Holy Fire.[93] According to Gregory, the "...Temple of the Resurrection which is in Jerusalem was dug up from its roots (or, foundations), and all its furniture was looted." He then observes that

> ...this persecution began through a certain man who hated the Christians. He told Hakîm the Khalîfah a story [to the effect that] 'the Christians, when they assemble in the temple of Jerusalem to celebrate the festival of Easter, deal cunningly (or, deceitfully) with the overseers of the church, and they anoint with oil of balâsmôn (balsam) the iron wire on which hangeth the lamp over the tomb. And when the governor of the Arabs sealeth the door of the tomb, the Christians from the roof light a fire at the top of the iron wire, and the fire runneth down to the wick of the lamp and kindleth it. And then they cry out "Kûrîâ Laysôn" (Kyrie Eleeson) and weep, pretending that they see the light which descendeth from heaven upon the tomb, and they are confirmed in their Faith.'[94]

The extreme violence of al–Hakim's campaign attests to the fact that his intentions were not merely political, and it well may be that the widespread popularity of and belief in the annual miracle of the Holy Fire provoked in him a fit of religious intolerance and destructive fury. Nonetheless, H. T. F. Duckworth asserts that "El–Hakim's mother was a Christian, and under her protection Christians had prospered in Egypt in the reign of El–

Jew"), he was a celebrated thirteenth–century scholar, fluent in Greek and Arabic and the author of books on philosophy, religion, medicine, and grammar.

93 Let us point out, however, that al–Hakim did not limit his campaign of destruction to the Church of the Resurrection or other Christian edifices. According to Peters, he also destroyed many synagogues; nor was his wrath directed simply at the Christian population. As Peters writes, "...his repressive measures against Muslims in Cairo provoked such a reaction that by 1020 he had to reconcile himself to the Jews and Christians to find any support" (Peters, *Jerusalem,* p. 260).

94 Gregory Abûl Faraj [Bar Hebræus], *The Chronological and Political History of the World from the Creation to the Year A.D. 1286: Part I,* trans. Ernest A. Wallis Budge (London: Oxford University Press, 1932), Vol. I, pp. 184–185.

Hakim's father Aziz."[95] He points out that there are a number of motives attributed to al–Hakim for taking the measures that he did. Thus,

> ...according to one story, which was put in circulation immediately after the event, the Jews of Orleans bribed an apostate Christian to carry, secreted in a staff, a letter addressed to the Khalif and warning him that the Franks were preparing to invade Palestine.[96]

Saul Colbi follows Duckworth's thinking, though he admits that al–Hakim used the miracle of the Holy Fire at least as a pretext for his destructive rampage:[97]

> Al–Hakim passed ordinances against the Christians; he banned pilgrimages, confiscated property, ordered crosses to be burned and small mosques to be built on the roofs of the churches. Hundreds of churches were pillaged and destroyed during his reign, among them the Church of the Holy Sepulchre itself, on the pretext that the annual miracle of the Holy Fire, celebrated in it on the Saturday before Easter, was an impious deception. ...Yet al–Hakim abandoned his un–Christian policy at the end of his reign: thousands of recent apostates were allowed to return to the Christian fold, Church property was returned to its owners, and the Greek Orthodox Patriarch Nikephoros was permitted to renew worship in the ruins of the Holy Sepulchre.[98]

Whether an act of religious intolerance or a pretext for the accomplishment of some unknown political aim, al–Hakim's destruction of the Church of the Resurrection was undeniably tied

---

[95] H. T. F. Duckworth, *The Church of the Holy Sepulchre* (London: Hodder & Stoughton, n.d.), p. 194.

[96] *Ibid.*

[97] Other contemporary sources also suggest that the miracle of the Holy Fire was but a pretext for al–Hakim to launch his anti–Christian campaign; see, for example, Teddy Kollek and Moshe Perlman, *Pilgrims to the Holy Land: The Story of Pilgrimage through the Ages* (New York: Harper & Row Publishers, Inc., 1970), p. 68.

[98] Saul P. Colbi, *A History of the Christian Presence in the Holy Land* (Lanham, MD: University Press of America, 1988), p. 34.

to the rite of the Holy Fire and attests to the fact that in his time it had become well–known as a Christian miracle.[99] Unfortunately, we do not have numerous other detailed or reliable accounts of the miracle from the remainder of the eleventh century.[100]

Twelfth Century. At the beginning of the twelfth century, an important event occurred which provides us with data—albeit, unreliable data, as we shall see—on the rite of the Holy Fire, its

[99] A great tragedy associated with the Church of the Resurrection is also reported in an historical chronicle by Matthew of Edessa, an Armenian monk who died *ca.* 1136. He claims that in the year 455 of the Armenian era (A.D. 1007), because "the whole Greek nations [*i.e.,* the Byzantines] fell into error concerning Holy Easter [celebrating it that year, Matthew claims, one week early]," a multitude of Christians was slaughtered by "infidel peoples who were in the city of Jerusalem" and "inside the church of the Resurrection...; thus, the holy sepulcher of Christ was filled with the blood of those praying"; see Ara E. Dostourian, "The Chronicle of Matthew of Edessa: Translated from the Original Armenian, with a Commentary and Introduction" (doctoral dissertation, Rutgers University, 1972), pp. 48–49. Matthew makes no mention of the Holy Fire as a cause for the slaughter in Jerusalem, which is in fact a reference to al–Hakim's anti–Christian campaign. This would lead one to question whether the association of al–Hakim's actions with the Holy Fire was widespread among scholars in the Eastern Christian world; however, as Dostourian notes, Matthew was not a *vardapet,* or from among the educated class of the Armenian clergy, but a simple clergyman. This may account both for his lack of details about al–Hakim's campaign and the rôle of the rite of the Holy Fire in it.

[100] Klameth includes in the eleventh–century witness a reference to the Holy Fire by Radulfus Glaber that he assigns to the year 1048, the year in which the reconstruction of the Church of the Holy Sepulchre, which began in 1046—a consequence of the treaty between al–Hakim's grandson, al–Mostanser–Billah and the Byzantine Emperor—, was completed (see Thomas Wright, ed., *Early Travels in Palestine,* p. xviii). Glaber, Duckworth tells us, was a Bishop and was also apparently a witness to the destruction of the Church of the Resurrection by al–Hakim (Duckworth, *Holy Sepulchre,* p. 197; Wilkinson identifies Glaber only as a monk of Cluny [*Jerusalem Pilgrims,* p. 14]). Glaber recounts the experience of a certain Odalricus Aurelianorum, who tells of a miraculous fire on Great Saturday which descends by Divine power at the Church of the Holy Sepulchre and which is passed by the believers from hand to hand. Except for its reference to the miraculous nature of the Holy Fire, this reference is unremarkable.

miraculous nature, and the importance that it held both for the Greek Orthodox and the Latin rulers of Jerusalem. In 1101 the Holy Fire failed to appear at the appointed time. O. Meinardus summarizes Fulcherius' history of the Crusades:

> Fulcher de Chartres (1101 A.D.) confirms that the Holy Fire usually appeared at the 9th hour, and that the Latins received it from the Greek Patriarch. In 1101, however, the Holy Fire did not descend as expected..., and the Patriarch[101] ordered everyone to leave the church. On the following day, on Easter Day, after much praying, the long–expected light did appear in one of the lamps in the Holy Sepulchre. And after the Celebration of the Holy Mass, at which the King assisted, wearing according to royal custom, the crown upon his head, Baldwin gave a banquet in the Temple of Solomon. And while the banquet was in progress, it was announced that the Holy Fire had again appeared in two of the lamps suspended in the Holy Sepulchre, and the king with his guests returned to the church to see the new miracle.[102]

Meinardus' summary, while rich in details, is unfortunately taken from a suspect manuscript of Fulcherius' history of the Crusades.[103] Sister Frances Ryan, in her English translation of Fulcherius' account, notes that this manuscript "...purports to be a text of Fulcher and has those characteristics in the beginning. However in Book II the author of Codex L [Cambridge University Codex 2079] begins to show an independent point of view and...adds some extra details, *including a long section about the Holy Fire of 1101* [emphasis ours]."[104] Though Bertonière and

---

[101] This would have to have been the Latin bishop in Jerusalem, since the Greek Patriarch had already gone into exile in Cyprus; see A. Martinos, ed., Θρησκευτικὴ καὶ Ἠθικὴ Ἐγκυκλοπαιδεία (Athens: 1966), *s.v.* "'Ιερουσαλήμ," by I. D. Zizioulas, col. 836.

[102] O. Meinardus, "The Ceremony of the Holy Fire in the Middle Ages and Today," *Bulletin de la Société d'Archéologie Copte,* Vol. 16 (1961–1962), p. 244.

[103] Fulcherius [Foucher] of Chartres, "Gesta Francorum Hierusalem Peregrinantium," Codex 2079, University of Cambridge.

[104] *Idem, A History of the Expedition to Jerusalem,* trans. Frances Rita Ryan

Klameth accept this version of the manuscript, there is little doubt that it is at odds with Fulcherius' attitude in other manuscripts, where he is laconic and noncommittal about the events of 1101:

> On Easter Sunday everyone was much disturbed because the Holy Fire failed to appear at the Sepulcher of the Lord. When the Easter solemnity was over, the king [King or Prince Baldwin] went back to Joppa.[105]

There is no mention here of a ceremony or of the appearance of the Holy Fire at a time later than usual. Whatever the case, Fulcherius' shorter account does establish that the Holy Fire was, in his time, considered miraculous, since he reports its failure to appear, something which would have no meaning had the rite entailed a symbolic flame.

Bernard Hamilton observes that in 1101 Prince Baldwin had, for the first time, excluded the Greeks from the celebration of the rite of the Holy Fire (an allegation contradicted, of course, by the Cambridge manuscript of Fulcherius' history, which portrays the Greek Orthodox Patriarch as playing an important part in the rite), and for this reason the Holy Fire did not occur.[106] Clearly his suggestion is, of course, that the Latins did not know how to produce the Fire through artificial means. But he does admit to the political importance of the rite. In fact, he notes that the Prince was careful to offer the visiting Russian Abbot Daniel, a few years later, the honor of joining the royal party at the Paschal celebrations. This was undoubtedly, he opines, because of the readmittance of the Orthodox to prominence in the Church of the Resurrection after the failure of the Holy Fire to appear at the appointed time in 1101.[107]

(Knoxville, TN: University of Tennessee Press, 1969), p. 21.

[105] *Ibid.*, pp. 151–152; for the Latin text, see Fulcheri Cartoniensis, *Historia Hierosolymitana*, ed. Heinrich Hagenmeyer (Heidelberg: Carl Winter's Universitätsbuchhandlung, 1913), pp. 395–397.

[106] Bernard Hamilton, *The Latin Church in the Crusader States* (London: Variorum Publications, 1980), p. 171.

Archimandrite Chrysostomos (Papadopoulos), in his history
of the Church of Jerusalem, also makes note of the events of 1101.
He contends that, while it is doubtful that the Greeks and Latins
normally concelebrated in the Church of the Resurrection
(where separate services, he asserts, were done by the Greeks and
Arabs according to the Greek *typikon* and alternately in the language of each[108]), in that year the Greek and Latin clergy together conducted the rite of the Holy Fire. Apparently he believes that as a result of the participation of the Latins, the Holy
Fire did not appear on Holy Saturday as usual.[109] He bases his
analysis on "the Latin witness Poulcharios [Πουλχάριος]"[110] (by
whom he undoubtedly means Fulcherius), using the same ex-
panded commentary as the Cambridge Codex. It is thus that he
establishes that the service was concelebrated by the Greeks and
Latins (though this is only implied by the text). At any rate, Papadopoulos goes on to say that the Holy Fire appeared only after
the Greeks prayed in the absence of the Latins, on the Sunday of
Pascha, when the Church of the Resurrection became filled with
light. The Latins then came to take light from the Greeks. On
the basis of this, he concludes, "...during the Crusader era the
rite of the Holy Fire remained a purely Greek celebration"[111]—
an important claim, since it helps us to understand the survival
of the rite to this day principally in the Greek Churches.

The next significant witness to the Holy Fire is the Russian
Abbot Daniel, who visited the Holy Land from 1106 to 1107. He
describes the descent of the Holy Fire as it was celebrated during
the first decade of the Crusader dominance over the Holy Land:

---

[107] *Ibid.*, p. 170.

[108] Chrysostomos Papadopoulos, Ἱστορία τῆς Ἐκκλησίας τῶν Ἱεροσολύμων (Jerusalem and Alexandria: 1910), pp. 388–389.

[109] *Cf.* Hamilton, who reports that the *absence* of the Greek clergy, not
the presence of the Latin clergy, was thought to have impeded the manifestation
of the Holy Fire (*Latin Church*, p. 171).

[110] Papadopoulos, Ἱστορία, pp. 389–390.

[111] *Ibid.*, p. 390.

The following is a description of the Holy Light which descends upon the Holy Sepulcher.... Many pilgrims relate incorrectly the details about the Holy Light. Some say that the Holy Spirit descends upon the Holy Sepulcher in the form of a dove; others that it is lightning from heaven that kindles the lamps above the Sepulcher of the Lord. This is all untrue for neither dove nor lightning is to be seen at that moment; but the divine grace comes down unseen from heaven and lights the lamps in the Sepulcher of our ' Lord. I will only describe it in perfect truth as I have seen it.

On Holy Friday, after Vespers, they clean the Holy Sepulcher and wash all the lamps there and fill them with pure oil, unmixed with water, and having put wicks in them, they do not light them. Seals are put on the Tomb at two in the morning and at the same time all the lamps and candles are extinguished in all the churches of Jerusalem....

I went joyfully to buy a large glass lamp, and...I brought it to the Holy Sepulcher toward evening.... The guardian opened the door for me, told me to take off my shoes, and with bare feet, alone with my lamp, which I was carrying, he let me enter the Holy Sepulcher and bade me put the lamp down on the Tomb of the Lord. I did so. ...The lamp of the Greeks was placed toward the ' head and that of St. Sabbas and the other monasteries near the breast, since this was the annual custom. By the Grace of God, all three of these lamps were subsequently lit, while none of the lamps of the Franks [*i.e.,* the Latins], which were suspended above the tomb, was lit.

After I had put my lamp on the Holy Tomb and venerated this holy place with kisses of compunction and the tears of piety, I left the Holy Tomb with great excitement and retired to my cell. The next day, at the sixth hour of Holy Saturday, everyone assembles at the Church of the Resurrection, people from everywhere, ...in numbers that are difficult to estimate. The crowd filled the space around the church, [and]...only the priests were inside, and everyone, clergy and laity, awaited the arrival of the prince and his court.

When they arrived, the doors were opened and the crowd rushed in, jostling and elbowing each other in terrible fashion and filled the entire church and its galleries. ...A large number were left outside. ...People were everywhere, and all they could cry was 'Lord, have mercy on us,' and the cry was so powerful that the whole building shook with it. The faithful wept torrents of tears. ...Even Prince Baldwin had a contrite and humble countenance. Torrents of tears rolled from his eyes, and his courtiers, who surrounded him, stood in great recollection near the main altar before the Tomb.

Earlier, about the seventh hour of Saturday, Prince Baldwin had left his residence.... I went with him. ...We reached the western door of the Church of the Resurrection, but the crowd was massed so tightly that we could not enter. Then Baldwin ordered his soldiers to disperse the crowd and open a passage. So they did and made a path to the Tomb, and that is how we got through the crowd.

We reached the eastern entrance of the Holy Sepulcher of the Lord, and the prince, following after took his place. ...The prince ordered...me to go...above the doors of the Holy Sepulcher, opposite the great altar, so that I could see past the doors of the Tomb, three of them, all sealed with the royal seal. As for the Latin clergy, they remained at the great altar.

At the eighth hour, the Orthodox clergy, which was above the Holy Sepulcher, together with all the other clerics, monks, and hermits, began to chant vespers; on their side, the Latin clergy muttered along in their peculiar fashion. While this chanting was in progress, I stood in my place and kept my gaze on the doors of the Tomb. When the chanting reached the lections for Holy Saturday, the bishop [the Latin Patriarch], followed by the deacon, left the great altar during the initial lesson and approached the doors, looked through the grillwork into the interior, and when he did not see the light, returned to his place. He returned at the sixth lesson and still saw nothing. Then everyone began to cry out *'Kyrie, eleison,'* which means 'Lord, have mercy.' At the end of the ninth hour, when they began to sing the passage *'Cantabo Domino,'*[112] a small cloud coming from the east suddenly came to rest over the open dome of the church and a light rain fell upon the

---

[112] "I will sing unto the Lord" ("῎Ασωμεν τῷ Κυρίῳ" in the Septuagint, or literally "Let us sing unto the Lord"), the first of the nine Biblical Odes ("The Song of Moses"), sung at the end of the sixth reading (Exodus 13:20–15:19) in the Paschal Vigil.

Holy Sepulcher, and upon us who were above the Tomb. It was then that the Holy Light suddenly illumined the Holy Sepulcher, stunningly bright and splendid. The bishop, followed by four deacons, then opened the doors of the Holy Sepulcher and went with the candle he had taken from Prince Baldwin, the first to be lit from this Holy Fire. ...It was from the prince's candle that we lit ours, which were then used to pass the fire to the rest of the people in the church.

This Holy Fire is not like an ordinary flame but burns in a quite extraordinary way and with an indescribable brightness and with a red color the likes of cinnamon. Thus all the people then stood with lit candles in their hands and repeated loudly and with excitement, 'Lord, have mercy on us.' ...Someone who has not shared in the excitement of that day cannot possibly believe that all that I saw is true. Only the truly wise and believing who being of full faith to the truth of this narrative will hear with delight the details of the event. Even the lukewarm will be somewhat moved, but to the evil man and the doubter, the truth always seems distorted.

But let us return to where I digressed. Scarcely had the light shone out in the Holy Sepulcher than the chanting ceased and the whole crowd, crying *'Kyrie, eleison'* and cupping the candles in their hand against the draft ran out of the church in great excitement. Everyone went back to his own place and with his candle lit the lamps of the churches and completed vespers there, while only the clergy stayed behind and finished vespers in the great church of the Holy Sepulcher....[113]

There are many noteworthy points in this passage. First, as Bertonière observes, there are two services ("vespers") being celebrated in conjunction with the rite of the Holy Fire, one by the Greeks, the other by the Latins.[114] Daniel simply states that the Latin bishop and his deacons go to the Sepulchre, at first finding it dark, and then return, at the ninth hour, to open the Sepul-

---

[113] Peters, *Jerusalem*, pp. 264–267; also see the text in Callistos, "Holy Fire," pp. 13–15.

[114] Bertonière, *Easter Vigil*, p. 19.

chre and to ignite their candles from the light that has finally
appeared. From these candles Prince Baldwin lit his own and
then those of his entourage and the visiting Russian clergyman.
This is either an erroneous account of the rite of the Holy Fire or
a temporary enactment of the ceremony in the absence of a
presiding Greek Bishop.

Second, the miracle itself is carefully described. Abbot Daniel cites other accounts of the miracle of Great Saturday, naming
different actual experiences of the event—the descent of a dove, a
flash of light, an Angel, a hand like fire, *etc.*—, and either dismisses them as false, if one reads his words literally, or purports,
if his words are placed in context, that they do not apply to the
"moment" of the descent of the Holy Fire, but may be phenomena attendant to it. He attributes no specific significance to the
small cloud and light rain which he saw just before the appearance of the Holy Fire, but they are interesting and unusual ad-
ditions to the phenomena reported in other accounts. Third, a
spirit of contrition is clearly present in the rite, manifested not
only in the chanting, but in the heartfelt expressions of piety
among the believers. And fourth, while the Holy Fire does man-
age to come before the end of the vesperal readings, the behavior
of the clergy evidences their familiarity with its irregularity.[115]
Finally, the Abbot takes note of the "quite extraordinary way"
that the fire burns, as well as its unusual brightness and color.

There are several incidental references to the Holy Fire in
the twelfth–century accounts of pilgrimages to the Holy Land
collected in the *Patrologia Græca* which have been overlooked by
scholars. Though they are undetailed, they do attest to a widespread knowledge of the miracle in the Christian world of that
century. The first of these is from Perdikos, a *protonotarios*[116]
from Ephesus who visited the Church of the Holy Sepulchre
sometime in the twelfth century. Describing the Holy Sepulchre,
Perdikos says that miracles came forth from it, both to believers
and unbelievers, and that on the feast of the universal Resurrec-

[115] See Meinardus, "Ceremony," p. 244.

[116] A chief notary either in ecclesiastical or imperial service.

tion of Christ a light came forth and illumined all.[117] The second of these references is from an anonymous twelfth–century pilgrim who reports that "...at the time of Vespers on Holy and Great Saturday, the Holy Fire descends and alights upon [προ-σεγγίζει] the Holy Sepulchre of Christ and immediately lights the lamps of the Holy Sepulchre."[118]

Finally, at the end of the twelfth century, the *Itinerarium regis Ricardi* recounts the visit of the Saracen Saladin to the Holy Sepulchre on Great Saturday, 1192. The author of this chronicle tells us that

> Saladin, with his retinue, paid a visit to the Holy Sepulchre of our Lord, to assure himself of the truth of a certain fact, namely, the coming down from heaven of fire, once a year, to light the lamp. After he had watched for some time, with great attention, the devotion and contrition of many Christian captives, who were praying for the mercy of God, he and all the other Turks suddenly saw the divine fire descend and light the lamp, so that they were vehemently moved, while the Christians rejoiced, and with loud voices praised the mighty works of God. But the Saracens disbelieved this manifest and wonderful miracle, though they witnessed it with their own eyes, and asserted that it was a fraudulent contrivance. To assure himself of this, Saladin ordered the lamp to be extinguished; which, however, was instantly rekindled by the divine power; and when the infidel ordered it to be extinguished a second time it was lighted a second time; and so likewise a third time.[119]

Thirteenth Century. Included in the foregoing references are several selections from the historical record found in F. E. Peters, who, in his history of Jerusalem from eyewitness sources, is one of the few contemporary authorities to have written at any length about the Holy Fire.[120] Peters is not sympathetic to "...the re-

---

[117] Migne, *Patrologia Græca,* Vol. 133, col. 965.

[118] *Ibid.,* col. 976.

[119] Quoted in Harry Charles Luke, *Ceremonies at the Holy Places* (London: Faith Press, 1932), pp. 30–31; *cf.* Monsignor Mislin, *Die Heiligen Orte: Pilgerreise nach Jerusalem* (Wien: Staatsdruckerei, 1860), p. 331.

markable annual miracle called 'the Descent of the Holy Fire,' an act that dazzled—and later appalled—Christian visitors to the Holy Sepulcher down to the twentieth century."[121] His post–thirteenth–century portrayal of the phenomenon (reaching well into the nineteenth century), therefore, is a somewhat unbalanced and historically limited collection of accounts, reflecting what he apparently considers a less credulous, modern approach to it. The accounts following, including materials from the thirteenth to the twentieth century, are meant to address this historiographical foible—and one not peculiar to Peters—and to show that the same diversity of reactions to the Holy Fire, from credulity to outrage, that we have found in the pre–thirteenth–century witness persists to this day. In fact, this diversity can be observed among a variety of witnesses, equally distributed among both the naïve and the sophisticated. It is only by understanding this diversity that we can objectively understand the phenomenon of the Holy Fire itself.

In the thirteenth century we find, unfortunately, only a very limited number of references to the rite of the Holy Fire, few of them noteworthy. Two of these, however, deserve our attention. The first is the life of Saint Meletios the Confessor, a thirteenth–century monk of the famous Mount Galesion, the Byzantine Mount Athos in Asia Minor, where Saint Lazarus the Stylite (†1054) established a number of monasteries.[122] During his visit to the Holy Land, according to the Saint's life, Saint Meletios

---

[120] See Peters, *Jerusalem.*

[121] *Ibid.,* p. 261.

[122] Though Saint Meletios is called a *"Galesiotes,"* or a monk of Mount Galesion, this is not, as most authorities assume, because he was first a monk at one of the monasteries on Mount Galesion. Archbishop Chrysostomos of Etna has argued that he was, in fact, tonsured a monk on Mount Sinai; see Bishop [Archbishop] Chrysostomos, book review of Saint Meletios the Confessor, *On Prayer* (Mount Athos: Prophet Elias Skete, 1991), in *Orthodox Tradition,* Vol. 9, No. 1 (1992), p. 24. *Cf.* the life of Saint Meletios in Μέγας Συναξαριστὴς τῆς Ὀρθοδόξου Ἐκκλησίας (Athens: 1978), Vol. 1, p. 459, which supports Chrysostomos' contention.

...went to Jerusalem, where he worshipped at the Holy Sepulchre and was found worthy to behold the grace–filled light which in those days continually radiated from the Life–bearing Tomb.[123]

It is interesting to note in this passage a miraculous light associated with the Holy Sepulchre, in this case a "grace–filled" light which continually emanates from it. It is impossible to determine whether the writer of the life is confusing a report by the Saint of seeing the Holy Fire with a continuous emanation of light from the Tomb; at any rate, these anecdotal data may provide us with a unique piece of evidence that miraculous light in the Holy Sepulchre was not, perhaps, at least in the thirteenth century, exclusively associated with the rite of the Holy Fire.

The other thirteenth–century reference of interest to us is a bull issued by Pope Gregory ix on March 9, 1238. In this pronouncement, Gregory explicitly forbids any participation in the rite of the Holy Fire, which he condemns as a fraud.[124] This entry of three lines gives us no description of the ceremony, except to note that the supposed miracle is accomplished by deceitful means. The importance of the bull lies in the fact that it tells us that the rite of the Holy Fire was well enough known in the thirteenth century to attract the attention of Papal authorities. It also represents the first official condemnation of the ceremony by a Latin churchman, perhaps reflecting the fact that Latin influence had waned in Jerusalem by the mid–twelfth century. The Pope's condemnation of the rite also signals in general the end of any sympathetic Western reactions to the Holy Fire.

Fourteenth Century. The fourteenth century witnesses to the rite of the Holy Fire are not numerous, but several of them give us clear details about a general awareness of the phenomenon and the celebration of the rite in that century. In 1322, for example, Sir John Maundeville, an English knight who travelled ex-

---

[123] Saint Meletios the Confessor, *On Prayer*, p. 1.

[124] Augustus Potthast, ed., *Regesta Pontificum Romanorum* (London: Berolini, 1874), Vol. 1, p. 893; *cf.* Lucien Auvray, ed., *Les Registres de Grégoire ix: Recueil des Bulles de ce Pape* (Paris: Librarie des Écoles Françaises d'Athène et de Rome, 1907), Vol. 2, col. 911.

tensively in the Levant and Asia from 1322 to 1356, writes about his visit to Jerusalem. In the midst of a somewhat curious description of the Edicule of the Holy Sepulchre, he notes that "...there is one lamp which hangs before the sepulchre which burns bright; and on Good Friday it goes out of itself, and lights again by itself at the hour that our Lord rose from the dead."[125] Maundeville has added, in his account of the miracle of the Holy Fire, an element which is elsewhere absent: the miraculous extinguishing of the lamp at the Tomb on Great Friday. We can only otherwise conclude that he was not a witness to the ceremony of the Holy Fire, but simply learned of it from secondhand accounts. This suggests that it was an event regularly recounted to Christian pilgrims to the Holy Places.

From the fourteenth century we have a manuscript of the travels of the Franciscan monk, Fra Niccolò da Poggibonsi. He tells in some detail his own story about the Church of the Holy Sepulchre, which he visited in 1347:

> Prior to the sixth hour, of Good Friday, all the generations of Christians...assemble at the holy chapel of the Holy Sepulchre [*i.e.,* the Edicule], and the patriarchs, bishops and friars in surplice with holy cross in hand, all vested according to their mode; each congregation of people and each nation separate; and encircling the holy chapel, they sing aloud, each congregation in its own tongue; and as varied the tongues, so varied the chants; and one sings with his mouth, and another with his hands, that is, makes strange gestures with his hands; and some in one key and some in another; and the procession in like manner; and thus they go round many times; and each people keeps behind its own generation, little and big, male and female, and all crying at the top of their voices: *Kyrie eleison, Christe eleison,* and gazing aloft to the windows above to see the holy fire; and this continues for a space of two hours. The lamps within the Holy Sepulchre are all extinguished, and the Saracens stand before the door and allow no Christian to enter. And, through the above–mentioned window, I saw a dove coming, which alighted upon the chapel of the Holy

---

[125] Wright, *Early Travels,* p. 123.

Sepulchre: and then a great light appeared within the Holy Sepulchre, with a great brilliance, and then he holds himself the happier
who can first get hold of that light...[;] and so everybody takes his
torch, or even candles, so that the church really seems afire from
the great glow, and then each congregation returns to its altar and
attends the service in its own rite.[126]

It is noteworthy that Niccolò says that the ceremony of the Holy
Fire occurred on Great Friday rather than Great Saturday. He also suggests that the faithful, during their processions by sect and
age, expected the Holy Fire to descend from a window above the
Church. In fact, he tells us that he saw a dove descend from this
window just before the manifestation of the Holy Fire. Interestingly enough, we still see in this account no evidence of the Patriarch or a Bishop present in the Tomb itself when the Holy
Fire descends, as a witness a century and a half later reports. Niccolò simply says that a "great" light appeared suddenly in the
Holy Sepulchre and that those present rushed to take from it.

Shortly after mid–century, in 1360, Emperor John VI Kantakouzenos (Cantacuzeni, *ca.* 1295–1383), one of the more erudite
Byzantine rulers, wrote his fourth apologetic treatise on the
Moslem faith. In it, he refers to the miracle of the Holy Fire as
an argument for the truth of the Christian religion. Scholars have
ignored this significant reference to the phenomenon, which
attests to the ceremony's eminence in the Byzantine world.
Addressing himself to the Moslems, the Emperor notes that

> ...in Jerusalem each year during Paschaltide, a miracle occurs in the
> Tomb of Christ. ...At the hour that the Christians are gathered
> there reciting hymns to the Resurrection of Christ, a light from
> Heaven comes down and lights three lamps found in the Tomb of
> Christ.[127]

Rhetorically, the Emperor addresses his Moslem reader: "Did
Christ falsely say that he was God and the Son of God? And is it

---

[126] Fra Niccolò da Poggibonsi, *A Voyage Beyond the Seas,* trans. T. Bellorini and E. Hoade (Jerusalem: Franciscan Press, 1945), pp. 23–24.

[127] Migne, *Patrologia Græca,* Vol. 154, col. 517.

falsely that Christians so believe?" He answers:

> How, then, at the time that we are singing hymns, as we said, to
> Christ God, the Son of God, the Creator of all..., does light come
> down from Heaven and light these aforementioned lamps in the
> tomb of Christ?[128]

Again, while there are few remarkable references to the actual
ceremony of the rite of the Holy Fire in Kantakouzenos' treatise
and while he does not claim to have seen the miracle personally,
he refers to it as though it were something well known in his
time.

In 1375 the Russian pilgrim Archimandrite Arsenius visited
the Holy Places and made the following interesting observations.
The Moslems were then in control of Jerusalem, as they had
been since 1244:

> According to custom, ...the Patriarch celebrates a litia near the
> Holy Sepulchre at noon on Great Saturday for the sake of the
> Holy Fire. The Patriarch came and with him Metropolitan Ger-
> manos from Egypt and Bishop Mark of Damascus...and Abbot
> Stephen from St. Sabbas (Monastery) with all the clergy. They
> went around the Tomb of the Lord twice and after the third cir-
> cling there appeared above the Holy Sepulchre a small cloud of
> smoke. Then they opened the Tomb (the Kuviklion [*sic*]) and the
> Patriarch went in with the Armenian bishop, for the cave was filled
> with holy Light and all the lamps which had been extinguished
> and prepared since Holy Friday were lit. The Patriarch lit candles
> from the Holy Fire and from the Patriarch the entire church and a
> mighty cry arose from the entire church at the appearance of the
> Light. After a short time the candles which everyone keeps as a
> blessing were put out. Then the Patriarch began the Liturgy of
> Great Saturday.[129]

The small rain cloud earlier reported by Abbot Daniel is described here by Father Arsenius as a cloud of smoke. The circumambulation is also noteworthy, since it appears in the more

[128] *Ibid.*
[129] Callistos, "Holy Fire," p. 16.

modern testimony and in the pre–ninth–century testimony. The service "for the sake of the Holy Fire" appears now to stand independent of the Vespers–Liturgy Vigil service as part of what Arsenius mistakes for a *"litia,"* or Lity. He properly assigns the ceremony of the Holy Fire to Great Saturday, unlike one of the earlier fourteenth–century witnesses, who placed it on Great Friday. Finally, we should note that, while the Patriarch once again plays an important part in the ceremony, he is not *inside* the Tomb at the time of the descent of the Holy Fire, as in modern times.

Fifteenth Century. Fifteenth–century accounts of the rite of the Holy Fire are limited to one pilgrim, a certain Paul Walther, an Englishman who visited the Holy Places in the late fifteenth century. The catastrophe that befell the Byzantine Empire in the mid–1400s and the attendant hostilities no doubt in part account for the silence of Orthodox and other Christian pilgrims during this century. While clearly a disbeliever in the "error" of the Holy Fire, Walther nonetheless recorded some important details about the ceremony. What follows is Meinardus' summary of Walther's account:

> In 1481, it was the custom to have the doors of the Church of the ꞌ Resurrection opened by Muslims, and three priests or bishops entered the Sepulchre of Christ. One was from the Greeks, the other from the Armenians and the third one from the Ethiopians, and they were shut up in the Sepulchre for the time during which one could recite the *Placebo,* approximately fifteen to twenty minutes. The next thing, which Walther noticed, was an Armenian bishop coming out of the Holy Sepulchre with a burning light, and after all lights were lit, the 'nations' made their procession three times around the Holy Sepulchre.[130]

We have in Walther's account, most importantly, for the first time an unambiguous description of the celebrants (three, here) closed up inside the Holy Sepulchre to receive the Holy Fire, a practice that has survived in modern times and which is either

---

[130] Meinardus, "Ceremony," p. 247.

unclear or absent in earlier reports. The procession reportedly followed the descent of the Holy Fire, whereas it is more commonly portrayed as preceding the descent in other sources. Though he identifies Greek clergy as being present at the rite, he oddly notes that an Armenian bishop distributed the Holy Fire. He perhaps confused the Greek and Armenian clergy or saw the distribution of the Fire to the Armenians by their own prelate, having missed an initial distribution by the Greek Prelate, to whom such privilege was clearly granted by this time.

Sixteenth Century. At the beginning of the sixteenth century, Fra Francesco Suriano wrote a treatise on the Holy Land. Published in 1524, it contains a description of the rite of the Holy Fire that is apparently taken from the accounts of others and not from Suriano's own experiences. The monk writes that

> ...as I have read in the Ordinary of the Divine Office[,][131]...on Holy Saturday each year about the hour of terce...fire descended visibly from heaven on the holy Sepulchre, and lighted all the lamps including the Easter Candle. I omit the preparation which was made by the person deputed for the service of the said divine fire, and the crying and weeping of the people, when this gift was granted by God to them. I waive the tears shed from compunction and consolation. Likewise I omit the shouts to heaven, the laments and the groans which resulted when, as customary, it delays in descending, and the people consider themselves as unworthy of so great a grace. At present the Christians of that country still hold in practice to that style and usage of old. And they assemble from Egypt, Syria, Pamphylia, Mesopotamia, Cappadocia, Greece, Armenia, and the Lebanon, men and women, for the said solemnity and feast of Holy Saturday, which they call Id el Nar, the feast of ˅ Fire. The said fire, however, does not descend in truth (and in the opinion of us Friars), although all the nations, save us Friars, feign this falsehood to be true. I think that the privation of such a grace

---

[131] A footnote in the translation of the manuscript points out that "...in the Breviary of Barletta mention is made of the holy fire and of the accompanying service"; see Fra Francesco Suriano, *Treatise on the Holy Land,* trans. Fr. Theophilus Hoade and Fr. Bellarmino Bagatti (Jerusalem: Franciscan Press, 1949), p. 47, n. 3.

is due to the sins and heresy of these nations.[132]

Suriano's report demonstrates that Latin clergy were still aware of the rite of the Holy Fire in his day, though his mention of an "Easter Candle" shows his unfamiliarity with the details of the ceremony (unless, of course, he is suggesting that the Latins lit their Paschal candle—a rite which we will discuss in Chapter 11 —from the Holy Fire). His comments seem to suggest that the Eastern Christians ("these nations"), deprived of grace because of "sins" and "heresy," believed, at his time, in a false miracle that in earlier times was indeed a true miracle.[133]

At the end of the sixteenth century we have quite a different kind of report about the ceremony of the Holy Fire from an Orthodox source. A reportedly miraculous event occurred that would prove to be the impetus for a new element in the rite: a triumphant and noisy, albeit somewhat chaotic, commemorative procession by the local (primarily Arabic) Orthodox Christians. Here is a description of the event, widely reported but here succinctly summarized by Archimandrite Callistos:[134]

> In 1580, during the time of the Patriarch of Jerusalem Sophronius, the following most glorious miracle occurred on Great Saturday.

---

[132] *Ibid.*, p. 48.

[133] If Suriano believed that the rite of the Holy Fire was once a true miracle, but that it had degenerated into trickery in the hands of Eastern Christians, his opinion is consistent with the assessment of the phenomenon which Meinardus attributes to the post–thirteenth–century Latin West: "It is generally held that following the Muslim occupation of Jerusalem in 1244, the Latin Church abstained from participating in the Ceremony. The conclusions at which the Catholic Church arrives are that the Holy Fire was a miracle indeed so long as the Catholic Church had control of the Ceremony, but since it fell into the hands of the schismatic Orthodox, it has been nothing but a barefaced trick and imposture. Thus, according to Catholic theory, the work of God degenerated into the sacrilegious work of imposters" (Meinardus, "Ceremony," p. 256).

[134] Callistos bases his summary partly on comments on this incident by the seventeenth–century Archbishop of Nazareth, Gabriel, which comments are worthy of note ("Holy Fire," p. 18).

The Holy Fire came out of a split (stone) column, which is visible even now next to the doors of the church, for the following reason. The Armenians at that time were ill–disposed towards the Orthodox. They promised to give the governor of Jerusalem a sufficient sum of money so that he would interfere and prevent the Orthodox Patriarch from entering the Church of the Resurrection on Holy and Great Saturday. The governor, out of greed, obeyed and ordered that it be so. Thus only the Armenians, with great glee, entered the church hoping to receive the Holy Fire, while the Orthodox stood with the Patriarch outside in the courtyard and in their sorrow prayed to God with contrite hearts that He might manifest the mercy of His compassion. During their prayer the above–mentioned column split and the Holy Fire came out from it.[135] Seeing this, the Patriarch quickly went up and with reverence lit the candles which were in his hand and distributed the fire to the Orthodox for their sanctification. When they saw the miracle the Mohammedan gate–keepers immediately opened the gates of the church. The Patriarch and the vast multitude with him entered the church singing: 'What God is as great as our God...' and the Liturgy was celebrated. As a consequence of this miracle, one of these gate–keepers of the church loudly confessed Christ to be the Son of God and believed in Him. But his (former) co–believers, when they heard this, waxed wroth and burned him in the sacred courtyard;[136] in this manner he received a martyr's death.[137]

To this day the local Arab Orthodox Christians commemorate this event with a tumultuous procession, proclaiming the victory of their religion over those who would have stolen the Holy Fire from its rightful custodians. This folk element of the rite of the Holy Fire has come to dwarf the more stately liturgical processions around the Edicule that have been associated with the ceremony since the earliest reports. We shall see this fact confirmed

---

[135] This fractured column can still be seen at the *Anastasis* to this day; see a photograph of the fissure in Tsekoura, *Tὸ Ἅγιον Φῶς*, p. 92.

[136] Tsekoura asserts that the relics of this Martyr are to be found today in the Megale Panaghia Convent in Jerusalem (*ibid.*, p. 93).

[137] Callistos, "Holy Fire," p. 17; see also the fascinating account of this event in Tsekoura, *Tὸ Ἅγιον Φῶς*, pp. 91–93.

in a number of subsequent accounts, which concentrate more on the raucous behavior of some of the believers attending the rite than on the liturgical elements of the ceremony.

Seventeenth Century. The first significant seventeenth–century source for our study of the Holy Fire is a codex of the Patriarchate of Jerusalem, "Account of a Miracle Concerning the Holy Fire," dated A.M. 7142 (A.D. 1634)[138] and studied by A. Papadopoulos–Kerameus.[139] This document tells of events which occurred in that year "between the Romans [*i.e.*, the Greeks] and Armenians in Jerusalem." According to the codex, the Greeks had calculated Pascha according to the Eastern formula, while the Armenians calculated that the feast would fall eight days later. At first, the Copts in Jerusalem followed the Greek calculation. But the Armenian prelate, a certain Karkour (Καρκούρ), threatened the Copts with punishment if they did not follow the Armenian formula, which the Copts, "poor and few in number," out of fear agreed to do. Thus, after the Greeks had begun the Great Fast, the Copts, "both monks and lay people," ate lamb together with the Armenians.[140] "This," the narrative continues,

> ...was the start of the scandalous things which Karkour did. The second week, then, they fasted with all the other peoples; later, he [Karkour] came to our monastery and said: 'Celebrate your Pascha according to your custom, and your services; and we will celebrate ours the next week; do your services and receive the Holy Fire, and He who gives you that gift perhaps will give it to us also.' However, his words to the Greeks [literally, "Ρωμαίους'] (who thought that he was speaking the truth and who believed his words without suspicion) were not at all [true] but completely deceitful and false.[141]

---

[138] According to the Byzantine reckoning, the year A.D. 1992 is the year A.M. 7500, or the seven thousand five–hundredth year of the world from the time of Creation; hence, A.M. 7142 = A.D. 1634.

[139] See his study of the document and the Greek text in A. Papadopoulos–Kerameus, "Διήγησις Θαύματος περὶ τοῦ Ἁγίου Φωτός," *Pravoslavnii Palestinskii Sbornik* (St. Petersburg), Vol. 38 (1894), pp. 13–17.

[140] *Ibid.*, pp. 13–14.

The Greeks celebrated the week of Palm Sunday, the narrative says, alone in the Holy Sepulchre, since the Armenian prelate had forbidden his people to participate, it being only the fifth week of Lent for them. On Great Friday, they opened the Church of the Holy Sepulchre and celebrated the usual service of Christ's Burial ("τοῦ ἐπιταφίου"). In the meantime, however, Karkour had paid the local Moslem authorities to prevent the Greeks from entering the Holy Sepulchre on Great Saturday. Guards were placed on and around the Edicule, some of them eating and "drinking wine." However, at the ninth hour, the earth began to shake and three loud bangs came from within the Holy Sepulchre. Then, like a flash of lightning, the Holy Fire appeared to all, and "...the Orthodox faithful began to cry out 'Lord have mercy.'" Again the earth shook, and many of the guards "fell on their faces from fear." Amidst great turmoil, all said: "The Faith of the Christians is true." Karkour, seeing all of this, then told the soldiers to prevent the people from lighting their candles.[142]

Archimandrite Callistos cites from the Russian literature a letter from Patriarch Theophanes of Jerusalem (1608–1645) to the Russian Tsar Michael Romanov (1596–1645) which repeats very much the same narrative as the codex which we have cited. However, he states that the Patriarch is relating events from the year 1643. The similarity of the passages in every detail and a clear reference in the codex to Patriarch Theophanes[143] leads us to the conclusion that the dating in the Russian text is incorrect (1634 was accidentally transcribed as 1643, perhaps). The Patriarch ends his account with an accusation that, when the Holy Fire appeared from the closed and guarded Tomb, "...the Armenians, in order to hide their shame gave out money to the infidels to keep silent about this manifestation."[144]

---

[141] *Ibid.,* p. 14.

[142] *Ibid.,* pp. 15–16.

[143] *Ibid.,* p. 15: "...τοῦ μακαριωτάτου πατριάρχου Ἱεροσολύμων κυρίου Θεοφάνους."

[144] Callistos, "Holy Fire," p. 17.

Callistos cites a further passage from the seventeenth century which, while brief, contains a fascinating description of the Holy Fire. The author is Archbishop Gabriel of Nazareth, who had gone to Russia to collect funds for his work in the Holy Land. The work from which the description is taken, *A Guide to the Holy and God–visited Places in the Holy City,* was published in Moscow in 1650 and became a popular source for pious reading among the Russian Faithful:

> On Great Saturday the Turks come early and put out all the lamps in the church and, locking the doors of the Holy Sepulchre, they seal it and, sitting at the doors, keep guard. The faithful pray to the Lord with tears, calling for help from on high. At the ninth hour of the day the Patriarch vests with all the clergy, and they celebrate a litany three times around the Holy Sepulchre. At that moment the Turks open the doors of the Kuvuklion and the Patriarch goes in and receives the Fire from the Tomb like flames of dew and gives it out to the faithful. Then the Liturgy of St. Basil the Great is celebrated.[145]

The descriptive image, "flames of dew," brings together once again elements of fire and water (recall the cloud and rain in Abbot Daniel's foregoing account), and will be echoed in subsequent testimony.

Another seventeenth–century source is cited by Kyriakos Simopoulos in his accounts of foreign travellers to Greece from 333 to 1700, in this case an account by a French traveller to the Greeks of Jerusalem.[146] In 1651[147] the French cleric J. Doubdan visited Jerusalem, witnessed the ceremony of the Holy Fire, and wrote about it in an extensive journal of his travels in the Holy Land.[148] As Simopoulos notes, Doubdan did not believe in the

---

[145] *Ibid.,* p. 18.

[146] Kyriakos Simopoulos, Ξένοι Ταξιδιώτες στὴν Ἑλλάδα· 333 μ.χ.–1700 (Athens: 1981), Vol. I.

[147] Simopoulos' text mistakenly sets the year at 1561 (*ibid.,* p. 549).

[148] J. Doubdan, *Voyage de la Terre Sainte, contenant une véritable description des Lieux plus considérables que notre Seigneur a sanctifié de sa présence* (Paris:

miracle, which he felt had ceased to be genuine after Latin participation in it came to an end, following the Crusades. Nonetheless, he gives us a useful picture of the ceremony. Arriving at the Church of the Sepulchre on "the afternoon of Great Saturday, 27 April 1651,"[149] Doubdan joined what he describes as thousands of other worshippers for the ceremony. Waiting for the Patriarch, the Arabic believers among the crowd engaged in the same raucous behavior to which we have earlier referred. Some three hours later, the Patriarch arrived in the Church:

> Afterwards, twenty–five or thirty archbishops, metropolitans, and priests dressed in rich chasubles of the Greek type and holding in one hand a small Cross and, in the other, a bundle of candles tied with multi–colored silk cords. Walking among them were many lay people carrying candles. There followed four deacons, walking backwards, continually censing the patriarch.... The patriarch was vested in gold–embroidered vestments with a silver–looking chasuble and had a gold mitre on his head. In his left hand he was holding a small Cross and in his right hand a staff. He was accompanied by two or three Bishops, also in rich vestments....
>
> Finally, the patriarch and only five of the metropolitans approached the Holy Sepulchre, where they removed their chasubles to enter. At that moment pandemonium arose anew. There were such thunderous echoes that one could not hear the strongest thunderbolt. Thousands of mouths crying out crazily and bellowing 'Mercy!' 'Mercy!'
>
> ...Amidst this clamour, the patriarch entered the Holy Sepulchre. The militia strictly guarded the entrance, so that no one would see what was happening inside. Therein, with a flint, the patriarch lighted the lamps and a bundle of candles which he was holding in his hand.
>
> ...Seeing...[the Patriarch]...come out with the much beloved light, the crowd shouted with happy voices, with cries of joy, ...and the people flung themselves on him, in order to light their candles from his.[150]

1666).

[149] Simopoulos, Ξένοι Ταξιδιώτες, p. 549.

[150] *Ibid.*, pp. 551–552.

While this account gives us few details about the rite of the Holy Fire itself and accuses the Patriarch of deception, it does give an overall impression of the service as it is celebrated even to this day. We see the procession of the clergy, the cries of "Lord, have mercy" (or, as reported by Doubdan, "Mercy!"), the entry into the Holy *Kouvouklion,* the Patriarch present *in* the Tomb when the Holy Fire descends, and the distribution of the light to the Faithful.

Arsenius Sukhanov, a Russian Orthodox pilgrim in the Holy Land, provides us with a useful description of the rite of the Holy Fire during his visit to Jerusalem in 1652:

> On the evening of Great Saturday the Patriarch and his suite enter the Church (of the Resurrection) and there he rests in his cell. Soon two Moslems (the door–keepers of the Church) appear and, when he has rested some, they proceed to the Holy Sepulchre with the Greek monks and extinguish all the lamps in it; when then they go out, they seal it. A litany is celebrated around the Kuvuklion: the Orthodox go first and after them the Armenians, followed by the Copts, Ethiopians, and Nestorians. After the third circling, Patriarch Paisius,[151] standing opposite the doors of the Holy Sepulchre, divested himself of his sakkos [the primary vestment of an Orthodox Bishop, much like a tailored chasuble and worn under the *omophorion* (a stole similar to the Latin *pallium*)[152]] and mitre, as did the Armenian Patriarch who came up and remained near our Patriarch who was standing by the closed doors of the Kuvuklion. A Turk came and unsealed the doors. Patriarch Paisius, after taking two bunches of candles[153] and opening the doors, went inside and again closed the doors, not daring

---

[151] Patriarch of Jerusalem from 1645 to 1661.

[152] For a description of Eastern Episcopal liturgical attire, see Archimandrite [Archbishop] Chrysostomos, *Orthodox Liturgical Dress* (Brookline, MA: Holy Cross Orthodox Press, 1981), pp. 45–51, 61–64.

[153] About these bunches of candles or torches we have read a great deal. In modern times, in which we have the only reliable data on the matter, these consist of thirty–three small candles tied together, representing the years of the earthly life of Christ.

to allow the Armenian Patriarch in. Paisius remained locked in the Tomb a quarter of an hour and then, opening the doors, came out holding in each hand a bunch of lighted candles. Patriarch Paisius stood on a raised place where the holy table [Altar] of the Serbs is under the so–called great chamber, opposite the Holy Kuvuklion, and here all the people lit their candles from his. And when all were lit the Patriarch left this place and went into the catholicon ⸱ [main Church], vested in his sakkos and mitre, and celebrated the Liturgy of St. Basil.[154]

Sukhanov's account is noteworthy, since he identifies many of the elements of the rite of the Holy Fire as we see them in modern times. He describes a procession around the *Kouvouklion,* the unsealing of the Tomb, and the Patriarch's enclosure therein. Although four decades later, in the next account from the seventeenth century, we see the Greek and Armenian Patriarchs sealed in the Tomb together, this is absent from Sukhanov's account.

Peters cites, in his treatment of the Holy Fire, a late seventeenth–century account of the phenomenon by the English chaplain Henry Maundrell, who visited Jerusalem in 1696.[155] Maundrell was, according to Peters, a prime example of the "new learning" exemplified by the recently founded (1660) Royal Society:

He [Maundrell] saw his own time as one in which men, 'having removed the rubbish of ages' and liberated themselves from 'the charms of vain apparitions,' could by investigation and experiment finally reach the truth, since now 'every man is unshaken at those tales at which his ancestors trembled: the course of things goes quickly along, in its own true channel of causes and effects.'[156]

---

[154] Cited by Callistos, "Holy Fire," p. 16.

[155] Colin Thubron assigns Maundrell's visit to the year 1697 and characterizes his comments about the service of the Holy Fire as "caustic." Nonetheless, Thubron himself associates the rite "even in recent times" with what he considers scenes of "pagan frenzy"; see Colin Thubron and the editors of Time–Life Books, *The Great Cities: Jerusalem* (Amsterdam: Time–Life Books, 1976), p. 100.

[156] Peters, *Jerusalem,* p. 516.

Maundrell's remarks on the Holy Fire are not unlike many of those which we find in Orthodox and non–Orthodox sources from the Enlightenment through the nineteenth and twentieth centuries. He describes the ceremony by pointing out that the worshippers

> ...began their disorders by running round the Holy Sepulcher with all their might and swiftness, crying out as they went *Huia!* which[a] signifies [in Arabic] 'This is he' or 'This is it,' an expression by which they assert the verity of the Christian religion. After they had by these vertiginous circulations and clamors turned their heads and inflamed their madness, they began to act the most antic tricks and postures, in a thousand shapes of distraction. Sometimes they dragged one another along the floor all round the sepulcher; sometimes they set one man upright on another's shoulders and in this posture marched round; sometimes they took men with their heels upward and hurried them about in such an indecent manner as to expose their nudities; sometimes they tumbled about the sepulcher after the manner of tumblers on the stage.
>
> In this tumultuous frantic humor they continued from twelve to four of the clock. The reason for this delay was because of a suit that was in debate before the [Moslem] chief justice between the Greeks and the Armenians; the former endeavoring to exclude the latter from having any part in this miracle. Both parties having expended, as I was informed, 5,000 dollars between them in this foolish controversy, the judge at last gave sentence that they should enter the Holy Sepulcher together, as had been usual at former times. Sentence being thus given, at four of the clock both nations went on with their ceremony. The Greeks first set out, in a procession round the holy sepulchre, and immediately at their heels followed the Armenians. In this order they compassed the holy sepulchre thrice.... Towards the end of the procession a pigeon came fluttering into the cupola over the sepulcher, at sight of which there was a greater shout and clamor than before. This bird, the Latins told us, was purposely let fly by the Greeks to deceive the people into an opinion that it was a visible descent of the Holy Ghost.

The procession being over, the suffragan of the Greek patriarch (he being himself at Constantinople), and the principal Armenian bishop, approached to the door of the sepulchre, and, cutting the string with which it is fastened and sealed, entered in, shutting the door after them....

The Greek and Armenian Patriarchs having entered the Tomb, where all the lamps had been extinguished, the doors were sealed behind them by the Turks:

The two miracle mongers had not been alone a minute in the Holy Sepulcher when the glimmering of the Holy Fire was seen, or imagined to appear, through some chinks of the door. And certainly Bedlam itself never saw such an unruly transport as was produced in the mob at this sight. Immediately after out came the two priests with blazing torches in their hands, which they held up at the door of the sepulcher, while the people thronged about with inexpressible ardor, everyone striving to obtain a part of the first and purest flame. The Turks in the meantime with huge clubs laid them on without mercy. But all this could not repel them, the excess of their transport making them insensible of pain. Those that got the fire applied it immediately to their beards, faces and bosoms, pretending that it would not burn like an earthly flame. But I plainly saw none of them could endure this experiment long enough to make good that pretension. So many hands being employed, you may be sure it could not be long before innumerable tapers were lighted. The whole church, galleries and every place seemed instantly to be in a flame. And with this illumination the ceremony ended....

It must be owned that those two within the sepulcher performed their part with great quickness and dexterity; but the behavior of the rabble without very much discredited the miracle. The Latins take a great deal of pains to expose this ceremony as a most shameful imposture and a scandal to the Christian religion; perhaps out of envy that others should be masters of so gainful a business. But the Greeks and Armenians pin their faith upon it and make their pilgrimages chiefly upon this motive. And it is the deplorable unhappiness of their priests that having acted the cheat so long already, they are forced now to stand to it for fear of endangering the apostasy of their people.[157]

In this account, the Greek and Armenian Patriarchs are both enclosed in the Holy Sepulchre for the reception of the Holy Fire. This is consistent with the modern ceremony, in which a representative of the Armenian clergy is closed into the Holy *Kouvouklion* with the Greek Patriarch. We also read detailed claims regarding the unearthly nature of the flame and its un-consuming properties: that its application to the face, beard, chest, *etc.* has no ill effect. And in the comments about the re-lease of a pigeon, the author provides us with a possible explana-tion of Abbot Daniel's assertion, in an earlier description, that many believed the Great Saturday miracle to involve the descent of the Holy Spirit in the form of a dove.[158]

Eighteenth Century. The very sparse references to the Holy Fire from the eighteenth century well testify to the increasingly negative Western assessment of the phenomenon. Thus Elzear Horn (1690?–1744), a Franciscan cleric and resident of the Holy Land from 1724 to 1744, in describing the Edicule of the Tomb, notes that its door was constantly open, except for the "…quarter of an hour, while the Greeks and Armenians produce their su-perstitious fire."[159] In 1784, another eighteenth–century skeptic, the French historian Constantine Volnez, visited Jerusalem in the course of his research program in the Near East. He remarks on the great numbers of pilgrims to Jerusalem from Orthodox lands and the sharp decline in Western Christian pilgrims. Of the Orthodox pilgrims whom he saw, he has the following to say. Though his words also reflect a profound misunderstanding of

---

[157] Maundrell's text is found in Wright, *Early Travels,* p. 462ff.

[158] We should note here that the practice of releasing a dove is not nec-essarily an artifice meant to deceive the Faithful. Even today in the Orthodox Church, especially during the service of the Great Blessing of the Waters on Theophany, when rivers, lakes, and oceans are blessed in an elaborate celebra-tion, it is customary to release doves or pigeons as a *symbol* of the descent of the Holy Spirit.

[159] Fr. Elzear[ius] Horn, o.f.m., *Ichonographiæ Monumentorum Terræ Sanctæ (1724–1744),* trans. Fr. E. Hoade, o.f.m. (Jerusalem: Franciscan Press, 1962), p. 42.

Eastern Christian theology and customs, in which there has never been a theology of merits and indulgences, they are typical of the trend which we have mentioned towards a disavowal by Westerners of the ceremony of the Holy Fire as little more than open deceit:

> Faithful to the spirit of the past, they continue to regard a journey to Jerusalem as an act of the greatest merit. They are even scandalized at the Frankish falling–off in this regard and they say that they have all become heretics or infidels. Their priests and monks, who find this fervor useful, never leave off encouraging it. The Greeks in particular stress that pilgrimage merits plenary indulgences, and not only for the past; they are also applicable for the future; and that it brings absolution not only from murder, incest, and pederasty but even from the violation of a fast or a holy day, which they regard as far more serious cases.[160]

Volnez's cursory remarks on the Holy Fire follow suit. "The Easterners still believe in this miracle, although the Franks have recognized that it is the priests, concealed in the sacristy, who bring it about by the most natural of means."[161] Here again, though without details, we have a clear indication that the clergy are enclosed in the Tomb at the time of the reception of the Holy Fire.

We must make mention, at this point, of the assessments of the Holy Fire by post–Byzantine Greek sources, which first appear in the eighteenth century. Despite the positive portrayal of the rite of the Holy Fire by Russian Orthodox pilgrims and commentators and the great popularity of the ceremony among Orthodox Greek believers to this day, post–Byzantine Greek thinkers viewed the phenomenon with suspicion and, at times, outright disgust. The legacy of this post–Byzantine attitude is a general disdain for the rite among many contemporary Greek intellectuals. Representative of this legacy are the comments of a contemporary Greek scholar, Kyriakos Simopoulos. He contends that in 1118 the Islamic rulers of the Holy Land granted ecclesias-

---

[160] Peters, *Jerusalem,* p. 552.

[161] *Ibid.,* p. 553.

tical primacy to the Orthodox, and

> ...the Eastern Church inherited from the Franks the lucrative rite [of the Holy Fire] and exploited in like manner the simple goodness, the ignorance, the naïveté, and the piety of the Orthodox to such an extent that, with the passing of the years, the 'miracle of the Holy Fire' has been transformed into a religious hoax.[162]

This "hoax," he further remarks,

> ...the well known ceremony of the 'false miracle' of Divine Light from Heaven on the afternoon of Great Saturday at the *Kouvouklio[n]* of the Holy Sepulchre has for centuries constituted a folk celebration in the Church of the Resurrection and the occasion for harsh polemics by Latin travellers against the Eastern Church and the Greeks of Jerusalem.[163]

Simopoulos' claims are the very ones made by a number of eighteenth–century Greek sources.

In 1775, the celebrated Greek theological thinker Nikephoros Theotokis (1731–1805) wrote a letter to the nobleman Michael of Larissa, who had asked him about the Holy Fire. In his reply, Theotokis writes that the Holy Fire "...comes neither from Heaven nor does it gush forth from the Tomb," but the Hierarch celebrating the service takes it from a lamp left burning in the Holy Sepulchre and distributes it to the people.[164] Theotokis, we should note, while facile in the scientific knowledge of his age and educated in Italy and Germany, was not, of course, a religious skeptic taken by the spirit of science. In fact, as Professor Constantine Cavarnos notes, he sought "...at every opportunity to show the inadequacy not only of science, but also of 'external philosophy,' and the absolute need of religious faith."[165] None-

---

[162] Simopoulos, Ξένοι Ταξιδιῶτες, pp. 548–549.

[163] *Ibid.*, p. 548.

[164] See the Greek text of this letter in K. Dyobouniotes, "Περὶ τοῦ ἐν Ἱεροσολύμοις ἁγίου φωτός," in Ἐπετηρὶς Ἑταιρείας Βυζαντινῶν Σπουδῶν (Athens: 1936), p. 5.

[165] Constantine Cavarnos, *Modern Greek Thought* (Belmont, MA: Insti-

theless, his assessment of the rite of the Holy Fire rests not on personal experience, but conforms to the prevailing attitude of his age of scientific realism and skepticism.

There is no better representative of post–Byzantine scholars of the Enlightenment than Adamantios Koraes (1748–1833), a classical philologist and theological writer.[166] Though Koraes, like Theotokis, was also an outspoken opponent of the religious skepticism of his time, nonetheless he believed that religion must be seen through the "prism" of the scientific discoveries of his age.[167] The miracle of the Holy Fire, therefore, was an effrontery to his systematic approach to religious phenomena. In a long tract on the Holy Fire, actually an animated dialogue,[168] he argues against the rite on the basis of his understanding of religious phenomenology and the silence of Scripture and Patristic reference with regard to a miraculous occurrence of this kind in the Tomb of Christ. In a telling display of his wide knowledge of Scripture and the Greek Fathers, he cites allusion after allusion to the Holy Sepulchre and the Resurrection to establish the foundation of his rejection of the "πραγματικότης," or "actuality," of the Holy Fire. He also contends that the rite "probably" originated with the Latin clergy of Jerusalem at the beginning of the ninth century as a ruse to increase the decreasing numbers of pilgrims going to the Holy Land. And the monk Bernard, "a *Western* monk," he further claims, was the first witness to use "the appellation 'Holy Fire.'"[169]

The scholarship of the Greeks under Turkish rule presents a

---

tute for Byzantine and Modern Greek Studies, 1986), p. 40.

[166] See a sketch of Koraes' scholarly works in Constantine Cavarnos, *The Hellenic–Christian Philosophical Tradition* (Belmont, MA: Institute for Byzantine and Modern Greek Studies, 1989), pp. 58–59.

[167] A. Martinos, ed., Θρησκευτική καὶ Ἠθικὴ Ἐγκυκλοπαιδεία (Athens: 1968), *s.v.* "Κοραῆς, Ἀδαμάντιος," by A. K. Papaderos, col. 821.

[168] This dialogue was published in 1836, three years after Koraes' death, under the title "Διάλογος περὶ τοῦ ἐν Ἱεροσολύμοις ἁγίου φωτός [A Dialogue on the Holy Fire in Jerusalem]" in Ἄτακτα, Vol. 3, No. 3, pp. 329–381.

[169] *Ibid.*, p. 377.

number of general problems beyond those peculiar to scholars of the Enlightenment. First, the post–Byzantine *intelligentsia* often tended to be consciously anti–Latin.[170] Bishop Kallistos of Diokleia has argued that at least some of the intellectual and theological positions taken by these writers are the consequence of deliberate efforts to distance themselves from anything which is "Latin," thus leading to a certain confusion in their positions.[171] While I have pointed out that Kallistos' assertion is one that he often applies unfairly and too generally,[172] we *can* see in Koraes, at least with regard to his suspicion of the Holy Fire on the basis of its supposed "Latin" origins, an unfounded polemical attitude towards the Latin Church—and the pre–Schism Latin Church at that. It is also true, as Kallistos observes, that the post–Byzantine Greeks suffered under political isolation, religious persecution, and Western influence. As a result, despite their general sympathy towards issues theological, they were perhaps subconsciously eager to dispel as ludicrous anything that might place them outside the current of Western thought or invite ridicule—a common phenomenon among captive peoples or minorities;[173] thus the strong rhetoric of Koraes in reaction to the rite of the Holy

---

[170] The exceptions to this rule are actually fewer than one might think. One such exception, the fifteenth–century humanist Georges de Trébizonde, was, among the Greeks, a virtual pariah in his and subsequent times because of his Latin sympathies and his curious desire for the establishment of a Christian hegemony under his Moslem captors. One of the few contemporary books on this Byzantine renegade is John Monfasani, *George of Trebizond: A Biography and a Study of his Rhetoric and Logic* (Leiden: 1976).

[171] Timothy [Bishop Kallistos] Ware, *Eustratios Argenti: A Study of the Greek Church Under Turkish Rule* (Oxford: Clarendon Press, 1964), p. 140.

[172] Bishop Auxentios, "Latin Purgatory and the Orthodox View of the Soul after Death and Prayers for the Dead," paper presented at the Second International Symposium on Orthodoxy and Islam, 6–8 May 1992, University of Athens, Greece, p. 7.

[173] Archbishop Chrysostomos of Etna and Archimandrite Akakios have discussed this phenomenon among Orthodox Christians in "The Old Calendarists: A Social Psychological Profile of a Greek Orthodox Minority," *Pastoral Psychology,* Vol. 40, No. 2 (1991), pp. 83–91.

Fire: "The place of Christ [has become] the place of Satan."[174]

In view of what we have said about the eighteenth–century
Greeks and the Holy Fire, we must point out that there is little
evidence to support Koraes' contention and that of the contemporary Greek scholars who follow his thought that the rite of the
Holy Fire is of Latin origin. As we noted above, Papadopoulos
argues that the phenomenon has always been associated with the
Greeks.[175] Indeed, the services in the Holy Sepulchre and in the
Church of the Resurrection, as many Greek scholars have convincingly argued in response to the assertions of some Western
authorities,[176] were primarily under the control of the Greeks
even under the Latin Kingdom established by the Crusades.[177]
Moreover, it is not certain that in the account of the monk Bernard we first find the appellation "Holy Fire" applied to the
flame in the lighting ceremony in the Holy Sepulchre; we have
also an early Jerusalem *typikon* (*HS 43*), copied in the twelfth
century but describing Jerusalem practices in the ninth century
and probably earlier, where the term is also used.[178]

Furthermore, Scripture and the Patristic witness are not necessarily wholly silent about the phenomenon of the Holy Fire, if,
as some theological writers do, we find in it parallels to certain
Biblical and Patristic images of the Divine (fire, clouds, light,
dew, *etc.*)—a matter which we will discuss in Chapter IV. A case

---

[174] Koraes, "Διάλογος," p. 369.

[175] Papadopoulos, Ἱστορία, p. 390.

[176] See, for example, Bertonière, who says, on the basis of the twelfth–
century account of the Holy Fire by the Abbot Daniel, that the services of the
Latins "clearly occupy the place of honor" in the Latin Kingdom (*Paschal Vigil*,
pp. 19–20). Bertonière's reading of the text is speculative at best, since the Abbot only describes the eminent rôle given to the Latin dignitaries in attendance,
not a similar liturgical rôle; see Callistos, "Holy Fire," p. 15. In fact, Hamilton
says that "...in the kingdom of Jerusalem in the twelfth century the Orthodox
enjoyed a privileged position" (*Latin Church*, p. 169).

[177] See Papadopoulos, Ἱστορία, pp. 388–389, and Zizioulas, "Ἱερουσαλήμ," col. 836.

[178] See the text of *HS 43*, with this appellation, in Callistos, "Holy Fire,"
p. 9.

for the total silence of these two sources of Tradition can be argued only if one ignores the exegetical science, a leap inconsistent with Christian theology both Eastern and Western. And finally, setting aside exegesis, while it is true that the pre–ninth–century historical witness establishes but the most tenuous links between the the lamp–lighting ceremonies of the Church of Jerusalem and later accounts of the ceremony of the Holy Fire, it is perfectly possible that the ceremony as it developed after the ninth century and later constitutes something distinctly new and different—whether of miraculous character or not—from the former rites. Therefore, if we set aside their anti–Latin bias, the silence of the pre–ninth–century historical witness does not justify the post–Byzantine polemicists in their argument against the integrity of the ceremony of the Holy Fire on the grounds that it is not found in antiquity. It is not an argument of Orthodox theology that authenticity derives only from age or that Tradition precludes new manifestations of the Divine.[179]

There are, we should point out, two noteworthy exceptions to the negative assessments of the rite of the Holy Fire in the eighteenth–century post–Byzantine witness. At the very beginning of the century, in 1727, Patriarch Paisios of Constantinople, apparently in reaction to negative accounts of the Holy Fire, threatened with excommunication anyone who impeded the Faithful from making pilgrimages to the Holy Sepulchre by implanting in them "satanic and destructive impiety or disbelief and malevolence."[180] The Athonite monk Neophytos Kafsoka-

---

[179] Thus Father Florovsky has said that: "'Tradition' in the Church is not a continuity of human memory, or a permanence of rites and habits. ...Ultimately, tradition is a continuity of the abiding presence of the Holy Spirit in the Church, a continuity of Divine Guidance and illumination. The Church is not bound by the 'letter.' Rather, she is constantly *moved forth* by the 'Spirit' [emphasis ours]" ([Protopresbyter] Georges Florovsky, *Bible, Church, Tradition: An Eastern Orthodox View* [Belmont, MA: Nordland Publishing Co., 1972], p. 106).

[180] See excerpts from his statement in Simopoulos, Ξένοι Ταξιδιῶτες, p. 557.

lybites, who died in 1784, also wrote a treatise on the Holy Fire in which he treats the phenomenon in an objective way.[181] Neophytos was one of the so–called *Kollyvades,* a group of exceptionally well–educated monks on Mount Athos who supported the practice of frequent communion, spurned the commemoration of the dead on Sundays (hence, *"Kollyvades,"* from the wheat which is blessed in commemoration of the departed), and helped revive interest in the mystical traditions of the Eastern Orthodox Church.[182] He examines the witness of Scripture, that of the Church Fathers, and the rite itself in an objective manner, beginning with a clear statement that he had heard from reliable sources both that the Holy Fire was produced by mechanical means and that it was not.[183] Neophytos was thus obviously aware of the arguments against the Holy Fire, as Dyobouniotes also observes in his introduction to the treatise,[184] and these arguments undoubtedly form the framework for his description of the ceremony and the arguments both for and against the actuality of the Holy Fire. His comments are often quoted out of context by those either arguing for or against the integrity of the rite, but on the whole his witness is important because it represents a fundamentally neutral counterbalance to the polemical writings against the Holy Fire by the majority of eighteenth–century and subsequent post–Byzantine Greek intellectuals.

Nineteenth Century. One of the first nineteenth–century Western observers to comment on the Holy Fire was Ulrich

---

[181] Neophytos Kafsokalybites, "Περὶ ἐπιταφίου φωτός," Codex 1457, University of Athens, Greece. This Codex has been edited and studied by K. Dyobouniotes in his "Περὶ τοῦ ἐν Ἱεροσολύμοις ἁγίου φωτός," in Ἐπετηρὶς Ἑταιρείας Βυζαντινῶν Σπουδῶν (Athens: 1936); the edited Greek text is found on pp. 6–18.

[182] The controversy provoked by their movement was an issue of great concern in the last three decades of the eighteenth century and continued into the first two decades of the nineteenth century; see Constantine Cavarnos, *St. Macarios of Corinth,* Vol. 2 of *Modern Orthodox Saints* (Belmont, MA: Institute for Byzantine and Modern Greek Studies, 1972), pp. 19–24.

[183] Dyobouniotes, "Περὶ τοῦ ἁγίου φωτός," p. 6.

[184] *Ibid.*

Seetzen, who visited the Holy Land in 1806, two years before a fire that devastated the Church of the Resurrection. His general comments about Jerusalem reflect the spirit of his day and perhaps his own commitment to the Protestant work ethic. Of Jerusalem in general he says:

> Judging from the number of ecclesiastical buildings, one would expect to encounter many truly pious people. What I found is exactly the opposite. All the Christian inhabitants have their children educated in the convents, but all they learn is the repetition of empty prayers where both soul and heart are neglected. Failing to go to church and breaking their fast is reckoned by them a great sin, yet to me they seemed to have no character and appeared mean, insincere, and liars, people one can never rely upon. The mindless charity of the monasteries makes them idle, and by taking the pilgrims as their example, they thoroughly indulge themselves in inactivity. This is why a wealthy man is so rarely found among the Christians. The Armenians, so it is said, are the most prosperous among them.[185]

Following are Seetzen's remarks on the ceremony of the Holy Fire itself, which he also observed in the same year on Great Saturday:

> [The Armenians]...were composed, while the Greeks behaved in a most indecent manner and were so noisy that my ears rang. The constantly growing crowd consisted of men of all ages. The younger ones pushed, shoved, and scuffled. Three or four fell upon another and carried him around the Sepulcher whether he wished it or not, while a mob followed after them screaming and shouting wildly. They had barely completed one round when they did it again with someone else. It was a carnival, and instead of a Christian celebration one seemed to be attending a Bacchanalian feast.
>
> Young Muslims mingled with the frolicsome crowd and added to the tumult so that it became complete chaos. It seems that the Greeks are incapable of making a pilgrimage without such wild outbursts of joy. From the gallery I also noticed some women pilgrims.

---

[185] Seetzen's account is quoted in Peters, *Jerusalem*, p. 570.

The Descent of the Holy Fire is a triumph for the Greeks, by which the Armenians, Copts, etc., should also be convinced. They pride themselves a great deal on this, and in order to humiliate their chief enemy, the Armenians, they tell the following story. Once, it seems, the Armenian clergy paid a large sum of money to the governor of the city in order to obtain permission to be the recipients of the Holy Fire. The Armenian bishop had already entered the Tomb and everyone was in a ferment of expectation. Then, after a long period of waiting, the Armenian clergy came out again, ashamed and afraid, and explained that they could not obtain the Holy Fire through their prayers. Then the Greek bishop entered the Tomb and in a few minutes the Holy Fire appeared. Angry with the audacity of the Armenians, the governor had them seized and forced them to eat something which politeness does not permit me to name. This is the reason for the abusive name of 'Sh–teaters' given to the Armenians by the Greek rabble. It is amazing what religious fanaticism can do to men![186]

There are two noteworthy elements in Seetzen's description of the Holy Fire. First, he provides us with a vivid account of the clamorous celebrations that began with the humiliation of the Armenians in 1580. He also observes that the Holy Fire descended while a recipient was waiting in the Tomb, an observation consistent with all other subsequent sources. Peters says of Seetzen's witness that it is a

> ...moral judgement, a deep European sigh at the debasement of a religious ceremony which had passed from an act of piety into something that a Westerner could no longer commend nor even comprehend.[187]

Circa 1832, the Coptic Patriarch Peter VII (Butrus al–Jawli) of Alexandria (1809–1852), according to a record of miracles at-

---

[186] *Ibid.*, pp. 571–572; Seetzen may be referring to the events of 1580 or 1634. His details are too muddled to identify definitely his account with either event. At any rate, his comments add a footnote to the saga of the Holy Fire which has at least the gloss of novelty.

[187] *Ibid.*, p. 572.

tributed to him, travelled to Jerusalem at the order of the governor of Syria, Ibrahim Pasha, who had challenged him to prove that "...a heavenly spark illuminates the Holy Sepulcher at Easter":[188]

> Following the success of his Syrian campaign in 1832, Ibrahim Pasha, son of Muhammed 'Ali, desired to ascertain for himself the truth of the apparition of the Holy Light. He sent for Pope Peter vii (Butrus al–Jawli) and disclosed his intention to him. Accordingly the Church of the Resurrection was vacated, and the congregation was replaced by Ibrahim's soldiers, while other guards were stationed outside. The Holy Sepulcher was thoroughly searched, and so were the Coptic and Greek Orthodox patriarchs, who, incidentally, had been fasting and praying for three consecutive days. Prayers commenced as usual when, at the appointed time, the light suddenly burst into the Sepulcher and, passing through the pillars, appeared outside the church. Ibrahim Pasha was exceedingly amazed.[189]

This report is ambiguous. It gives us no details about the ceremony of the Holy Fire. In fact, we can determine only by circumstantial evidence (the fact that the Faithful were gathered in the Church and then removed by the Pasha's soldiers) that the appearance of light reported here is indeed the Holy Fire. The report is, however, clear evidence of a wide knowledge of the phenomenon even in the Islamic world of the nineteenth century.

In 1834, a tragedy occurred when panic broke out during the ceremony of the Holy Fire and, in the ensuing stampede and the unleashing of Turkish bayonets, some three hundred pilgrims lost their lives. This often cited event was witnessed by the traveller Robert Curzon. The Faithful having gathered for the ceremony of the Holy Fire a number of hours earlier, Curzon reports, they

---

[188] See details about the life of this patriarch in Aziz S. Attiya, ed., *The Coptic Encyclopedia,* (New York: MacMillan Publishing Co., 1991), *s.v.* "Peter vii," by Mounir Shoucri.

[189] Quoted *ibid., s.v.* "Holy Fire," by Archbishop Basilios.

...were by this time become furious; they were worn out with standing in such a crowd all night, and as the time approached for the exhibition of the Holy Fire, they could not contain themselves for joy. Their excitement increased as the time for the miracle in which they all believed drew near. At about one o'clock a magnificent procession moved out of the Greek chapel. It conducted the patriarch three times around the Tomb, after which he took off his outer robes of cloth and silver, and went into the sepulcher, the door of which was then closed. The agitation of the pilgrims was now extreme: they screamed aloud; and the dense mass of the people shook to and fro, like a field of corn in the wind.

There is a round hole in one part of the chapel over the sepulcher, out of which the Holy Fire is given, and up to this the man who had agreed to pay the highest sum for this honor was then conducted by a strong guard of soldiers. There was silence for a minute; and then a light appeared out the Tomb and the happy pilgrim received the Holy Fire from the patriarch within. It consisted of a bundle of thin wax candles, lit, and enclosed in an iron frame, to prevent their being torn asunder and put out by the crowd; for a furious battle commenced immediately; everyone being so eager to obtain the holy light, that one man put out the candle of his neighbor in trying to light his own....

This was the whole of the ceremony; there was no sermon or prayers, except a little chanting during the processions, and nothing that could tend to remind you of the awful event which this feast was designed to commemorate.

Soon you saw the light increasing in all directions, everyone having lit his candle from the holy flame: the chapels, the galleries, and every corner where a candle could possibly be displayed immediately appeared to be in a blaze. The people in their frenzy put the bunches of lighted tapers to their faces, hands, and breasts to purify themselves from their sins. The patriarch was carried out of the sepulcher in triumph, on the shoulders of the people he had deceived, amid the cries and exclamations of joy which resounded from every nook of the immense pile of buildings. As he appeared in a fainting state, I supposed that he was ill; but I found that it is the uniform custom on these occasions to feign insensibility, that the pilgrim may imagine that he is overcome with the glory of the

Almighty, from whose immediate presence they believe him to have returned.[190]

A lengthy and gruesome description of the panic that broke loose and the consequent tragedy follows. We resume Curzon's report on the Sunday of Pascha:

> The day following the occurrences which have been related, I had a long interview with Ibrahim Pasha, and the conversation turned naturally to the blasphemous imputations of the Greek and Armenian patriarchs, who for the purposes of worldly gain, had deluded their ignorant followers with the performance of a trick in relighting the candles which had been extinguished on Good Friday with fire which they affirmed had been sent down from heaven in answer to their prayers. The pasha was quite aware of the evident absurdity which I brought to his notice....[191]
>
> It was debated what punishment was to be awarded to the Greek patriarch for the misfortunes which had been the consequence of his jugglery, and a number of the purses which he had received from the unlucky pilgrims passed into the coffers of the pasha's treasury. I was sorry that the falsity of this imposture was not publicly exposed, as it was a good opportunity of so doing.
>
> It seems wonderful that so barefaced a trick should continue to be practiced every year in these enlightened times.... If Ibrahim Pasha had been a Christian, probably this would have been the last Easter of the lighting of the Holy Fire; but from the fact of his religion being opposed to that of the monks, he could not follow the example of Louis xiv, who having put a stop to some clumsy imposition which was at that time bringing scandal on the Church, a paper was found nailed upon the door of the sacred edifice the days afterwards, on which the words were read:
>
>> Du part du roi, défense à Dieu
>> De faire miracle en ce lieu.

---

[190] Robert Curzon [Zouche], *Visits to Monasteries in the Levant* (London: Arthur Barker, Ltd., 1955), pp. 197–199.

[191] Curzon's portrayal of the Pasha's assessment of the Holy Fire seems to be at odds with his reaction to the miracle reported in the life of the Coptic Patriarch Peter VII several years earlier.

The interference of a Muhammadan in such a case as this would only have been held as another persecution of the Christians; and the miracle of the Holy Fire has continued to be exhibited every year with great applause, and luckily without the unfortunate results which accompanied it on this occasion.[192]

We find no new elements to the rite of the Holy Fire reported here, but we do find confirmation of a practice that was probably established centuries earlier: the ceremony is now completely independent of the Vespers–Liturgy Vigil service (which now comes after the ceremony of the Holy Fire). It is worthy of mention that the narrator, confessing his pure Christian concerns about the tragedy which he observed, should have found a kindred spirit in Ibrahim Pasha—whose soldiers played a major rôle by bludgeoning and bayoneting the Christian believers—, while reviling the Eastern Christians who were its victims. This fact is evidence of the growing alienation between Eastern and Western Christians that seems to be so much a characteristic of at least early nineteenth–century Christianity.

It was in the 1830s that A. W. Kinglake travelled throughout the East and returned to England to publish an account of his travels, in 1844, in a book with the title *Eöthen: Or Traces of Travel Brought Home From the East.* During his travels, he visited the Holy Land and, in his accounts of that visit, writes about the Holy Fire. This must have been in the year 1835, since he speaks of the tragedy described by Curzon as having occurred "...the year before that of my going to Jerusalem."[193] He was not, as he notes, a witness to the ceremony, but his remarks are of interest. He begins his narrative with a description of the Holy Places under Turkish rule, circumstances under which, he claims, the various Christian sects were constantly squabbling:

> In this strife the Greek Church has of late years signally triumphed, and the most famous of the shrines are committed to the care of

---

[192] *Ibid.,* pp. 206–208.

[193] A. W. Kinglake, *Eöthen: Or Traces of Travel Brought Home From the East* (London: Sampson Low, Marston, & Co., 1913), p. 177.

their priesthood. ...Although the pilgrims perform their devotions at the several shrines with so little apparent enthusiasm, they are driven to the verge of madness by the miracle displayed before them on Easter Sunday. Then it is that the heaven–sent fire issues from the Holy Sepulchre. The pilgrims assemble in the great church, and already, long before the wonder is worked, they are wrought by anticipation of God's sign, as well as by their struggles for room and breathing space, to a most frightful state of excitement. At length the Chief Priest of the Greeks, accompanied (of all people in the world) by the Turkish governor, enters the Tomb. After this there is a long pause, but at last, and suddenly, from out of the small apertures on either side of the Sepulchre, there issue long, shining flames. The pilgrims now rush forward, madly struggling to light their tapers at the holy fire. This is a dangerous moment, and many lives are often lost.[194]

Kinglake provides no details about the ceremony of the Holy Fire, beyond noting that the Turkish authorities and the Greek Patriarch ("Chief Priest") take part in it; that the Patriarch is in the Tomb when the fire descends; and that the Holy Fire is taken from apertures in the Edicule. He also assigns the celebration to the Sunday of Pascha rather than Great Saturday.[195] His account does, however, give us evidence that the ceremony unquestionably belonged in his time to the Greek Church.

An English pilgrim, W. H. Bartlett, visited Jerusalem in the summer of 1842 and described the Holy Sepulchre, "...the centre of attraction for the devoted but ignorant multitude."[196] He notes that the descent of the Holy Fire, "that stock 'miracle' of the Greek church,'" takes place there and then provides a very vivid account of the rite from an anonymous article from a contemporary periodical, *The New Monthly Magazine,* which apparently adequately captures his own experiences. The article begins

[194] *Ibid.,* pp. 176–177.

[195] We can assume from other sources that the ceremony of the Holy Fire was, indeed, held on Great Saturday at this time.

[196] W. H. Bartlett, *Walks about The City and Environs of Jerusalem* (London: George Virtue, 1844), p. 191.

with the Faithful gathered at the Holy Sepulchre on Great Saturday:

> The tumult had now continued from eight o'clock in the morning
> until past two, and every moment had been augmenting in vehe-
> mence, when at last, when it seemed to have reached its climax, the
> Turkish governor, taking compassion on the multitude, suddenly
> entered with his suite, and took his seat by the side of the kady....
> The crowd and rush were now excessive; every one tended to the
> orifice on the right side of the sepulchre, and the Turkish topgis
> and tchoushes...could scarcely open a passage with their long whips
> for the person who had purchased the right (he was an Armenian,
> as may be expected) of having the first spark of the holy fire. The
> kady at last, at the suggestion of the governor, gave the signal with
> his rod, and the last imploring litany commenced. The papas
> [Priests] proceeded with lights and banners, and in their large loose
> silk embroidered dalmatics [*phelonia,* the Priests' outermost vest-
> ment], which brought one back to the Chrysostomos and Con-
> stantinople, made several circuits with their archbishops round the
> sepulchre.
>
> The preliminary ritual was gone through, and the archbishop
> having taken off his cope and mitre, and now and then glancing up
> at the kady, broke the seals, and without any attendance entered
> the chapel of the sepulchre. This was the moment of suspense, at
> least for the pilgrims; but those who know what a good under-
> standing there is between them, might have already seen the mira-
> cle in the countenance of the governor. In a minute or something
> less, the person who stood at the orifice already mentioned, drew
> forth a large torch, or staff, with a grated receptacle at the end. The
> fire was communicated in a similar manner, but a few seconds lat-
> er, from the entry of the sepulchre, and in rear to the small a-
> ttached chapel of the Copts. It is quite impossible to describe, with
> adequate effect, the scene which immediately followed; there were
> eight thousand pilgrims in the church: one universal shout rose si-
> multaneously from the whole congregation. ...The archbishop now
> left the sepulchre in the same undress in which he had entered, but
> had no sooner crossed the threshhold [*sic*] than he was taken up in
> triumph by four stout papas, and carried horizontally, in this state,

upon their shoulders. ...The governor...kept...his Mahommedan [*sic*] face with great propriety, and reserved, probably, his congratulations at their mutual success for a private interview with the good archbishop.[197]

In this description we see a number of elements of the rite of the Holy Fire that are consistent with other reports: the circumambulation of the Edicule, the breaking of the seals on the doors of the entrance to the Holy Sepulchre, and the entrance of the chief Greek clergyman, here an Archbishop, into the Tomb to receive the Holy Fire. We also see for the first time the strange accusation that the ceremony involved the collaboration of the Greek Church authorities with their Moslem rulers. It is significant, perhaps, that we see no prayers of supplication by the Patriarch within the Tomb, but the manifestation of the Holy Fire almost immediately after his entrance into it.

Yehoshua Ben–Arieh, in his portrait of nineteenth–century Jerusalem, retells the accounts of two visitors to Jerusalem in that century, one from 1845, the other from 1851. With regard to the first account, he writes that:

> Before, during, and after the Holy Fire ceremonies, the church rang out with noise and confusion. The Turkish guards could barely restrain the enthusiastic pilgrims by using their rifle butts. Every year, the Turkish pasha was present at the ceremony; it began only when he arrived. The clerics were able to circle the Holy Sepulchre only twice, despite the strenuous efforts of the Turkish soldiers. Large sums of money were paid for the privilege of receiving the Holy Fire from the patriarch. The Armenians had long wanted to abolish this evil; the Greek Orthodox were opposed, because they did not wish to cast aspersions on their predecessors and because abolishing a practice that held so prominent a place in the popular faith might cause a decline in the number of pilgrims. Until the time of the ceremony, large numbers of men, women, and children lived at the church, eating, drinking, and sleeping there.[198]

---

[197] *Ibid.*, pp. 194–195.

[198] Yehoshua Ben–Arieh, *Jerusalem in the 19th century: the Old City* (New

The second visitor he quotes as saying that the

> ...rite of the Holy Fire attracted crowds of Jerusalemites, from
> Greeks to Muslims, whose behavior was hardly in keeping with the
> sanctity of the place. If they were not laughing and shouting, they
> were dancing and eating. ...Distinguished guests who wished to
> watch the ceremony were seated on the balcony. Of course, there
> were armed Turkish guards at hand; without them, there might
> have been bloodshed. The ceremony usually continued until two
> p.m., at which time the Armenian and Greek bishops received the
> Holy Fire (from the heavens) and relayed it to the Chapel of the
> Angel adjoining the Holy Sepulchre. At this point the crowd
> would become ecstatic.... The Holy Fire was used to light their
> candles, either directly or from candle to candle.[199]

In both of these reports, we have confirmation of many of
the same elements of the ceremony in later nineteenth– and
twentieth–century reports. There is reference to a procession
three times around the Edicule (though it was apparently inter-
rupted) in the first account, and in the first and second accounts
we see the Greek Patriarch distributing the Holy Fire from within the Tomb, where he is accompanied, in the second instance,
by the Armenian Bishop. In both reports we see the same raucous behavior—shouting, eating, and drinking—about which
visitors repeatedly remark. In the second account, we also learn
that the ceremony takes place at about two in the afternoon.
Secular authorities are again in attendance.

The Russian Monk Parthenius visited Jerusalem at about the
same time as the sources cited by Ben–Arieh, witnessing the
celebrations of Great Week and Pascha in 1846. Parthenius is an
important source, since he was an experienced traveller and a
careful observer. Indeed, a five–volume collection of his various
reminiscences from pilgrimages across Russia and the Near East
was widely read and circulated in pre–Revolutionary Russia.[200]

York: St. Martin's Press, 1984), p. 218.

[199] *Ibid.*, p. 218.

[200] His accounts of Holy Week and Pascha in Jerusalem are contained in
the second volume of this collection; see Monk Parthenius, *Report of the Wan-*

His lengthy account of the ceremony of the Holy Fire provides us with the most detailed view available of the ceremony in the mid–nineteenth–century:

When dawn [of Great Saturday] came, they began to put out the fires and lamps [in the Church of the Resurrection] and nowhere was a lamp left burning. The Turks opened Christ's Sepulchre and put out all the lamps. Then the Turkish authorities and the Pasha himself came: a host of armed soldiers stood around Christ's Sepulchre. In the church everything had changed; everyone had become melancholy and the Arabs had become hoarse and weak. The church was unusually crowded and stuffy. Above, all the balconies were crammed with people in four rows. All the iconostasia and the domes were full of people. All were holding thirty–three candles in both hands in remembrance of the years of Christ's life. There was nothing lit anywhere.

The Patriarch went up to the main iconostasis with the consul. Meletius, the Metropolitan of Trans–Jordan, sat in the altar with the rest of the bishops, all melancholy and hanging their heads. In the church the Moslems with their weapons of war were giving orders; the Arabs had already stopped running about, but stood lifting their hands to heaven and uttering compunctionate cries; the Christians were all weeping or continually sighing. And who at that time could withhold his tears, beholding such a multitude of people from all countries of the world weeping and wailing and asking mercy from the Lord God? It was joyous to see that now, although unwillingly, the rest of the Christians were showing some respect for the Orthodox Greek Faith and for the Orthodox themselves, and that they were looking upon the Orthodox as though upon the brightest of suns, because everyone was hoping to receive the grace of the Holy Fire from the Orthodox. The Armenian patriarch went to the altar with two bishops and the Coptic metropolitan, and they bowed to Metropolitan Meletius and the rest of the bishops and asked that when we receive the grace of

derings and Journeys across Russia, Moldavia, Turkey, and the Holy Land, Vol. 2 (Moscow: 1855). An English translation of these accounts is found in Monk Parthenius, "Holy Week and Pascha in Jerusalem," *Orthodox Life,* Vol. 34, No. 2, pp. 25–38.

the Holy Fire, that we grant it to them also. Metropolitan Meletius answered with humility and told them to pray to God. They went to their own places. Then the royal gates were taken off and were replaced with others with a special opening.

It is not possible to describe what was then happening in the church. It was as though all were waiting for the Second Coming of the King of Heaven. Fear and terror fell upon all, and the Turks became despondent. And in the church there was nothing to be heard except sighings and groans. And Metropolitan Meletius' face was wet with tears. Then the Turkish Pasha came with the other authorities, and they went into Christ's Sepulchre to make sure that nothing remained alight there. When they came out they sealed the Sepulchre, but previously they had placed a large lamp inside, filled to the very brim with oil. In it floated a large wick. They put the lamp in the middle of the Tomb of Christ. Now there were no Christians near the shrine, but only the Turkish authorities. And from the balconies they let down on ropes hundreds of wires with bunches of candles attached.

At eight o'clock according to Russian time (two in the afternoon), they began preparing for the procession with the Cross. The bishops, priests, and deacons, having dressed in all their sacred vestments, each took thirty–three unlit candles. Then from the altar, through the royal doors, were handed twelve banners, and whoever could took them. The soldiers cleared the way, and the chanters went behind the banners. From the altar through the royal doors came the deacons, priests, abbots, and archimandrites, two by two, then the bishops, and behind all of them, Metropolitan Meletius. They went to the Lord's Sepulchre, and went around it three times chanting, 'Thy Resurrection, O Christ Saviour, the angels hymn in heaven; vouchsafe also us on earth with pure hearts to glorify Thee.'

Having finished the procession, all the clergy went quickly into the altar with the banners. Metropolitan Meletius stayed alone at the entrance of the Sepulchre in the hands of the Turks. The Turks divested him, and the authorities searched him. Then they put the omophorion on him, opened the Sepulchre of Christ, and let him go inside. Oh, what fear and terror fell upon all them that were there at the time! All were silent and moaning and asking the

Lord God that He not deprive them of the grace of His heavenly
Fire. Some time passed, I do not know how long, for we were all
beside ourselves from a kind of fear. But all of a sudden from near
Christ's Sepulchre there shined a light. Soon light also appeared
from the altar in the royal doors in the opening. And it flowed like
two rivers of fire, one from the west, from Christ's Sepulchre, and
another from the east, from the altar. Oh, what joy and exultation
there was in the church then! Everyone became as though drunk or
besides himself, and we did not know who was saying what, or who
was running where! And a great noise rose in all of the church. All
were running around, all were crying out in joy and thanksgiving
—most of all the Arab women. The Turks themselves, the Moslems, fell on their knees and cried, 'Allah, Allah,' that is, 'O God,
O God!' Oh, what a strange and most wonderful sight! The whole
church was transformed into fire. Nothing could be seen in the
church besides the heavenly Fire. Above and below, and round all
the balconies the Holy Fire was being poured forth. And afterwards
there was smoke about the whole church. And a good half of the
people went out with the Fire and carried it about Jerusalem to
their own homes and to all the monasteries.

In the Great Church Vespers began, and then the Liturgy of
St. Basil the Great. The Metropolitan served with the priests, and
he ordained a deacon. The people stood through the Liturgy with
candles. When the Metropolitan of Trans–Jordan goes into the
Sepulchre, he finds a large lamp standing on the Grave of Christ
which has been lit by itself; sometimes it lights itself unexpectedly
while he is there. However, he himself has never seen it light. In
Jerusalem, I heard from many people with whom the Metropolitan
himself had spoken about it openly: 'Sometimes I go in and it is already burning; then I take it out quickly. But sometimes I go in
and the lamp is not yet burning; then I fall down to the ground
from fear and begin with tears to beg mercy from God. When I get
up the lamp is already burning and I light two bunches of candles
and I carry them out and distribute them.' The Metropolitan
carries the fire out into the vestibule and puts the bunches of the
candles into iron holders and gives them out from the Sepulchre
through openings made for that purpose, with the right hand to
the Orthodox and the left hand to the Armenians and the rest. The

Orthodox Arabs stand in a crowd near the opening. As soon as the Metropolitan shows the Holy Fire, one Arab, laying hold of it, runs straight to the altar and there through the royal doors it is distributed to the people; but one is hardly able to light his candles in the openings. Then the Metropolitan again returns to Christ's Sepulchre and lights another two bunches and goes out of the door of the Sepulchre. The strongest Arabs stand at the doors of the Sepulchre and await him. As soon as he goes out holding in his hands the thirty–three burning candles, the Arabs, taking him in their hands, carry him directly to the altar. All the people rush toward him. They all desire to touch his clothing. And with great difficulty, they are barely able to carry him into the altar. They sat him on a chair, and he sat through the whole Liturgy as though beside himself, with his head bowed; he did not look up and did not say a word; and no one disturbed him. As soon as they carried him out of the Sepulchre, the people rushed in to venerate it. And I was deemed worthy to do the same. The whole of Christ's Sepulchre was wet, as though dampened by rain; but I could not find out what it was from. In the middle of the Grave stood the large lamp which lit itself and a great flame was burning.[201]

Monk Parthenius' account contains essentially every element of the fully developed rite of the Holy Fire, even as the rite is performed in our day. These elements are:

Extinguishing and preparation of lamps in the
Holy Sepulchre and surrounding Churches

***

Gathering of the Faithful in the *Anastasis*

***

Procession three times around the Edicule
of the Tomb at about 2 *p.m.*

***

Patriarch (in this instance, a Metropolitan
representing the Patriarch) divested

***

Seals of the Tomb broken and the Patriarch
(or his appointed representative) enters

---

[201] Parthenius, "Holy Week," pp. 32–34.

***

Light suddenly appears from the Tomb and the Altar of the
Anastasis, eventually filling the entire Church

***

Light distributed from apertures in the Edicule and then by the
Patriarch from the door of the Holy Sepulchre
to the Orthodox and the Armenians

***

Great tumult among the Faithful (even the Moslems)

Something of particular interest in this report is Father Partheni-us' reference to the actual reception of the Holy Fire by the Pa-triarch, Metropolitan Meletius having indicated that at times it came quickly and at times only after prayer. The prayer for the reception of the Holy Light which, as we shall see subsequently, is an integral part of the ceremony in modern times was, there-fore, apparently absent from the ceremony in Parthenius' time; or perhaps it was used only when there was a delay in the descent of the Fire. The remarkable thing about Monk Parthenius' ac-count, though, is not only its wealth of detail about the ritual as-pects of the ceremony of the Holy Fire, but its portrayal of the religious content of the rite. We find no traces of the polemical or skeptical; rather, his account heartily testifies to a profound experience, embracing contrition, supplication, fear, awe, joy, and thanksgiving on the part, it would seem, of nearly all present at the enactment of the rite—including the Moslem observers. And this experience he considers consonant with the Paschal Mystery being commemorated. Thus, late in the evening of Great Saturday, at the beginning of Paschal Matins, Parthenius reflects:

> We all stood around the Grave of our Saviour and were glorifying
> His glorious Resurrection from the dead. In truth, all things were
> now filled with light; then the canon of Pascha became for us real
> and clear. For that which we were chanting, we were seeing with
> our own eyes.[202]

---

[202] *Ibid.,* p. 37.

In the mid–1800s, shortly after the visit of the Russian Monk Parthenius, Colonel Sir Charles W. Wilson, "the foremost explorer of Jerusalem,"[203] as one writer calls him, and a Royal Engineer in the British Army, also wrote about the Holy Fire. Like many of the well–placed Englishmen of his day, Wilson was thoroughly familiar with the ceremony.[204] He was also, typically, critical of it, noting that "...no description of the Church of the Holy Sepulchre would be complete without some notice of the ceremony of the 'Holy Fire,' which, to the disgrace of Eastern Christianity, is enacted at the present day."[205] Wilson does not indicate, in his travel accounts, whether he actually saw the ceremony of the Holy Fire. He simply tells us that he "...cannot do better than quote the words of Dean Stanley" (Arthur P. Stanley [1815–1881], Professor at Oxford and Dean of Westminster, who lectured widely and wrote on the Eastern Church). Wilson's negative reactions to the ceremony are apparently based on Stanley's testimony:

> The Chapel of the Sepulchre [the Edicule] rises from a dense mass of pilgrims, who sit or stand wedged around it; whilst round them, and between another equally dense mass, which goes around the walls of the church itself, a lane is formed by two lines, or rather two circles, of Turkish soldiers stationed to keep order. For the spectacle which is about to take place, nothing can be better suited than the Rotunda [the *Anastasis*], giving galleries above for the spectators and an open space below for the pilgrims and their festi-

---

[203] Samuel Heilman, *A Walker in Jerusalem* (New York: Summit Books, 1986), p. 251.

[204] For example, in the so–called "official journal" (the document is actually a personal diary, as the editor of the diary avers) of the wife of the British Consul in Palestine, James Finn, we see a calendar entry, among other important engagements, for "Holy Fire Day." This entry also attests to the official status of the ceremony among political dignitaries in nineteenth–century Jerusalem. See Arnold Blumberg, *A View From Jerusalem 1849–1858: The Consular Diary of James and Elizabeth Anne Finn* (Cranbury, NJ: Associated University Presses, 1980), p. 286.

[205] Colonel Sir Charles W. Wilson, *Jerusalem: The Holy City* (Jerusalem: Ariel Publishing Co., 1975), p. 23.

val. ...[From] the night before, and from this time forward for two hours, a succession of gambols takes place, which an Englishman can only compare to a mixture of prisoner's base, football, and leap–frog, round and round the Holy Sepulchre. ...Gradually the frenzy subsides or is checked, the course is cleared, and out of the Greek Church on the east of the Rotunda a long procession with embroidered banners, supplying in their ritual the want of images, begins to defile round the Sepulchre.

...Thrice the procession passes round, at the third time the two lines of Turkish soldiers join and fall in behind. ...The presence of the Turks is thought to prevent the descent of fire, and it is at this point that they are driven, or consent to be driven, out of the Church. ...The procession is broken through, the banners stagger and waver. ...In one small but compact band the Bishop of Petra (who is on this occasion the Bishop of 'the Fire,' the representative of the patriarch) is hurried to the Chapel of the Sepulchre, and the door is closed behind him.

...At last the moment comes. A bright flame as of burning wood appears inside the hole—the light, as every educated Greek knows and acknowledges, kindled by the bishop within—the light, as every pilgrim believes, of the descent of God Himself upon the Holy Tomb. Any distinct feature is lost in the universal whirl of excitement which envelops the church as slowly, gradually, the fire spreads from hand to hand, from taper to taper, through that vast multitude, till at last the whole edifice, from gallery to gallery and through the area below, is one wide blaze of thousands of burning candles.

Such is the Greek Easter—the greatest moral argument against the identity of the spot which it professes to honor—stripped, indeed, of some of its most revolting features, yet still, considering the place, the time, the intention of the professed miracle, probably the most offensive imposture to be found in the world.[206]

Stanley's portrayal of the rite of the Holy Fire provides little useful information. While his description of the crowds is consistent with that of other nineteenth–century observers, he interestingly enough makes no mention of the sealing of the

---

[206] *Ibid.*, pp. 23–28.

Tomb, the breaking of the seals, or the divesting of the Patriarch, features which we see in other accounts from his era and in the twentieth–century sources. However, he does offer a comment about the Holy Fire which is worthy of note: he compares it to a bright flame "as of burning wood," as though it were, indeed, distinct in character from the light of a lamp or a bundle of candles.

Monsignor Mislin, a clergyman in Hungary writing in the 1860s about the phenomenon, gives us a clear view of how Roman Catholic scholars in the mid–nineteenth century looked at the Holy Fire. He comments that the majority of the participants in the ceremony are Russians and pilgrims from Greece and the Near East. And while the pilgrims take the Holy Fire back home with them as a sacred memento from their pilgrimages, the "Greek Priests" in Jerusalem "...believe as little in the miracle as the Catholics."[207] Another Catholic observer, Johann Nepomuk Sepp, writing in 1863, describes the ceremony of the Holy Fire as a *"Volksfest,"* with scenes reminiscent of the Hippodrome. As he describes it, about three o'clock in the afternoon, the flame is produced by the Patriarch, "...who has rubbed his hands with some kind of phosphorous–like substance." He then passes this to the Faithful, who produce a great tumult.[208] In both of these references we see evidence of the general skepticism about the Holy Fire that prevailed throughout nineteenth–century Catholic Europe and which persists to this day. It had obviously by the time of these two writers lost any element at all that might have commended it as a worthwhile ceremony to Latin Christianity. Victor Guerin, another Catholic pilgrim who visited Jerusalem and attended the ceremony of the Holy Fire in 1854 and again in 1863, summed up this state of affairs well:

The ceremony of the Holy Fire [*feu sacré*]...[,] this feigned mira-

---

[207] Mislin, *Die Heiligen Orte*, p. 333.

[208] Johann Nepomuk Sepp, *Jerusalem und das Heilige Land: Pilgerbuch nach Palästina, Syrien, und Aegypten* (Schaffhausen, Switzerland: Fr. Hurter'sche Buchhandlung, 1863), pp. 402–403.

cle..., I could describe in every aspect and speak of such scandals...; but I prefer to take my reader far from such din and turmoil...to the retinue of the Reverend Franciscan Fathers [of Jerusalem].[209]

The last important reference to the Holy Fire in the nineteenth–century comes from Karl Baedecker, the publisher of a number of popular guidebooks for travellers, including one on Jerusalem. About the Holy Places and the Church of the Holy Sepulchre in particular he writes that at them one may encounter "...many disorderly scenes which produce a painful impression."[210] Among the most painful impressions for Baedecker, apparently, was the ceremony of the Holy Fire, which he saw in the year 1876. He describes the events of Great Saturday at about two o'clock in the afternoon:

> A procession of the superior clergy moves round the Sepulchre, all lamps having been carefully extinguished in view of the crowd. The patriarch enters the chapel of the Sepulchre [the Edicule], while the priests pray and the people are in the utmost suspense. At length the fire which has come down from heaven gleams from the Sepulchre, the priests emerge with a bundle of burning tapers, and there now follows an indescribable tumult, every one endeavouring to be the first to get his taper lighted.[211]

Baedecker's mention of the Holy Fire contains no novel details as such about the ceremony itself. Nonetheless, his description is succinct and lacks any elements dissonant with the service as it is celebrated today, suggesting that what he saw was very much the same ceremony that one would see in present–day Jerusalem.

Twentieth Century. Interest in the Holy Fire waned with the turning of the century, either because it came to be so foreign to Western Christians or because pilgrimages by the same came to be more greatly limited than in the nineteenth century. John

---

[209] Victor Guerin, *La Terre Sainte: son histoire, ses souvenirs, ses sites, ses monuments* (Paris: 1883), n.p.

[210] Quoted in Martin Gilbert, *Jerusalem: Rebirth of a City* (London: Hogarth Press, 1985), p. 160.

[211] *Ibid.*

Kelman wrote a book about the Holy Land in 1912. In it, he makes mention of the ceremony of the Holy Fire at the Church of the Holy Sepulchre. While he treats the idea of its miraculous character with scorn, he nonetheless looks for a religious meaning behind it—a search curiously absent from the polemical accounts of nineteenth–century witnesses to the event. We do not know, from his account, whether Kelman actually ever saw the ceremony himself:

> And there [in the Holy Sepulchre], on Easter Eve, the sham mira-
> cle of the 'Holy Fire' has been enacted annually for at least a
> thousand years. Who can miss the underlying truths behind these
> legends? They are, for all but the ignorant and the gross, symbols
> of the eternal healing and quickening power that the love and sac-
> rifice of Christ exert on humanity and even on His enemies. The
> torch–bearers, who kindle their fires at the blaze on Easter Eve, and
> speed thence to Bethlehem and other towns to light from it the
> candles waiting on many altars, tell their own exhilarating les-
> son.[212]

In the year 1926, on Great Saturday, a remarkable event occurred in the Holy *Kouvouklion* that is the subject of a recent
book, published in Greek, with the title *I Saw the Holy Light,* by
Archimandrite Savvas (Achilleos).[213] This volume recounts the
experiences of a monk in Jerusalem, the ascetic Father Metrophanes (Papaioannou), still alive and an octogenarian at least two
years prior to its publication.[214] In 1926, Metrophanes, according to his own account as recorded by Archimandrite Savvas, hid
himself on a small shelf formed by an arch in the *Kouvouklion,*
just behind a lamp.[215] Barely able to conceal himself, he was
nonetheless able to escape the various investigations of the Tomb
before it was sealed. From this vantage point, he could see the

---

[212] John Kelman, *The Holy Land* (London: Adam & Charles Black, 1912), p. 155.

[213] Archimandrite Savvas Achilleos, Εἶδα τὸ Ἅγιον Φῶς (Athens: 1982).

[214] *Ibid.,* p. 10.

[215] *Ibid.,* p. 105.

manifestation of the Holy Fire. Finally, seeing the silhouette of the Patriarch in the Tomb, he relates,

> ...at precisely that moment, when my agony had come to the point of fearful strain [from his confinement to the small niche] in that boundless, dead silence..., I heard a weak whistle. It was similar to a light wisp of wind. And immediately—an unforgettable sight—a blue light filled the whole confines of the Holy Tomb. ...In the midst of this light I saw clearly the Patriarch, from whose face were rolling huge beads of sweat.[216]

At this point, Father Metrophanes continues, the Patriarch began to read from the prayer book containing the prayer for the reception of the Holy Fire, which had been earlier placed on the Tomb. As the blue light in the Tomb spread, moving about here and there—even settling for a moment above the Patriarch's head—, it eventually took on a white color. Then, in full view, the lamp placed on the Holy Tomb lighted by itself. The Patriarch then rose, venerated the Holy Tomb, and went into the Chapel of the Angel.[217]

Father Metrophanes' fascinating account gives us little insight into the liturgical aspects of the ceremony of the Holy Fire. It affords us, however, a rare look at the phenomenon itself from a perspective that can be found in no other source. Of particular interest are, first, the monk's description of the light itself: a blue light which seems, with time, to take on a more brilliant, white color. The idea that the properties of the Holy Fire change over time is important, since we have examined accounts which assert that the Holy Fire is first an unconsuming flame, but later takes on the normal properties of fire. Also of interest is the fact that Father Metrophanes saw a blue light in the Sepulchre prior to the manifestation of the Holy Fire at the spontaneous lighting of the oil lamp placed on the Tomb, following the prayers of the Patriarch. Thus, not only did the light in the Tomb change in color, but it was transformed from a vague, animated light to ac-

---

[216] *Ibid.*, p. 127–128.

[217] *Ibid.*, p. 128–129.

tual flame.

Sir Harry Charles Luke, a British diplomat and the author of several books on the Holy Land, provides us with an interesting early twentieth–century account of what he calls, in one place, the "astounding Saturnalia of the Holy Fire"[218] in his sketches of the various religious groups in Palestine and Syria. Though obviously unsympathetic to the ceremony, his observations, published in the 1930s, afford a reasonably vivid picture of the rite at the beginning of that decade. His words attest to the fact that the ceremony was almost exclusively associated with Eastern Christianity:

The annual ceremony, or 'miracle,' of the Holy Fire, performed on the Saturday before Orthodox Easter...[,] [attracts] pilgrims of all nations and of all ages, with Russians and Copts, with Orthodox Arabs from every part of Palestine, Syria, and Trans–Jordan, with tottering old men and women who have come to leave their bones in the Holy Land, with sucklings in their mothers' arms. ...At ten o'clock, the bells of the Holy Sepulchre break out into that clang of strange and unforgettable rhythm, which is the signal that the Orthodox Patriarch is leaving the Patriarchal palace on his way to the Sepulchre; and the crowd both inside and out the Church becomes tense with anticipation. ...Although the Rotunda [the *Anastasis*] is so closely packed that it seems impossible that it should hold another person, there forces its way into it from the east a procession of 'young men,' the *shâbab,* wild–looking young peasants of the neighbourhood, worked up into a state of the highest excitement. ...At their head, standing on the shoulders of two of his fellows and swinging his body in every direction, is borne their leader, a frenzied individual with kohl–blackened eyes, who, as he brandishes his sword furiously about him and finally executes a sword–dance on the heads of his companions, suggests a Persian devotee at Muharram rather than a participant in a Christian service. ...Soon the vanguard of the ecclesiastical procession is seen to emerge from behind the iconostasis of the Chorus Dominorum, the banners and their bearers swaying from side to side as

218 Harry Charles Luke, *Prophets, Priests, and Patriarchs* (London: Faith Press, 1927), p. 24.

the police with great difficulty force a way for them through the solid mass of humanity. Somehow or other they reach the Rotunda and pass thrice round the Tomb, first the choir, then the priests and Archimandrites, then the Archbishops, and finally the Patriarch.[219] After the third circuit the Patriarch is led to the door of the Tomb, at which, following the precedent of his Turkish predecessor, the British District Commissioner of Jerusalem has taken up his position with his staff. Here he [the Patriarch] is divested of cope and mitre, while the seals of the Tomb—previously affixed by the gate–keeper in the presence of the Commissioner as a visible precaution against fraud—are broken. Hastily the Patriarch and an Armenian *vartaped* (it should be explained that the Armenians participate with the Orthodox in the ceremony) are pushed inside, all lights are extinguished, and there ensues a pause of painfully strained expectancy, not unmixed with apprehension. ...In a minute or two a shout of triumph goes up from the crowd. A brand, lit by the fire which the vast majority of those present believe to have come down from heaven, is being pushed by a shaking hand —the Patriarch's and the Armenian *vartaped's*—through a small orifice on each side of the Tomb, and those who are near struggle desperately and regardless of each other's safety to be the first to light their taper from it and thus to ensure eternal salvation. In the twinkling of an eye the fire has passed from hand to hand..., and the Church, hitherto in semi–darkness, is in an instant a–flicker and ablaze.[220]

The details of Luke's description of the rite of the Holy Fire are consistent with the contemporary ceremony and the general witness of the nineteenth century. A tumultuous display by the Arab Faithful takes place, followed by the threefold circumambulation of the Edicule by the clergy. The Greek Patriarch is then divested in the presence of secular authorities (here the British) and enters the Tomb, on which the seals closing it have

---

[219] According to a calendar published by Luke in 1934, this procession begins at 12:00 noon; see Sir Harry Luke and Edward Keith–Roach, eds., *The Handbook of Palestine and Trans–Jordan* (London: Macmillan & Co., 1934), p. 214.

[220] Luke, *Ceremonies,* pp. 26–31.

been broken. He is accompanied by a representative of the Armenian clergy. The Holy Fire is distributed from within the Tomb to the Faithful.

In a narrative published in 1939, the Russian Archbishop Meletii writes of his pilgrimage to the Holy Land, which "...did not coincide with those great days when the inhabitants of the Holy Land, in anticipation of the Bright Resurrection of Christ, piously prepare for the reception of the Blessed Fire which yearly comes down upon the cave of the Lord's Tomb on Great Saturday."[221] Nonetheless, he cites a description of the phenomenon published in 1926 by another Russian Bishop, Aleksei. This report is of interest, in the first place, because it describes the modern ceremony of the Holy Fire; more importantly, however, because it gives us evidence of the fact that the pious reaction of the Russian Orthodox pilgrims to nineteenth–century celebrations of the rite also marked their reactions earlier in this century:

> When they had finished reading Small Compline, around one o'clock p.m., the Patriarch, vested in an inner cassock and having taken off his mitre, went into the Tomb of the Lord in the company of the Armenian Bishop. The Armenian Bishop remained in the Chapel of the Angel, and Patriarch Damian disappeared through the door of the cave to the Lord's Tomb. The people, as if by order, became silent and still. And kept strained attention on the doorway to the Tomb, from whence the Patriarch would appear with the Holy Fire.
>
> Soon after one o'clock, the Patriarch emerged from the cave of the Lord's Tomb with a bundle of candles, thirty–three in number, according to the years of the Savior's earthly life. He had hardly succeeded in coming through the door, when there arose such a din and began such movement, that one feared for the life of the elderly Patriarch. All pressed toward him, in order to receive from his hands the Blessed Fire.[222]

Thomas A. Idinopulos, a writer of Greek descent and an

---

[221] Arkhiepiskop Meletii, *Zariski Palomika Na Svyatuyu Afonskuyu Goru i vo Svatuyu Zemlyu* (Harbin, China: 1939), p. 33.

[222] *Ibid.*, p. 34.

American college professor, gives us a more timely glimpse of the Holy Fire in the description of his visit to Jerusalem in 1981.[223] Describing his visit to Jerusalem, he writes:

> This past year I observed an Easter[224] ritual in Jerusalem that will be repeated soon, exactly as it has been performed each year for centuries—the Miracle of the Holy Fire. It is celebrated at midday on Easter Eve in the Church of the Holy Sepulchre, on the site that church tradition holds to be Christ's burial place. The event consists of the sending down of fire by God, the bursting forth of flame at the sacred Tomb and the lighting of the candle held in the hand of the Greek Orthodox patriarch of Jerusalem.[225]

This somewhat inaccurate description of the rite is followed by a description of the history of the Holy Fire which is, if not inaccurate, at least compromised by its selective use of references and by its brevity.[226] Idinopulos then tells of a conversation which followed his attendance at the rite of the Holy Fire. His narration reflects what one finds in many of the more polemical references to the phenomenon, including the occasional acknowledgment of an element of piety amidst deceit:

> The ritual of the Holy Fire lasted about an hour. As we made our way through the soul of the Old City to Jaffa Gate, my companion, a super–Sabra who studied mathematics and philosophy at Hebrew University, asked me the inevitable question.
> 'How do they do it?'
> 'How do they do what?' I replied.
> 'How do the Greeks make the fire?'
> 'The Greeks don't make it; God does.'
> She paused. 'You mean the Greeks *believe* that God sends the

---

[223] Thomas A. Idinopulos, "Holy Fire in Jerusalem," *The Christian Century*, 7 April 1982, pp. 407–409.

[224] The use of the term "Easter" instead of "Pascha" is either in compliance with Western convention or shows the author's lack of facility in Orthodox ecclesiastical nomenclature, a shortcoming to be found in other parts of his account.

[225] *Ibid.*, p. 407.

[226] *Ibid.*, p. 408 *pass.*

fire?'

'Right.'

'But who really produces the fire? How is it done?'

'I don't know.'

Exasperated, she pressed me. 'Don't give me that. You teach theology. You know how it's done.'

Another long pause and then I replied, 'The patriarch does it with a cigarette lighter.'

She glanced at me with a mildly derisive smile on her face, and said, 'You think the people know this?'

'I doubt it. But if they did, it wouldn't matter to them.'

'Really? Then the miracle is not the fire but their faith.'

'You got it.'[227]

In a popular book about his wanderings in Jerusalem in the 1980s, Samuel Heilman, a non–religious Jew, tells of meeting a Greek Orthodox monk, "Brother Cornelius,"[228] who became his guide into the world of the Orthodox Christian places of the Holy Land. Heilman's negative portrayal of Christian monasticism through the monk Cornelius includes an interesting reference to the Holy Fire, attributed to Cornelius himself, which casts the rite in a very negative light. His general description of the Feast of the Resurrection sets the tone for this "conversation" with Cornelius about the Holy Fire:

> As there is disagreement among Christians over when Christmas falls, so too believers are at odds about the precise day on which their Saviour rose. ...A week after the Catholics and Protestants of Jerusalem celebrate Easter, the Greek Orthodox have their own commemoration of the Resurrection.[229]

---

[227] *Ibid.,* p. 409.

[228] Heilman, *Walker,* p. 244. "Brother" is a title used to designate novices in the Orthodox Church; all professed monks, in every grade from the Rasophore to the wearer of the Great Schema, are called "Father." Heilman's lack of familiarity with this basic element of Eastern Christian monasticism calls into question his general familiarity with Orthodox customs.

[229] *Ibid.,* pp. 291ff. The issue of the celebration of the Feast of the Resurrection in Christian Jerusalem today has little to do with any disagreement over

In his broken English, standing on the edge of the roof of the Church of the Resurrection, "Brother" Cornelius confides to Heilman the "true source" of the Holy Fire:

> 'This is where I pass the holy fire to the Patriarch,' Cornelius explained. 'Everybody thinks it's a miracle, that the fire come from Heaven. But'—he laughed—'the miracle begin here with me.'[230]

In 1985, Eugene Zavarin, a Russian Orthodox professor of chemistry at the University of California, Berkeley, visited Jerusalem and observed the rite of the Holy Fire. His comments give us some insight into the assessment of the phenomenon by a modern believer with training in the natural sciences:

> I had heard about the Holy Fire and was, when I made my trip to Jerusalem for Pascha, not disbelieving. I found the idea that such a phenomenon existed interesting, and I wanted to see it for myself. What I saw *was* interesting. We had to go early to the Church and wait for hours for the ceremony, which began when the Patriarch came and went with the clergy in a procession around the Tomb. The Church was crowded beyond description. Before the manifestation of the Holy Fire, the Arabs created a tremendous scene, proclaiming the correctness of their Faith and running here and there through the Church, some with others standing on their shoulders. They were wildly enthusiastic and yet one could see that they were expressing some sort of religious sentiment. They were not being raucous for the sake of being raucous. Then the Holy Fire was brought out by the Patriarch. During this time, I could see what appeared to be flashes of blue–colored light bouncing off the walls of the dome of the Church and through the galleries. There was an electric quality to the air, almost like static electricity. Others, who had been closer to the flame as it was brought, report-

---

the "precise day" of Christ's Resurrection. The Orthodox hold to the calculation of the First Œcumenical Synod, held in Constantinople in 325, which simply universalized the commemoration of the Resurrection. The fact that the Orthodox in Jerusalem follow the Old, or Julian, Calendar also accounts for the variation in dates for the Nativity Feast among the various Christians in that city.

[230] *Ibid.*

ed to me that it did not at first burn, as they handled it.[231]

Ioanna Tsekoura's study of the phenomenon of the Holy Fire provides us with the latest available data about it. She has collected a number of fascinating accounts by contemporary pilgrims of their experiences at the ceremony of the Holy Fire. Once again, they are not accounts which tell us anything about the liturgical aspects of the ceremony *per se,* but are descriptions of the Holy Fire itself and of its purportedly miraculous effects. These are anonymous personal testimonies collected by Ms. Tsekoura during her research at the Holy Sepulchre in 1990. For the sake of brevity, there follows a synopsis, from her own words, of each report:

a) 1990: Pilgrims looking at the façade of the Holy *Kouvouklion* when the Holy Fire appeared saw a lamp which is over the outside door of the...Tomb ignite.

b) 1990: The same Pascha, one person was standing on the north side of the...Tomb. When the Holy Fire appeared, he saw the lamps suspended next to the doors of the Holy *Kouvouklion* near the entrance to the Church of the Resurrection ignite.

c) 1990: Again [the same Pascha] the Holy Fire appeared outside the Church on a balcony near the Church of Saint Constantine and ignited the candles of two pilgrims.

d) 1987: At the time of the [manifestation] of the Holy Fire, pilgrims saw it come forth from the outside door of the Holy Tomb and flood its façade with light.

e) 1985: The Holy Fire...ignited the candle of a Russian nun.

f) 1985: The Holy Fire...descended from the dome of the Church of the Resurrection as a cloud of a superb blue color.

g) 1984: The Holy Fire ignited the candle of a young man. [In the same year]...the Holy Fire manifested itself as a fire and light, igniting the candle of yet another pilgrim.[232]

Tsekoura also compiled a catalog of other manifestations of the Holy Fire as it has been described by various individuals whom

---

[231] Professor Eugene Zavarin, interview by author, 13 October 1985, San Francisco, transcript, Center for Traditionalist Orthodox Studies, Etna, CA.

[232] Tsekoura, *Τὸ Ἅγιον Φῶς,* pp. 57–61.

she interviewed. They include its appearance as a "small, shining star," "a small, shining triangle," "bright...snow," "a Cross of light," "a dove," "flames of...fire," "strikes of lightning," "a blue light," and "a blue light which gradually increases in intensity and becomes white."[233] Many of these same manifestations we have seen in even the earliest accounts of the rite of the Holy Fire.

Finally, it seems appropriate to conclude our historical consideration of the Holy Fire with the testimony of a principal contemporary participant in the ceremony, the present Greek Orthodox Patriarch of Jerusalem, Diodoros I. In an interview with the author, His Beatitude affirmed that, in his experience, the Holy Fire is indeed a supernatural phenomenon. The following comments are particularly pertinent:

> *Author:* Your Beatitude, as you know, there are a number of theological opinions with regard to the actuality [ὡσχετικῶς πρὸς τὴν πραγματικότηταῷ] of the Holy Fire.
> *Patriarch:* Yes.
> *Author:* In your experience, is the Holy Fire supernatural?
> *Patriarch:* The Holy Fire is *holy* fire [Τὸ "Αγιον Φῶς εἶναι ἅγιον φῶς].
> *Author:* In other words, is it a miracle?
> *Patriarch:* ...It is a true miracle, a true miracle [...Εἶναι ἀληθινό, ἀληθινό].[234]

It should be noted that the Patriarch's testimony stands in sharp contrast to the reports of a Scandinavian student of Semitics who visited Jerusalem in 1889, K. U. Nylander. Carl–Martin Edsman, taking note of his speculation that the Holy Fire, "a light which flashes from inside the Tomb," is ignited by spreading alcoholic spirits about the Tomb,[235] quotes Nylander as saying that "...the

---

233 *Ibid.*, pp. 62–66 *pass.*

234 Greek Orthodox Patriarch Diodoros I of Jerusalem, telephone interview by author, 26 March 1992, tape recording, Center for Traditionalist Orthodox Studies. Etna, CA.

235 Edsman, "Påskaftonens II," p. 6, n. 3.

Greeks themselves, the Patriarch of Jerusalem himself, answered my inquiry [about the actuality of the Holy Fire] that the service is not now as it was in past times, and that this fire is not sent by something supernatural, but that they are only keeping alive an old custom as well as they can."[236]

The disparity between the two foregoing reports perhaps captures the essence of the mystery of the Holy Fire: Are the lighting ceremonies of the Early Church the precursors of the rite of the Holy Fire, and is it an ancient phenomenon? Is the Holy Fire a symbol of the Resurrection of Christ, or is it a miraculous manifestation of Divine Fire and mystical light? In subsequent chapters we will try to treat with these matters. At present, however, we must acknowledge that the historical data are ambiguous and are compromised by witnesses polarized at the extreme ends of a spectrum from belief to disbelief. With regard to the ceremony itself, one can see a possible development from the ceremonies of the ancient Church to the fairly complete skeleton of the contemporary rite of the Holy Fire reported in the account of the Monk Parthenius in 1846. Yet most Western, as well as the post–Byzantine Greek, sources trace the contemporary rite only to the ninth century. There is also a remarkable similarity in reports with regard to the miraculous properties of the Holy Light. However, the vast majority of sources attribute the phenomenon to deceit and trickery.

In the end, one must look at the rite of the Holy Fire from a phenomenological perspective. If Christian liturgy has developed in a disjointed, haphazard way, such that the lighting ceremonies of the Early Church and the ceremony of the Holy Fire are separate and distinct entities, the unifying image of Resurrectional Light which prompts one to seek unity in that liturgical witness is worthy of consideration; it is a unique and valid phenomenon in and of itself. By the same token, if the Holy Fire is produced by normal means and the miraculous properties attributed to it by the Faithful are the product of imagination, naïve credulity, or social contagion—an imprudent assumption at best—, it is

---

[236] *Ibid.*, pp. 6–7.

nonetheless a phenomenon to which is attached a tremendous power to evoke what are remarkable visions and sensations of a largely immaterial kind, whatever their psychological or social etiology. If our survey of the historical witness entails a diversity of polarized historiographies and assessments of the Holy Fire, then, it also presents us with a phenomenon which transcends its own history and which deserves independent treatment.

CHAPTER II

*FIRE RITUALS, THE "NEW FIRE," AND THE PASCHAL
CANDLE: COMMENTS ON THEIR POSSIBLE NEXUS
WITH THE RITE OF THE HOLY FIRE*

Since the beginning of recorded time, fire has played a rôle
in religious rites. The ancient Chinese, the cultures of India, the
African natives, the Indians of North America, the ancient
Greeks, the primitive tribes of Europe and Scandinavia—all of
these and other ancient peoples have recorded fire rituals as part
of their cultural development: bonfires, the burning of sacred
wood, sacred flames that were kept burning at all times, the ceremonial lighting of the hearth fire, *etc.*[237] This fact is reflected in
the presence of various aspects of these rituals as they survive in
the religious ceremonies and symbols of today's major religions,
including Shintoism, Hinduism, Buddhism, Islam, and Christianity. Such instances are so "...ancient and constant, that they
present no problem from the standpoint of the history of religion."[238] In Christianity, according to some authorities, there
has always been a particular tendency to incorporate pagan symbols and images into the liturgical *corpus,* "purifying" and "rais-
ing" them, as Dom Odo Casel describes this process, "for the
Christian rites."[239] Just as the Church Fathers saw other symbols

---

[237] Carl–Martin Edsman, "Påskaftonens nya eld i Jerusalem, III," *Svenska
Jerusalemsföreningens Tidskrift,* Vol. 56 (1957), pp. 4–17. E. O. James also dis-
cusses the use of fire in ancient Indian and Greek religious ceremonies; see his
Christian Myth and Ritual (London: John Murray, 1933), pp. 105–108. One of
the most complete surveys of pagan fire ceremonies is Sir James George Frazer,
The Golden Bough: A Study in Magic and Religion, Part 7, *Balder the Beautiful:
The Fire–Festivals of Europe and the Doctrine of the Eternal Soul* (New York: The
Macmillan Co., 1935), esp. Vol. I, pp. 132–140.

[238] *Ibid.,* p. 10; *cf.* an article by Samuel Cheetham, "Kindling of Fire," in
William Smith and Samuel Cheetham, eds., *A Dictionary of Christian Antiquities* (Hartford: J. B. Burr Publishing Co., 1880).

and rituals in "pagan sacrifices" as "shadows, if misleading ones," of the "true mystery" of Christianity—"as the precursors of Christianity"[240]—, so it is possible that early Christians saw fire rituals as an appropriate expression of the Christian understanding of Christ as the God of light (St. John 9:5) and fire (Hebrews 12:29). Whether there was a conscious appropriation of these rituals by the Christian Faith is impossible to determine; their presence in some form in Christian liturgy, however, is undeniable.[241]

Certain fire rituals associated with Paschaltide in the Western church undoubtedly have their origins in the pagan bonfire. In rural Germany and Scandinavia, huge fires are still lighted on the eve of Easter,

> ...not only in churchyards but upon hilltops, where the young people gather around, dance, sing Easter hymns, jump over them, and sometimes light straw-wheels from their flames and set them rolling down the hill. Boys will run through the fields with flaming straw bundles from the fire, in the belief that such fields will become especially fruitful in the following year.[242]

---

[239] Odo Casel, *The Mystery of Christian Worship*, ed. Burkhard Neunheuser (London: 1962), p. 60.

[240] Bishop Auxentios of Photiki, "Fear and Trembling Language in Fourth– and Fifth–Century Liturgical Texts: From Bishop to Schmemann to a Corrected View," *Orthodox Tradition*, Vol. 9, Nos. 2 & 3 (1992), p. 48.

[241] We should make some comment here about the use of fire and light in Jewish worship in the Temple and in the pre–Christian synagogue. There are no credible data to establish a nexus between such worship and later Christian customs. In the *Apostolic Tradition*, for example, Saint Hippolytos of Rome († *ca.* 236) simply states that the Christians lighted lamps in the evening *agape*, in imitation of the Jewish practice of lighting a lamp on the eve of the Sabbath. He says nothing of any other ceremony, sacrificial or not, involving fire; see *Hippolytus: A Text for Students*, trans. Geoffrey J. Cuming (Bramcote, Nottingham: Grove Books, 1984), p. 23. It is also unlikely that the use of fire and candles for illumination in the catacombs accounts for such customs, since the catacombs were not normally used for public worship, even in times of persecution; see J. G. Davies, ed., *A New Dictionary of Liturgy and Worship* (London: SCM Press, Ltd., 1986), *s.v.* "Candles, Lamps, and Lights," by C. E. Pocknee and G. D. W. Randall.

This practice of lighting bonfires is also associated with Saint Patrick († *ca.* 461), the Enlightener of Ireland, who, according to E. O. James, "...records that as early as the sixth century large bonfires were lighted in Ireland on the Eve of Easter, apparently having been kindled from 'new fire' struck from flint."[243] There is no doubt that this practice is derived from the pagan Celtic rites of renewing the hearth from a new fire each spring and from the sacrificial fires lighted at that time by the Irish Druids.[244] In his suggestions for parish renewal in the contemporary Roman Catholic Church, Father William Baumann, interestingly enough, suggests that the kindling of the "new fire" of Pascha (with which we will deal subsequently and which is usually associated with more formal liturgical rite) should "...ideally...be a large bonfire which bursts into flame in the parking lot or suitable outdoor gathering place."[245] This is nothing less than a call for the preservation of the popular celebration of Easter that we have described.

In addition to bonfires, other kinds of fire ceremonies have been traditionally associated with the Easter season. Sir James George Frazer describes, for example, a curious fire ceremony which is popular in Mexico and which takes place on Easter Saturday morning:

> Ropes stretch across the streets from house to house, and from every house dangles an effigy of Judas, made of paper pulp [*i.e.,* a *piñata*]. Scores or hundreds of them may adorn a single street. They are of all shapes and sizes, grotesque in form and garbed in strange attire, stuffed with gunpowder, squibs and crackers, sometimes, too, with meat, bread, soap, candy, and clothing, for which the

[242] Alan W. Watts, *Easter: Its Story and Meaning* (New York: Henry Schuman, 1950), p. 112.

[243] James, *Christian Myth*, p. 108.

[244] See Geoffrey Keating, *The History of Ireland*, trans. John O'Mahony (New York: 1857), p. 300.

[245] Rev. William A. Baumann, *Lent and the New Holy Week* (Notre Dame, IN: Ave Maria Press, 1972), p. 71.

crowd will scramble and scuffle while the effigies are burning.[246]

This same kind of ceremony is seen elsewhere in South America:

> In Brazil the mourning for the death of Christ ceases at noon on Easter Saturday and gives place to an extravagant burst of joy at his resurrection. Shots are fired everywhere, and effigies of Judas are hung on trees or dragged about the streets, to be finally burned or otherwise destroyed. In the Indian villages scattered among the wild valleys of the Peruvian Andes figures of the traitor, made of pasteboard and stuffed with squibs and crackers, are hanged on gibbets before the door of the church on Easter Saturday. Fire is set to them, and while they crackle and explode, the Indians dance and shout for joy at the destruction of their hated enemy. Similarly, at Rio Hacha, in Colombia, Judas is represented during Holy Week by life–size effigies, and the people set fire at [*sic*, "to"] them as if they were discharging a sacred duty.[247]

In Florence, Italy, there is a bizarre fire ceremony each Easter day called

> ...the Ceremony of the Car, or *Scoppio del carro* [literally, "Explosion of the car"]. A dove ignited at the high altar of the Duomo, flies along a wire out at the western door, and is supposed to ignite [the fireworks in] the car [an ox–drawn cart], signifying the 'fruits of the earth.' If this is successful, prosperity in the harvest is ensured for the coming year, according to popular belief.[248]

As a final witness to the diversity of the fire rites associated with the Christian Feast of the Resurrection,[249] we have a custom in the Armenian Church which survives in many villages in modern times. While the rite is not directly attached to the Paschal ceremonies, it occurs on February 2, or Candlemas, in commemoration of the purification of the Virgin Mary and as a purification

---

[246] Frazer, *Golden Bough*, p. 127.

[247] *Ibid.*, p. 128.

[248] Ethel L. Urlin, *Festivals, Holy Days, and Saints' Days* (London: Simpkin, Marshall, Hamilton, & Kent, Ltd., 1915), p. 75.

[249] Frazer cites a fascinating array of these rites; see *Golden Bough*, pp. 126–131.

rite in preparation for the Resurrection. A bonfire is made by young couples who are to be married in the ensuing year. It is set ablaze by a local clergyman. The young men dance around the fire, while the prospective brides encircle it, praying to be preserved from disease and for a fruitful harvest. The ashes from the fire are considered to have protective qualities.[250]

There is no evidence that the foregoing folk rites have directly affected the development of Christian Paschal services *per se;* rather, they seem to have existed in past times, as they do today, alongside the formal worship of the Church under what Frazer calls "a thin cloak of Christianity."[251] There is no doubt whatsoever, however, that these rites express the universal theme of Paschal renewal—the eradication or burning away of sin and betrayal—and the triumph of light (fire) over darkness. To some extent, one might argue, they are not unlike the raucous frolicking during the rite of the Holy Fire in the Holy Sepulchre, in which the Arabic Christians of Jerusalem celebrate the humiliation of the Armenians in failing to usurp that ceremony from them. This argument is reinforced by the fact that, as one authority contends, "...at Jerusalem, at Easter, the belief is, that in obtaining fresh fire from the Holy Sepulchre, which is supposed to be kindled by a miracle, luck is ensured for the coming year"[252]—a contention supported even by early Moslem accounts of the rite of the Holy Fire. This is, notably enough, precisely the theme that we have observed in the Easter celebrations described above in Florence, Italy, and in Armenia. But again, there is not a direct liturgical link between these folk customs and liturgical customs in the East or West.[253] In general, the fire

---

[250] Manuk Abeghian, *Der Armenische Volksglaube* (Leipsic: 1899), pp. 72ff.

[251] Frazer, *Golden Bough,* p. 131.

[252] Urlin, *Festivals,* p. 73.

[253] We might, however, note an interesting feature of the "Ceremony of the Car" in Florence. The flame which ignites the fireworks in the cart is taken from the Paschal "new fire" (see *infra*), which in turn, according to Frazer, was in his time (the turn of the nineteenth century) "...elicited from certain flints which are said to have been brought...from the Holy Land" (*Golden Bough,* p.

rituals of Western Christianity are as informal as the colorful Arabic procession at the ceremony of the Holy Fire in Jerusalem and remain phenomena clearly distinct from the Church's worship.

There is one pagan ritual to which we have referred, however, that may have a liturgical connection to the Christian Paschal rites in the West: the renewing of the hearth fire each spring. This ritual, which was known in ancient Rome, in Celtic Ireland, and throughout pre–Christian Europe, is reflected in the Roman Catholic Church in the kindling of the so–called "new fire" by "means of a flint...[or] a burning glass,"[254] an established feature of pre–Vatican II Latin Paschal worship that is today variously and not invariably performed at the parish level. This rite of the "new fire," one writer tells us, "the spark obtained by friction," has "...from remote pagan times...symbolized regeneration and holiness, and now symbolizes the Resurrection."[255] In modern times, it is performed on the morning of Holy Saturday, whereas in ancient times it was performed on the eve of Easter.[256] According to one source, the rite, portions of which are of tenth–century Germanic origin, is not an integral part of the Western Paschal services and is performed outside, at the entrance of the church:

> [This]...introductory rite...[is]...a preparation for the Vigil rather than a part of it, and ideally...[it]...take[s] place outside the Church. Many of these rites are Gallican in origin. The formula for blessing the new fire originated in Germany in the 10th century, but the practice of kindling the new fire is found there as early as the 8th century. The Roman custom was to bring a light out of

126). For a description of the ceremony, see J. L. Weston, "The *Scoppio del Carro* at Florence," *Folklore,* Vol. 16 (1905), pp. 182ff.

[254] John Walton Tyrer, *Historical Survey of Holy Week: Its Services and Ceremonial,* No. 29 of Alcuin Club Collections (London: Oxford University Press, 1932), p. 149.

[255] Christina Hole, *Easter and its Customs* (New York: M. Barrows & Co., 1961), p. 52.

[256] Watts, *Easter,* p. 99; *cf.* James, *Christian Myth,* p. 109.

hiding for illumination Saturday night. ...For the whole first part of the service up to the Mass itself the celebrant wears the cope, the vestment for solemn rites outside of Mass. Nothing is done at the altar because these rites are not part of the sacrifice.[257]

We can see evidence of the informal character of the "new fire" in the ceremonies which are taken from it. In Bavaria, for example, the folk ritual of "burning the Easter man"—igniting a Cross wrapped in straw so as to represent a man with his arms outstretched—is carried out with "...a taper bearing New Fire from the church."[258]

The kindling of "new fire" at the entrance of the church does not seem to have been known in Rome before the twelfth century.[259] In ancient Rome, James observes,

> ...three large lamps were hidden away on Maundy Thursday during the consecration of the chrism, and kept alight by means of wicks until Holy Saturday. It was from these lamps that the candles and other lamps were lighted by a priest to illuminate the baptismal ceremony.[260]

What seems to have held forth in the Paschal services in Rome was something very much like the lamp–lighting ceremonies of the ancient Church. These were apparently later supplanted by the rite of the "new fire," as it developed in the non–Roman rites of the mass. Alan W. Watts thus suggests, in his inexact reconstruction of Latin Paschal services around the year 1000 (along with what appear to be later elements of worship in some places), that despite the practice in Rome, the Paschal services (held at this time on Saturday evening) began with the kindling of the "new fire" very much as we have referred to it in its modern form:[261]

---

[257] The Most Rev. William J. McDonald, ed., *The New Catholic Encyclopedia* (New York: McGraw–Hill Book Co., 1967), *s.v.* "Easter Vigil," by W. J. O'Shea, p. 10.

[258] Watts, *Easter,* p. 112.

[259] Davies, *New Dictionary, s.v.* "New Fire," by J. D. Crichton, p. 388.

[260] James, *Christian Myth,* p. 109.

Toward midnight they [the worshippers] hear the clink of steel striking on flint in the back of the church. From the rock comes fire; from the tomb, Christ. Sparks from the flint catch on tinder and are blown into flame.[262]

The kindling of the "new fire" is often equated by scholars with the ceremony of the Holy Fire at the Tomb of Christ in Jerusalem. Thus Frazer notes that:

Every year on the Saturday before Easter Sunday a *new* fire [emphasis ours] is miraculously kindled at the Holy Sepulchre in Jerusalem. It descends from heaven and ignites the candles which the patriarch holds in his hands, while with closed eyes he wrestles all alone in the chapel of the Angel. ...This is the sacred new fire; it is passed to the expectant believers.[263]

Ethel L. Urlin, curiously enough, in an unattributed and inexact quotation from Frazer, has the Greek Patriarch in the Chapel of the Angel "all night," waiting for the Holy Fire to descend. In this rite she sees "the old fire ceremonies," finding parallels between the Patriarch's supposed all–night vigil in the Tomb and a ditty sung on Easter Eve by English children as they bear "torches and a little black flag": "We fasted in the night/For this is the Light."[264] Mary Hamilton also suggests that the Paschal light which in the modern Greek Church is passed from the celebrant's candle to the candles held by the worshippers is nothing but a counterpart of the Western "new fire," its "full significance" realized only in Jerusalem at the ceremony of the Holy Fire.[265] A similar equation is made by John Tyrer in his consideration of the Paschal Vigil.[266]

While it is obvious that there are parallels between the kin-

[261] For a good sketch of the modern form, see Baumann, *Lent,* pp. 70ff.

[262] Watts, *Easter,* p. 99.

[263] Frazer, *Golden Bough,* pp. 128–129.

[264] Urlin, *Festivals,* p. 74.

[265] Mary Hamilton, *Greek Saints and Their Festivals* (Edinburgh and London: William Blackwood & Sons, 1910), pp. 134–135.

[266] Tyrer, *Holy Week,* p. 149.

dling of the "new fire" in the Western church's preparatory Paschal services and the pagan, springtime lighting of the hearth fire, the relationship of such a rite to the ceremony of the Holy Fire is tenuous at best. First, the Holy Fire has never been called a "new fire." Furthermore, like the ancient Paschal lighting ceremonies in Rome, the rite seems to derive from the lamp–lighting ceremonies of the Early Church, not from the customs associated with the kindling of the "new fire." Finally, the distribution of the Paschal light in Orthodox services has nothing whatsoever to do with the kindling of fire. Rather, the Paschal light is taken from the vigil lamp that is constantly kept lit over the Altar in Orthodox Churches.[267] The only direct link between the distribution of the Paschal light and the ceremony of the Holy Fire can be found solely in the Greek Churches—and that of late, as we shall see subsequently—and their conscious imitation of the rite in Jerusalem.

The rite of lighting a Paschal candle in the Western church, in which a candle, "...usually very big..., is solemnly blessed in the vigil service of Holy Saturday,"[268] is undoubtedly ancient. In the "...*Liber ordinum* of the fourth century, according to the Visigothic liturgy, there is preserved the lighting of the paschal candle from a lamp (*lucerna*)," probably a rite similar to that followed in Rome before the Paschal Baptismal ceremonies, though clear evidence for this is absent from the liturgical record.[269] As

---

[267] Frazer quite wrongly asserts, in what is at best an imaginative account of Paschal ceremonies in contemporary Greece, that: "At Athens a new fire is kindled in the cathedral at midnight on Holy Saturday. ...Theoretically all the candles [of the worshippers] are lit from the sacred new fire in the cathedral, but practically it may be suspected that the matches which bear the name of Lucifer share in the sudden illumination" (*Golden Bough*, p.130).

[268] Cardinal Giacomo Lercaro, *A Small Liturgical Dictionary*, trans. J. F. Harwood–Tregear (London: Burns & Oates, 1959), p. 63; a description of the Paschal candle can also be found in Martène, *De Antiquis Ritibus*, Vol. 4, p. 24. For a summary of the development of the shape and form of the candle, see Charles G. Herbermann, ed., *The Catholic Encyclopedia* (New York: Robert Appleton Co., 1913), *s.v.* "Paschal Candle," by Herbert Thurston, p. 516.

[269] Dom Fernand Cabrol and Dom Henri Leclercq, *Dictionaire d'Arché-*

we have noted, as late as the eighth century, it seems that lamps, rather than a candle, were the major focus of the Paschal lighting ceremony in Rome.[270] Nonetheless, outside Rome,

> ...the blessing of the paschal candle—usually a column of wax of very large dimensions—was an ancient custom, and so popular did it become that, according to the second edition of the *Liber Pontificalis,* it was sanctioned by Rome in the sixth century in the 'suburbicarium' diocese.[271]

The rite of blessing the Paschal candle is also traced to pagan influence by some scholars.[272] However, it is more likely that it, like the ceremony of the Holy Fire and the Paschal lighting custom in Rome, derives directly from the lighting ceremonies of the Early Church:[273]

> The explanation most favored today is that the candle comes from the ancient [Christian] practice of lighting and blessing a lamp (or lamps) in the early evening to provide light in the darkness. The

---

ologie Chrétienne et de Liturgie (Paris: Librairie Letouzey et Ané, 1938), *s.v.* "Pâques," by Henri Leclercq, col. 1567.

[270] Thus Tyrer affirms what we observed above with regard to ancient liturgical usage in Rome and the absence of the rite of the "new fire": "At Rome, as we know from Pope Zacharias (A.D. 741–52) in his 13th *Epistle* (to Boniface), three lamps of large size were hidden away in some remote part of the church during the consecration of the Chrism...and kept alight till required for use on Easter Even" (*Holy Week,* p. 149). Again, there is no firm evidence from the liturgical sources that a Paschal candle was lighted from these lamps even at this date. We simply know that the candles and lamps in the Church were lighted from these for the Baptismal service on Holy Saturday; *cf.* E. O. James, *Seasonal Feasts and Festivals* (New York: Barnes & Noble, Inc.,1961), p. 212.

[271] James, *Christian Myth,* p. 109.

[272] *Ibid.,* p. 108.

[273] Also in the ancient Christian churches of India we have evidence that the Paschal candle has its origins in the lighting of a lamp, since in the uncorrupted Paschal rubrics of these churches only the lighting of a lamp is appointed; see Varghese Pathikulangara, C.M.I., *Resurrection, Life, and Renewal: A Theological Study of the Liturgical Celebrations of the Great Saturday and the Sunday of Resurrection in the Chaldeo–Indian Church* (Bangalore, India: Dharmaram Publications, 1982), p. 67, n. 112.

ceremony, though practical in origin, became in time an elaborate rite called the *Lucernarium,* 'the lighting of the lamps,' accompanied by psalms, chants, and prayers. Because this service introduced Vespers, Vespers is itself called *Lucernarium,* as it is today in the Milanese rite. The light and blessing of the paschal candle on the greatest night of the year is thus both a survival and a development of a custom once observed every day. That this is probably the true origin of the paschal candle seems to be borne out by the fact that it is still the deacon who carries the candle into the church....[274]

James, attesting to the ancient Christian source of the Paschal candle, notes that, "...the Emperor Constantine, according to Eusebius, caused Jerusalem to be illuminated [by candles[275]] during the night of the Vigil of Easter, and St. Cyril refers to it as 'that night whose darkness is like day.'"[276]

As early as the eighth-century, the ceremonies for the lighting of the Paschal candle were transferred to Holy Saturday morning (where it remains to this day).[277] At the same time, according to James, the rite began taking on a more Eastern character, having been influenced by the Spanish and Gallican rites, which in turn had absorbed many elements of the Eastern liturgical tradition.[278] By the twelfth century, the lighting of the Paschal candle had become universal even to the rites of the Church in Rome. It also came to be attached to the rite of the "new fire," from which the Paschal light was lighted.[279] The symbolism of this ceremony is obvious: Light triumphs over darkness, or darkness is transformed into spiritual daylight. Thus the appropriation of the ceremony by the Church of Rome, along with the rite of the "new fire" and some of the Eastern elements of the Spanish and Gallican liturgical rites was a natural development. By way of this de-

---

[274] O'Shea, "Easter Vigil," p. 10.

[275] He refers to "κηροῦ κίονας," or "wax pillars."

[276] James, *Seasonal Feasts,* pp. 211–212.

[277] *Idem, Christian Myth,* p. 109.

[278] *Idem, Seasonal Feasts,* p. 212.

[279] *Ibid.*

velopment, we can see some interesting parallels between the ceremony of lighting the Paschal candle and the rite of the Holy Fire.

The Gallican Paschal customs,[280] from which the rite of the "new fire" derives, brought together the "new fire" and the blessing of the Paschal candle and gave final form to this pre–vigil Paschal ceremony as it survives in present times.[281] The Spanish rite, however, while it—like the other non–Roman rites—influenced the development of the service of blessing the Paschal candle in the Roman Church, entailed additional liturgical practices which have not survived. These practices are of interest to us, since they contained elements reminiscent of the ancient lamp–lighting service and the Paschal Vigil in Jerusalem that evoke images of the rite of the Holy Fire. Thus we have suggested in Chapter I that Egeria, who was probably a Spanish nun, was familiar with the Jerusalem Paschal Vigil (which she describes as being celebrated "quemadmodum ad nos," or "as we serve it at home"[282]), and that what she saw may have been an ancient form of the rite of the Holy Fire.

It was the practice in the Spanish (Mozarabic) rite for the Paschal Vigil to begin

> ...at the ninth hour; the clergy and the people repair to the church, and every one receives an unlighted taper from the Bishop. He, then, accompanied by the presbyters and deacons only, enters the sacristy, the doors and windows of which are covered with veils, so that it is dark inside. Arrived there, he strikes a fire with a flint and

---

[280] We are not, here, using the term "Gallican" to refer only to the rite used in pre–Carolingian France, but to the "family of non–Roman Latin rites," as R. C. D. Jasper and G. J. Cuming call them. The Spanish, or Mozarabic, rite is also often included under this generic term, though we have chosen to speak of its influence separately, in contrast to the composite influence of the other non–Latin, "Gallican" family of rites on Roman Paschal customs; see R. C. D. Jasper and G. J. Cuming, *Prayers of the Eucharist: Early and Reformed* (New York: Pueblo Publishing Co., 1987), p. 147.

[281] Tyrer, *Holy Week,* pp. 151-152.

[282] Gingras, *Egeria,* p. 114.

tinder; from this a lamp is lighted, and from the lamp the 'Paschal' [candle]. The Bishop thereupon proceeds to bless the lamp... which is held by...[the]...Deacon. ...Next, he blesses the 'Paschal'.... This done, he lights his taper from the 'Paschal,' all the clergy following his example, and the door of the sacristy is opened. Then come the thrice–repeated exclamation *Deo gratias* and the Antiphon *Lumen verum,* while Bishop and clergy walk in procession into the church. As they go along, the chief of the laity (*seniores populi*) light their tapers from the 'Paschal,' and every one else from theirs, so that there is soon a blaze of light.[283]

Tyrer's reconstruction of the Spanish Paschal rite as it was as early as the seventh century is consistent with the evidence found in Professor Rafael Puertas Tricas' collection of literary sources for the history of the Spanish Church. Under an entry from a seventh–century liturgical source, the *Antifonario de León,* we read that:

> En la vigilia pascual...el obispo, después de haber repartido cirios entre los clérigos, marchaba al *thesaurum,* después de haber tapado puertas y ventanas con velos, y procedía a encender la lucerna y el cirio y a bendecirlos [In the Paschal vigil...the Bishop, having distributed candles among the clergy, goes to the sacristy, the doors and windows thereof having been covered with veils, and proceeds to light the lamp and the (Paschal) candle and to bless them].[284]

It is impossible to miss the astounding similarities between the Spanish rite of the blessing of the lamp and the Paschal candle and the rite of the Holy Fire in Jerusalem. The Spanish clergy are enclosed in the sacristy, the doors and windows having been sealed. A lamp is lighted and from it candles are lighted. The doors of the sacristy are opened, the light is passed on to the Faithful, and the Church becomes illuminated. We have here the essential ingredients of the rite of the Holy Fire in its developed form: the Patriarch is enclosed in the darkened Holy Sepulchre,

---

[283] Tyrer, *Holy Week,* pp. 154–155.

[284] Rafael Puertas Tricas, *Iglesias Hispánicas (Siglos IV al VIII): Testimonios Literarios* (Madrid: Dirección General del Patrimonio Artístico y Cultural, Ministerio de Educación y Ciencia, 1975), pp. 144–145.

which has been sealed; the Patriarch reads a blessing for the reception of the Holy Fire; the lamp on the Tomb ignites; and the Patriarch lights candles from the lamp and passes the Holy Fire on to the worshippers, whose candles illuminate the darkened Church. One is tempted by this evidence to conclude that the Spanish Paschal rite is modelled after the ceremonies in Jerusalem; that what Egeria saw in Jerusalem was precisely what she saw at home; and, therefore, that it must have been the ceremony of the Holy Fire, conducted within the Holy Sepulchre, which she saw on her pilgrimage.

However, there are also difficulties with such a conclusion, though these difficulties, admittedly, are in the domain of skeptical scholars and little work against what a circumspect believer cannot help but take as something more than accidental similarities. First, we do not know in detail the form of services in Spain before the sixth or seventh centuries. Thus, we cannot assume that what Egeria saw in Jerusalem was what we see in seventh–century Spain. Second, there are no indisputable historical data to establish that the Spanish rite was an outright adaptation of Eastern liturgical usage. Even the assumption, though upheld by many scholars, that the Mozarabic rite was influenced by the liturgies of the East is based primarily on textual analysis, not on instances of clear collaboration and exchange.[285] Third, pre–ninth–century accounts of the Paschal ceremonies in Jerusalem do not consistently portray the same rites there that we observe in seventh–century Spain. Finally, while there are remarkable similarities between the Mozarabic rite which we have described and the fully developed ceremony of the Holy Fire, there are also similarities between the pre–twelfth–century Paschal customs in

---

[285] Jasper and Cuming, for example, contend that the non–Roman Latin rites "...tend to show more traces of Eastern influence than does the native Roman rite" (*Eucharist*, p. 147). Gregory Dix, on the other hand, while acknowledging such influence, argues that "...these eastern borrowings are relatively late and of superficial importance, matters of decoration rather than of substance"; see Dom Gregory Dix, *The Shape of the Liturgy* (San Francisco: Harper & Row Publishers, 1982), p. 549.

Rome and the earlier accounts of that ceremony. In Rome a lamp was "hidden away," and from it the Church's lamps and candles (albeit, originally the Baptismal candles) were lighted. Here, too, we have the custom of "bringing out" light from a hidden place (from the Holy Sepulchre, as Egeria says[286]) and using that light to conduct the Paschal Baptismal service and to illuminate the Church. As compelling as the similarities between the Mozarabic Paschal rites and the ceremony of the Holy Fire may be, it is always possible—at least for the skeptic or unbeliever— that these similarities are simply adventitious.

We must address one final question. If, indeed, the rite of the Holy Fire in Jerusalem has elements in common with the lighting ceremonies of the Christian West—whether those of Rome or those of the Gallican and Spanish rites—, which influenced which? Are the lighting ceremonies in Rome and Christian Europe a conscious imitation of an ancient miracle in the Tomb of Christ, or did the lighting ceremonies of the Early Church, common to Eastern and Western Christianity, develop into an elaborate ritual in post–ninth–century Jerusalem involving either the miraculous or sleight of hand? With regard to the question of who influenced whom, it is probably safe to say that, in most instances, the liturgical practices of the Western church ultimately derive from those of Eastern Christianity. One writer, Joan L. Roccasalvo, uses the following as a working axiom for her liturgical study of the Eastern Church:

> To a large extent the roots of Western culture can be traced to the ancient cultures of the East. Western studies in history, religion, philosophy, literature, and fine arts often begin with Greek culture and thought.[287]

With allowances for overstatement in this formula, we can follow her lead and say that it was from the East that the Paschal

---

[286] "The light...is taken from inside the grotto [the Holy Sepulchre]" (Gingras, *Egeria,* p. 90).

[287] Joan L. Roccasalvo, *The Eastern Catholic Churches: An Introduction to Their Worship and Spirituality* (Collegeville, MN: Liturgical Press, 1992), p. 5.

ceremonies of the West must have likely come.

The question of whether the Paschal ceremonies of the West constitute a reenactment of a miracle at the Tomb of Christ in Jerusalem is a different kind of question. Undoubtedly, at least in the pre–Schism Christian Church, the Holy Land was a center of devotion for both Eastern and Western Christians and there was a common attribution of supernatural significance to its Holy Places and rites. We have seen evidence, for example, that some pre–Schism Latin Christians once believed that the ceremony of the Holy Fire involved a miraculous descent of "fire" or "light" from Heaven. There is no reason to believe, therefore, that Western Paschal customs did not once commemorate such a belief. At the same time, we have no recorded evidence to support such a belief.[288] The question, it would seem, must remain unanswered, not because the historical record is wholly insufficient, but because any answer would have to account for the issue of belief in the miraculous. And again, this is a matter of religious psychology, not historical investigation. The skeptic would never admit to that which makes the historical record sufficient.

---

[288] There is, however, abundant evidence that pilgrims to Jerusalem brought back to the West images and impressions that affected at least Church architecture. In a recent book on the general influence of Jerusalem on both Eastern and Western Christian art and worship, Robert Ousterhout discusses the influence of the architecture in Jerusalem on the construction of Churches in the West; see his chapter, "Loca Sancta and the Architectural Response to Pilgrimage" in Robert Ousterhout, ed., *The Blessings of Pilgrimage* (Urbana and Chicago: University of Illinois Press, 1990), pp. 108–124.

CHAPTER III

CONTEMPORARY ASSESSMENTS OF
THE PHENOMENON OF THE HOLY FIRE

As we observed in Chapter I, the historical data regarding the rite of the Holy Fire are complex and problematic. This in part accounts for the fact that, while the phenomenon is perhaps better known to Eastern Christians, Christians in both the East and the West are on the whole rather unfamiliar with the enactment of the ceremony each year in Jerusalem. Moreover, not only has the Holy Fire been variously understood and treated by historical investigators, both as a miracle or as a deliberate hoax, but one finds in contemporary reference works a wide diversity of opinions about it. This diversity, again, is prompted by a lack of careful and objective historical study of the rite and by the relative obscurity of the phenomenon.

To capture a vision of the rite of the Holy Fire as it is understood in the contemporary Christian world, we will turn to various accounts from encyclopædic source books. Though perhaps not exhaustive, our sources constitute a fairly complete and unique collection of the very scant treatments of the subject that can be found in standard historical, liturgical, and theological reference works—further evidence, indeed, of the limited general and critical attention paid to the fascinating rite of the Holy Fire. The sources have been divided into those which view the phenomenon in a polemical tone, as a pious hoax; those which are skeptical about the phenomenon, but not polemical in their expressions of their skepticism; those which report on the subject objectively and remain neutral with regard to the authenticity of the miracle; and one source which accepts the phenomenon as a genuine religious miracle, this latter source with Eastern Christian sympathies and affiliations.

Polemical References. The view that the Holy Fire is a hoax and the product of trickery is reflected in an entry from a standard religious encyclopædia which condemns the phenomenon as a disgrace both to religion and human nature:

> The Greek and Armenian clergy combine on this occasion, and amidst processions, solemnities, an excited multitude, and scenes disgraceful not only to the name of religion, but to human nature, the expected fire makes its appearance from within an apartment in which a Greek and an Armenian bishop have locked themselves.[289]

The "apartment" to which the author of this citation alludes is, of course, the Edicule of the Holy Sepulchre, the Holy *Kouvouklion*. The purported combination of Greek and Armenian clergy is an overstatement of the passive rôle that the Armenian clergy play in receiving the Holy Fire from the Orthodox celebrants. The polemical tone of this citation is again consistent with the nineteenth– and early twentieth–century assessments of the Holy Fire on which the few more contemporary encyclopædic references to the phenomenon are often based.

Another standard encyclopædic reference dismisses the Holy Fire with equal disapproval:

> In the church of the Holy Sepulcher in Jerusalem until a few years ago[290] the pious fraud of the 'holy fire' was perpetrated by the Greek patriarch who presented from the sacred tomb three times a lighted taper or torch which he declared had been lighted by a miracle without human intervention. The spectators, wrought to great excitement, struggled to light their tapers at the miraculous fire, and then carried it throughout the Greek world. In the twelfth century Saladin is said by an early tradition to have witnessed this miracle and acknowledged its miraculous character....[291]

[289] The Rev. John M'Clintock and James Strong, eds., *Cyclopedia of Biblical, Theological, and Ecclesiastical Literature* (New York: Harper & Bros. Publishers, 1891), *s.v.* "Holy Fire," p. 305.

[290] The author was apparently under the impression that the ceremony of the Holy Fire had ceased to be celebrated in Jerusalem at the time that he was writing. This is, of course, untrue.

All of the elements of nineteenth–century, early twentieth–century, and most contemporary polemical assessments of the rite of the Holy Fire are also contained in this passage: the rite is a fraud—albeit a "pious" one—; involves unseemly behavior on the part of the believers; and belongs to the world of the Greeks.

Recounting the deeds of the eleventh–century despot al–Hakim and the destruction of the Church of the Holy Sepulchre in Jerusalem, *The Encyclopedia of Islam* makes reference to the Holy Fire in a polemical tone, noting that its fraudulent nature led to this unfortunate event:

> ...The destruction of the Church of the Holy sepulchre at Jerusalem; according to Ibu al–Kalanisi, this was because the caliph was indignant at a fraud practised by the monks in the miracle of the descent of the holy fire on to the altar.[292]

The descent of the Holy Fire did not take place, as suggested in this entry, on the Altar of the Church, but at the Sepulchre itself. The author is repeating an error of the chronicler al–Qalanisi.

Skeptical References. Several encyclopædic references express skepticism about the Holy Fire, neither maintaining a polemical nor a neutral position with regard to the phenomenon. One such example is from a Greek–language reference work, under the entry "Ceremony of the (Holy) Fire":

> Celebrated in Jerusalem on the afternoon of Great Saturday. In it, the Orthodox Patriarch of Jerusalem, along with his Bishops and a large number of Priests, Deacons, and Chanters, as well as the Patriarch of the Armenians, form a procession in the Church of the Resurrection. Extinguishing all of the lights of the Church, the Patriarch, in simple white vestments, enters into the Edicule of the Holy Sepulchre, sealed and dark up to this time, and, having prayed on the Holy Tomb, distributes the Holy Fire[293] from two

---

[291] Samuel M. Jackson, ed., *The New Schaff–Herzog Encyclopedia of Religious Knowledge* (Grand Rapids: Baker Book House, 1963), *s.v.* "Easter," by D. S. Schaff, pp. 45–46.

[292] B. Lewis *et al.*, eds., *The Encyclopedia of Islam: New Edition* (Leiden, Netherlands: E. J. Brill, 1971), *s.v.* "al–Hâkim bi–amr Allâh," by M. Canard.

[293] Here and elsewhere we have translated the Greek "Αγιον Φῶς" as

torches to those outside the Edicule. This rite derives from the lofty symbolism of the enlightenment of mankind by the Resurrection of Christ.[294]

While we see no polemics against the rite of the Holy Fire, it is clear from this entry that the Holy Fire is a symbolic expression of the light of the Resurrection. In fact, no mention is made of the claim that the Fire is of miraculous origin. This explanation of the phenomenon is representative of the legacy of what we have called the post–Byzantine Greek assessment of the Holy Fire among Greek intellectuals.

This same skeptical attitude we see in another standard, modern Greek reference work, *The Encyclopædia of Religion and Ethics,* under the entry "Holy Fire":

As is known to all, on the night of Great Saturday, shortly before the Liturgy of the Resurrection, the celebrant distributes to the Faithful the bright light of the Resurrection from the eternal lamp in the Altar [a lamp which usually hangs behind or over the Holy Table and which is kept lit constantly] with the words, 'Come and take from the unwaning light, glorifying Christ, Who is risen from the dead.' All of the lights are then lighted and the Church is made brilliant with abundant light, symbolizing the enlightenment of mankind by Christ's Resurrection. The distribution of this holy light commemorates the splendid ceremony of the Holy Fire in Jerusalem, during which the Orthodox Patriarch distributes to the faithful pilgrims the Holy Fire of the Resurrection.

This ceremony [in Jerusalem] is celebrated with great majesty on the afternoon of Great Saturday. During the ceremony, the Orthodox Patriarch and his Bishops and many Priests, Deacons, and Chanters go in procession to the Church of the Resurrection. All of the lights of the Church having been extinguished, the Patriarch alone, in simple, humble white vestments, enters into the Edicule of the Holy Tomb, until then darkened and sealed, and,

---

"Holy Fire," for the sake of clarity. It should be noted, however, that the actual Greek appellation means "Holy Light."

[294] Ἐγκυκλοπαιδικὸν Λεξικὸν Ἐλευθερουδάκη (Athens: 1931), *s.v.* "Φωτὸς ἁγίου τελετή," by D. I. Kouimoutsopoulos, p. 768.

after extended prayer, comes forth from the Edicule and distributes the Holy Fire of the Resurrection to the waiting Faithful from two torches. Pious pilgrims to the Holy Places during Paschaltide describe with wonder and contrition the ceremony of the Holy Fire, which, it is said, does not have the property of burning [those who handle it].[295]

This description of the Holy Fire is certainly not polemical, and worthy of note is the fact that the entry contains a reference to the allegedly miraculous properties of the Holy Fire. However, this reference is prefaced by the expression "it is said," which in Greek carries with it a tone of skepticism ("ὡς λέγουν," literally, "as they say"). Once again, too, there is no mention of its supernatural origin. It should be noted that the entry, written by Spyridon Makres, is almost identical to the foregoing entry by Professor D. I. Kouimoutsopoulos, save for a few added expressions. This is perhaps evidence of the fixed view that modern Greek intellectuals have of the phenomenon of the Holy Fire.

Finally, a relatively recent reference work contains an entry about the Holy Fire which, again while not polemical, expresses skepticism about the ceremony, which it attributes to a legend:

Holy Fire, a legend associated with the blessing of the new fire during the Easter Vigil is conducted according to the Orthodox rite in the Church of the Holy Sepulcher in Jerusalem. Early versions of the legend date from the 11th and 12th cent.... The legend varies in content, but the following may be regarded as the most widespread elements: (1) The fire is of miraculous origin, descending as the tongues of fire on Pentecost. Some commentators hold that this 'spontaneous flame' is caused by a chemically treated torch that ignites after a certain period of time or upon contact with water. This procedure may have been intended as a symbolic dramatization, but because of the widespread belief that it is a miracle some have viewed it as a deliberate deception. (2) The fire neither gives heat nor consumes. (Some Greek accounts describe it as *phos*, (light), not *pur*, (fire).) ...The fire is selective, bypassing the

---

[295] A. Martinos, ed., *Θρησκευτικὴ καὶ Ἠθικὴ Ἐγκυκλοπαιδεία* (Athens: 1968), *s.v.* "Φῶς, Ἅγιον," by S. G. Makres, cols. 13–14.

candles of all those who are not of the Orthodox faith. This aspect of the legend seems to have originated shortly after the schism of 1054.[296]

There are, of course, many inaccuracies in this report. The historical recounting of the development of the rite is misleading, since the first account of the ceremony dates to the ninth century. Also, the Holy Fire is never called "fire" in Greek sources, but is always called "light." Nor is it part of a ceremony of striking "new fire." Furthermore, as we have seen in the historical record, well after the Schism of 1054 there were non–Orthodox participants in the ceremony, many of whom are reported as taking the light from the Orthodox, as the Armenians and other non–Orthodox do to this day. This argues against the claim that a legend began around the time of the Schism that the Holy Fire bypassed the candles of non–Orthodox participants in the rite. Despite these weaknesses, however, the entry is not polemical in tone and leaves even the accusation of deception to an anonymous "some."

Neutral References. There are only several references to the ceremony of the Holy Fire which report the details of the phenomenon without polemical remarks and in a neutral tone. The first of these is from an early twentieth–century edition of the *Catholic Encyclopedia,* which simply mentions the phenomenon in passing in the course of an entry on the Holy Sepulchre: "In each of the side walls [of the Edicule] at the east end is an oval opening used on Holy Saturday by the Greeks for the distribution of the 'Holy Fire.'"[297] There is nothing remarkable or informative about this entry, but it is an interesting example of a reference to the Holy Fire—something rare in and of itself—which simply treats the ceremony as an event, rather than as an occasion for negative comments with regard to claims about its miraculous origins or properties.

---

[296] Paul Meagher, O.P., S.T.M., *et al.,* eds., *The Encyclopedic Dictionary of Religion* (Washington, DC: Corpus Publications, 1979), *s.v.* "Holy Fire," by R. H. Marshall, p. 1690.

[297] Charles G. Herbermann, ed., *The Catholic Encyclopedia* (New York: Robert Appleton Co., 1913), *s.v.* "Holy Sepulchre," by A. L. McMahon, p. 426.

A second neutral presentation of the rite of the Holy Fire is found in a standard, modern Greek encyclopædic reference. Under the heading "Holy Fire," we read the following:

Thus is called the light distributed by the Orthodox Patriarch of Jerusalem to the Faithful on Great Saturday. On the afternoon of Great Saturday, all of the lights of the Church of the Resurrection having been extinguished, the Patriarch enters the Edicule of the Holy Sepulchre and, after praying, distributes the Holy Fire to those outside from two torches. Much has been written about this Fire, comprised especially of commentaries about the celebration of the rite and its actuality.[298]

Sympathetic References. The single sympathetic encyclopædic reference to the ceremony of the Holy Fire is found in a Coptic reference work in an entry on the celebration of Holy Saturday:

Every year on Holy Saturday, the eve of Easter, the four Orthodox churches[299] in the Holy Land (Greek, Armenian, Coptic, and Syrian) participate in the Apparition of the Holy Light....

Early in the morning all sanctuary lamps inside the Holy Sepulchre are extinguished and refilled with new oil and new wicks. At about eleven o'clock, the entrance to the Holy Sepulchre is closed and sealed. ...At about half past twelve, the Greek Orthodox procession makes three circuits around the rotunda, after which the Greek patriarch or his representative, who presides over the celebration, enters the aedicula after undoing its seals.

At about one o'clock, following the celebration of the Apparition of the Holy Light, a Coptic priest and a Coptic layman take the light from the aedicula to the Coptic chapel adjacent to the

---

[298] Μεγάλη Έλληνική Έγκυκλοπαιδεία, 2nd ed. (Athens: 1926–1934), *s.v.* "Φῶς ἅγιον," by K. I. Dyobouniotes, p. 318.

[299] This term is often used by the non–Chalcedonian Oriental churches to refer to all non–Latin and non–Protestant Christian churches, whether Chalcedonian or non–Chalcedonian. It should not be understood as an indication that these various Churches are in communion with one another; nor is the term used here as it is by the various Churches which belong to the Constantinopolitan hegemony and call themselves, collectively, *Greek* or *Eastern Orthodox.*

Holy Sepulcher.... At the same time, another member of the Coptic community receives the light from the southern oval window of the aedicula and proceeds via the same route to the Coptic chapel, where the candle lamps are lit from the Holy Light and the congregation light their own candles.[300]

It is indeed as great a mystery as the phenomenon itself that a ceremony as old as that of the Holy Fire should be so seldom mentioned in encyclopædic historical, liturgical, and theological references. Moreover, it is surprising that so much of what is reported in the scant references available is marked by such little critical scholarship and by factual errors and historiographical prejudice. We have included in this survey several standard, modern Greek reference works, not only because there are so few secondary references to the Holy Fire in English, but because these Greek sources are reasonably well known to Western scholars. As well, they provide one with an opportunity to see that even in the Greek–speaking world, despite the popularity of the rite among religious folk, the ceremony of the Holy Fire is given but short shrift.

---

[300] Aziz S. Attiya, ed., *The Coptic Encyclopedia* (New York: MacMillan Publishing Co., 1991), *s.v.* "Holy Saturday," by Archbishop Basilios, p. 1248.

CHAPTER IV

THE PHENOMENON OF THE HOLY FIRE FROM A THEOLOGICAL PERSPECTIVE

Having looked with some care at the historical sources for the rite of the Holy Fire, its possible relationship to similar Paschal rites in the Latin Church, and the scant reference material on the ceremony, let us now look at the phenomenon in a wholly different way: from a theological perspective. Whatever its source, whether it is produced miraculously or by sleight of hand, and however obscure it may be to scholars East and West, the rite of the Holy Fire is, as we suggested earlier, worthy of further study simply as the *phenomenon* that it is. And taken simply as a phenomenon, it yields to theological treatment; in particular, the symbol of the Holy Fire itself and the various manifestations associated with it conform to the unifying imagery of the vision of God in the Eastern Christian understanding of Scripture and the Patristic witness. For the sake of brevity, we have compiled a statistical summary of the various manifestations of the Holy Fire and the effects associated with it from the post–ninth–century commentators and witnesses cited in Chapter 1. The data were entered independently of the subject's belief or disbelief in the Holy Fire and both from the reports of eyewitnesses and second-hand observers or chroniclers:

TABLE A

Various Manifestations of the Holy Fire

Manifestation	Number of Reports
Light from Heaven or holy light	14
White, blue, or violet light	6
Flash of light or lightning	5
Fire	4
Rain, dew, or snow	4

Cloud or smoke	4
Cross or triangle of light	2
Unconsuming flame	2
Angel	2
Dove	2

$$n = 45$$

Table B

Effects Associated with the Holy Fire

Effect	Number of Reports
Miraculous lighting of lamps	13
Miraculous lighting of candles	3
Loud noise or whistle	2
Earthquake	1

$$n = 19$$

In both of these tables, aside from specific supernatural manifestations and effects also contained in the *corpus* of Christian Scripture and the Patristic witness, as we will subsequently see, there is in general a remarkable frequency of reports of light imagery, which holds such a pivotal place in the Orthodox theological scheme. In Table A, the Holy Fire appears as a manifestation of light (including lightning and fire) thirty–three times, or, where n is the total number of reports entered, 73% of the time. In Table B, where $n = 19$, 84% of the effects associated with the Holy Fire are also associated with the production of light or a flame. In the first instance, accounting for the uneven and low frequency of non–light–related manifestations of the Holy Fire, a statistic of 73% actually deflates the power of our observation, since a light–related manifestation occurs more than eight times more frequently than the largest number of other reports taken separately and eleven times more frequently than the mean frequency of these reports together.

With regard to the Eastern Church's understanding of the

vision of God and light imagery, Jostein Børtnes provides a summary of what he calls the "light metaphysics of Christian Neo–Platonism...developed in the early Fathers of the Eastern Church," a metaphysics which he approaches from the æsthetic of the Icon:

> The origins of Orthodox light metaphysics are to be found in Dionysius the Areopagite's synthesis of Neo–Platonist philosophy and the light theology of the Fourth Gospel [of Saint John]. The metaphysics of light...is grounded on the idea that material light is an image of the pure, unintelligible Light, which is God in His transcendent glory. The light we perceive through our senses is the self–revelation of the transcendent godhead. Therefore, according to [the] Neo–Platonist aesthetics [of the Areopagite], light is the highest and most perfect manifestation of beauty, the reflection of divine beauty, truth, and goodness, which never reveals itself directly to man, but which 'sends forth a ray, incessantly and continuously produced in itself,[301] and transforms this ray through its goodness into natural radiance, which corresponds to individual finite beings. It raises those who are hit by the Holy Spirit up to itself according to their possibilities, lets them behold its reflection and partake of it, and teaches them to resemble itself as much as possible.'

The experience of God underlying this aesthetics of light is difficult to apprehend from a modern angle. It presupposes the medieval concept of analogy,[302] implying that all things have been

---

[301] We might point out that Saint Dionysios (†96) is not putting forth a theory of neo–Platonic emanationism with this imagery. As Father John Romanides contends: "It is the uncreated Logos Himself Who is sent and not a created imitation, and the relationship established between God and creation is real both ways and not mediated by subordinate creature–gods"; see the Rev. John S. Romanides, "H. A. Wolfson's Philosophy of the Church Fathers," *The Greek Orthodox Theological Review,* Vol. 5 (1959), p. 72.

[302] The idea of an analogy of being between God and man is, of course, foreign to the Greek Fathers. Thus, Father Florovsky writes that: "...there is no similarity between that which comes forth from nothing and the Creator Who verily *is,* Who brings creatures out of nothing"; see [Protopresbyter] Georges Florovsky, *Creation and Redemption* (Belmont, MA: Nordland Publishing Co., 1976), p. 48.

created in the image and likeness of the Creator, being in various degrees 'manifestations of God, images, vestiges, or shadows of the Creator....'

...Whereas in the Areopagite the opposition between the noetic reality of the divine and the world perceived by our senses is absolute, this is no longer so in post–iconoclastic aesthetics. Here, Christ through His Incarnation has become mediator between the two spheres. This Christocentric reinterpretation of Dionysian light mysticism was carried through by Saint Maximus the Confessor, the seventh–century theologian, according to which Christ is the prototype transforming each individual believer into his image and filling him with his energy, thus assimilating him to Himself. This process of assimilation, the return of the image to its prototype, of the thing to its logos, is what is meant by the term *theosis,* or deification[:] determined by the conception that light is the highest perceptible expression of the transcendent God in whom everything has its origin, a visible symbol of Christ. ...By becoming light, all men, indeed all things are transformed into images, or icons, of the Uncreated light which is God himself.[303]

There are some serious theological problems in Børtnes' statements, and, though they are not our specific concern in this chapter, we are obliged to comment briefly on them before drawing on his correct understanding of the rôle of light in Orthodox theology. In the first place, while he is correct in associating the Areopagite's theological understanding of light with a general Orthodox metaphysics of light, he is led into error by his assumption that Dionysian theology, if not the *corpus* of Orthodox thought, is neo–Platonic in origin. A number of scholars have challenged this assumption and argue that neo–Platonic concepts of God and the cosmos are at odds with Dionysian theology and the consensus of the Eastern Fathers, to which he belongs. For example, Andrew Louth has pointed out, with regard to Saint Dionysios and other Fathers, that

303 Jostein Børtnes, *Visions of Glory: Studies in Early Russian Historiography,* trans. Jostein Børtnes and Paul L. Nielsen (Oslo: Solum Forlag A/s, 1988), pp. 82–84.

...though we can see Patristic mysticism taking its cue from Platonist mysticism when it tries to achieve intellectual expression—and such is hardly surprising, it seems to me that at several points this intellectual background is modified.[304]

Louth goes on to consider three very important issues, namely, the concept of God, the soul's relationship to God, and the moral virtues, in which the Greek Fathers and the neo–Platonists are quite distant from one another in their thinking. In effect, he says, "...the Fathers...readily use Platonist language but it is transfigured by the context in which they use it."[305] Similarly, in very strong language, Louis Bouyer dismisses unqualified accusations of neo–Platonism against the Fathers, tracing these accusations to an "unjustifiable prejudice," wherein "...it...[has]...to be shown at any cost that any thinking in Christianity and also in Judaism, must necessarily be a foreign importation."[306]

Børtnes, basing his understanding of Orthodox anthropology and soteriology on the æsthetics of the Icon, also overstates the idea of human salvation as an appropriation of the image of Christ, the return of the image to its prototype, of the "thing to its logos." The anthropology and soteriology of the Eastern Fathers are far more complex than this. The *Logos*, or Christ, as a

---

[304] Andrew Louth, *The Origins of the Christian Mystical Tradition, From Plato to Denys* (Oxford: Clarendon Press, 1981), p. 194; *cf.* Vladimir Lossky's chap. "The Divine Darkness," in *The Mystical Theology of the Eastern Church* (Cambridge and London: James Clarke & Co., 1973), pp. 23–43, where he argues vehemently against the idea that Saint Dionysios, in particular, was a neo–Platonist.

[305] Louth, *Origins*, p. 198. This is not to say, however, that the human being cannot approach God, for the soul is, according to Saint Gregory the Theologian (Nazianzus, †390), also "...deified by its inclination to God"; see his "Oration xlv: The Second Oration on Easter," in *Nicene and Post–Nicene Fathers*, ed. Phillip Schaff, Vol. 7, 2nd ser. (Grand Rapids, MI: Eerdman's Publishing Co., 1978), p. 425.

[306] Louis Bouyer, Dom Jean Leclercq, Dom François Vandenbroucke, and Louis Cognet, *The Spirituality of the New Testament and the Fathers*, trans. Mary P. Ryan (New York: Seabury Press, 1963), p. 259.

manifestation of the transcendent God, of the Hypostasis of the Father, is not in Orthodox theology a mere "prototype." Børtnes uses this word in too imprecise a way. The restoration of the image of God in man is not one of identity—a union of image and prototype—, but of imitation and participation. Thus, θέωσις, or deification, is not a "return" of the human person to the *Logos* (or simply to some "prototype" of Christ, for that matter), but an appropriation of God's Energies in man—Grace—, which is contained in, but does not encompass or fully define, the Divine Person and *Logos* of Christ. Deification is a participation in the Grace, but not the Essence, of God, as Father Georges Florovsky observes:

> The source and power of human *theosis* is not the Divine essence [which the *Logos* is], but the 'Grace of God.' ...Χάρις is not identical with the οὐσία. It is θεία καὶ ἄκτιστος χάρις καὶ ἐνέργεια [Divine and Uncreated Grace and Energy].[307]

In describing the process of deification, Børtnes also makes a directional error. He speaks of man returning to his image. This is true only figuratively, for in actuality, as Florovsky avers, "...in his 'energies' the Unapproachable God mysteriously *approaches man*. And this Divine move effects encounter: πρόοδος εἰς τὰ ἔξω, in the phrase of St. Maximus."[308] Divinization, again, is not simply a return to some lost image; nor is it an "assimilation" by God: "...the soul is not absorbed into...[God]...," as Professor Cavarnos observes.[309] Rather, divinization entails the restoration of human nature in its encounter with God, by which the pre–Lapsarian image of God is restored and renewed[310] in the hu-

---

307 Florosvky, *Bible*, p. 117.

308 *Ibid.*

309 Constantine Cavarnos, *Byzantine Thought and Art* (Belmont, MA: Institute for Byzantine and Modern Greek Studies, 1968), p. 28.

310 As an incidental note, this idea of "renewal" is not just rhetorical; rather, the restoration of the human person to a proper, pre–Lapsarian relationship with God involves a new and fuller communion with God, rooted in the Light of the Resurrection. Thus, divinization is both a restoration and a literal "renewal." This point is clearly made in an essay by Father Gregory Telepneff,

man person, whose "...individuality is not only retained but enhanced."[311]

With specific regard to iconographic æsthetics, Børtnes' observations are in want of further critical treatment. He is wrong in his idea that in becoming light, the image being assimilated by its prototype, images are transformed into the Uncreated Light which is God Himself. This is a completely muddled statement of the basic theology of Icons. First, the relationship between an image and its prototype is hypostatic in nature, not one of mutual "absorption," as it were. That is, the Icon does not become a holy object by virtue of being literally "drawn into" the holiness of what it represents; rather, as Saint Theodore the Studite (†826) argues, every object having an *hypostasis* or an objective identity which is defined by its purpose, the objective hypostasis of a material Icon allows it to participate hypostatically in the holiness of what it represents, its prototype, simply because this participation is the natural intention of an Icon.[312] Commenting on the iconographic theology of Saint Theodore, Archbishop Chrysostomos of Etna, Father James Thornton, and I have explained this principle as follows:

...An icon, while material and while a mere image in some limited sense, nonetheless also exists in objective hypostasis, the image be-

"The Concept of the Person in the Christian Hellenism of the Greek Church Fathers: A Study of Origen, St. Gregory the Theologian, and St. Maximos the Confessor" (doctoral dissertation, Graduate Theological Union, Berkeley, 1991), pp. 152–154, 295–297, 355–360. He bases his argument on the thought of Saint Irenæus of Lyons († *ca.* 202), Saint Gregory the Theologian, and Saint Maximos the Confessor (†662). One must not, of course, overstate the theme of renewal, since we are speaking here of "degrees" of spiritual glory. Thus Saint Gregory Palamas (†1359) assures us that before the Fall, "Adam too participated in this divine illumination and radiance [τῆς θείας ἐλλάμψεως τε καὶ λαμπρότητος], and he was truly clothed in a garment of glory" (Saint Gregory Palamas, *The One Hundred and Fifty Chapters,* trans. R. E. Sinkewicz, c.s.b. [Toronto, ON: Pontifical Institute of Medieval Studies, 1988], p. 161).

[311] Cavarnos, *Byzantine Thought,* p. 28.

[312] See Saint Theodore the Studite, *On the Holy Icons,* trans. Catherine Roth (Crestwood, NY: St. Vladimir's Seminary Press, 1981), esp. pp. 102–108.

ing joined to its prototype, participating in the holiness of that which it depicts. One must not be presumptuous here and find neo–Platonic parallels in this iconic theory, as Western observers are wont to do. The theory stems from pure Christological theology. St. Theodore clearly argues that an icon cannot participate in the very essence of its prototype. There is thus no emanationism to be found in his argument. He simply points out that the hypostatic nature of an object allows for the material icon to participate in the holiness of its prototype, since this is the natural intention of an icon (intentionality, we should emphasize, being foreign to symbols, but natural to perceived images), part of its very identity. The veneration offered up to an icon reaches up to its prototype because it is implicit in the intrinsic character, in the hypostatic identity of an icon, that the veneration of the image should reach up to its prototype.[313]

Second, Uncreated Light is not "God Himself" essentially, but is a manifestation of God's Energies. Thus, an Icon does not become light, anymore than a person who experiences *theosis* literally becomes light; rather such a person is transformed by Grace and perceives even in a sensible way, as we shall see, the Divine or Uncreated Light attendant to and inseparable from Divine Grace. And finally, the objective hypostasis of an Icon cannot be equated with the hypostatic reality of the human person, who is not only transformed by Grace, but participates in It in a way that an inanimate object does not.[314]

Because of his failure to understand the Orthodox notion of the nature of God and because of his misunderstanding of the

[313] Hieromonk [Bishop] Auxentios, Bishop [Archbishop] Chrysostomos of Oreoi [Etna], and the Reverend James Thornton, "Notions of Reality and the Resolution of Dualism in the Phenomenological Precepts of Merleau–Ponty and the Orthodox Responses to Iconoclasm," *The American Benedictine Review*, Vol. 41, No. 1 (1990), p. 96.

[314] We should probably also note that the Icon is by nature subservient to the human person; it *serves* human spiritual development. Its intended purpose is to arouse "...our moral and spiritual zeal...and...[reinforce] our efforts to imitate the sacred persons and live in the light of religious truth" (Cavarnos, *Byzantine Thought*, p. 72).

hypostatic uniqueness of the human person, Børtnes wrongly summarizes the hesychastic doctrine of Saint Gregory Palamas. He does rightly portray Palamite theology as an exemplary expression of the unifying principle of a metaphysics of light in the Eastern Fathers. And he correctly observes that Saint Gregory Palamas' ascetic and spiritual tradition is a synthesis of ancient traditions, and that the teaching of Palamas' mentor, Saint Gregory of Sinai (†1346), "...in essence goes back to the traditional mysticism of the fifth–century Orthodox ascetics."[315] But in his faulty grasp of the Essence–Energy distinction which underlies Saint Gregory's ascetic *theology* (a distinction with equally ancient precedents[316]), Børtnes' limited understanding of Orthodox theology and anthropology comes to light. He thus fails to understand that the Essence–Energy distinction serves not only to explain how the simplicity of God is maintained in an apparent separation of His Energies (which can be perceived) from His Essence (which is transcendent and unknowable), but defines the limits and scope of the ascetic efforts by which the hesychasts achieved a vision of God.

Børtnes, following, among other scholars, the work of Father John Meyendorff,[317] suggests that there must have been "...several points of contact between Hesychasm and the [Bogomil] heretics,"[318] and thus attributes much of the ascetic theology of

---

[315] Børtnes, *Visions of Glory*, p. 110. This affirmation is supported by Father Florovsky's study, *The Byzantine Fathers of the Fifth Century*, trans. Raymond Miller, Anne–Marie Döllinger–Labriolle, and Helmut Wilhelm Schmiedel (Belmont, MA: Notable and Academic Books, 1987), though Father Florovsky goes on to say that these Fathers represent a theological tradition, a unity of thought, which reaches back to Scripture itself (p. 16).

[316] In a very persuasive manner, Florovsky has pointed out that the Essence–Energy distinction can be traced back at least to Saint Athanasios the Great (†373) and his distinction between God's absolute Essence and his "power and bounty," and clearly to the Cappadocian concept of God in "essence" and "action," as well as to other earlier Greek Fathers; see Florosvky, *Bible*, pp. 116–117.

[317] See John Meyendorff, *A Study of Gregory Palamas*, trans. George Lawrence (London: The Faith Press, 1975), esp. pp. 32–33.

the hesychasts to a disdain for the body. There is, however, no historical evidence whatsoever to support Meyendorff's claim that the hesychasts and Bogomils may have had "...traits of spirituality common to both of them."[319] If anything, contacts between the two groups resulted in the condemnation of the spiritual precepts and practices of the Bogomil heretics and their negative attitudes toward the body by the hesychasts.[320] Meyendorff's view of hesychastic spirituality is also compromised by a general philosophical misunderstanding of Palamite thought[321] and by certain misapprehensions and misstatements of Saint Gregory Palamas' theological positions. Thus, Børtnes, presumably influenced by Meyendorff, sees the ascetic tradition of the hesychasts in the light of a kind of neo–Platonic mysticism and fails to understand this tradition as an expression of the Greek Patristic consensus. Speaking of Palamas, Børtnes says that:

> Many of the ideas he took up and developed can be traced to the Areopagite, especially the latter's teaching about the Divine Light that illuminates the universe; further to Symeon the New Theologian and his light mysticism, to the apophatic theology which was developed by the Neo–Platonists in fifth–century Athens—the transcendent essence of the phenomena defined as silence and ab-

[318] Børtnes, *Visions of Glory*, p. 110.

[319] Meyendorff, *Study*, p. 33.

[320] Regarding the hesychasts' positive view of the human body, see Archimandrite [Archbishop] Chrysostomos, Hieromonk [Bishop] Auxentios, and Hierodeacon [Archimandrite] Akakios, *Contemporary Eastern Orthodox Thought: The Traditionalist Voice* (Belmont, MA: Nordland House Publishers, 1982), pp. 52–55.

[321] In a biting review of Father Meyendorff's study of Saint Gregory, Father John Romanides makes mention of the philosophical weaknesses in Meyendorff's arguments, citing, for example, his "...revolutionary claim...that Barlaam is both a nominalist and a Neo–Platonist or Platonist. ...Had Father Meyendorff," he continues, "explained how it is possible for one and the same person to be both a nominalist and a Platonist, he would have revolutionized our intellectual knowledge of the history of Europe"; see the Rev. John S. Romanides, "Notes on the Palamite Controversy and Related Topics," *The Greek Orthodox Theological Review*, Vol. 6 (Winter 1960–1961), pp. 187–188.

sence—and finally to the Patristic doctrine of *theosis,* man's deification and union with God through imitation of Christ and participation in His body in the mystery of the Eucharist and in the contemplation of His passion.[322]

We have already commented on the issue of neo–Platonism in
the Greek Fathers. The idea that hesychasm entails a primarily
sacramental and contemplative attempt to participate in Christ
—let alone in "His passion"—simply further obscures Palamas'
ascetic theology.

It is through a series of mistranslations and critical misinter-
pretations[323] that Meyendorff comes to the conclusion that Palamite mysticism rests in contemplation and sacramentalism, a
conclusion which apparently led Børtnes to his faulty assump-
tions about the hesychastic vision of God. What Father John
Romanides says of Meyendorff's error also applies to Børtnes:

> Whereas in the West a distinction is made between the contem-
> plative and the active states of the Christian life, in the East there is
> no such distinction. The quest for and the gift of uninterrupted
> prayer is not a life of contemplation and is not a seeking after ec-
> static experiences....[324]

The hesychastic vision of God, the product of uninterrupted
prayer, involves not in essence an attempt at literal union with
Christ—whether sacramentally or through the contemplation of
and participation in His Passion—, but an ontological purifica-

---

[322] We shall say more about the notion of "contemplation" and "meditation" below. At this point, however, we should point out that spiritual concen-
tration in the Eastern Christian Tradition rarely involves an envisioning of the
"passion" of Christ or a conjuring–up of religious images in general. "Φαντα-
σία," or the imagination, as Cavarnos remarks, is for the Eastern Fathers "one of
the lower faculties of man." It is properly applied with great precision, as an ac-
cessory to meditation, and is usually concentrated on the remembrance of death
and the Last Judgment; see Cavarnos, *Byzantine Thought,* p. 52.

[323] See, for example, Romanides' comments in "Notes on the Palamite
Controversy and Related Topics—II," *The Greek Orthodox Theological Review,*
Vol. 9 (Winter 1963–1964), esp. pp. 238ff.

[324] *Ibid.,* p. 230.

tion of the senses (if not the whole person) by active spiritual pursuits, through which one comes into communion with God's Grace.[325] The subtle conceptual contrast of the Essence–Energies distinction finds its counterpart in ascetic theology in the efforts of the human being to attain, through purification, invulnerability to the consequences of sin, while still acknowledging the potential dominance of sin over the flesh and the fallen world and his or her own essential imperfection.[326] With ascetic labor and the acquisition of human virtue,[327] one comes, by Grace, to union with God, *theosis,* and the vision of God as Uncreated or Divine Light through the purified or spiritually transformed senses.[328] It is this ontological purification in the active

[325] Cavarnos says of uninterrupted prayer, or "Prayer of the Heart," as it is often called in Patristic texts, that it "...first...is pleasant warmth (*therme*) of the heart, which purifies man of passions, effecting a state of passionlessness. This warmth is a manifestation of God..." (*Byzantine Thought,* p. 56).

[326] See Chrysostomos, *Contemporary Thought,* pp. 54–56.

[327] The virtues, according to the Greek Fathers, are closely linked to asceticism, which is thus something active, involving as it does *efforts* towards the acquisition of the virtues. As Cavarnos remarks: "This ascetic way of looking at the virtues appears frequently in the writings of Christian writers of the Hellenic East, from the early centuries of the Christian era to the present"; see Constantine Cavarnos, *The Hellenic–Christian Philosophical Tradition* (Belmont, MA: Institute for Byzantine and Modern Greek Studies, 1989), p. 32.

[328] Telepneff, "Concept of the Person," pp. 282–284, 345–348; cf. Cavarnos, who writes: "Through prayer and meditation, exemplary men and women, living an impeccable Christian life, ...[can] be transformed by the grace of the Holy Spirit and...achieve 'theosis' or 'deification'—what the Latins equated with the 'Vision of God' or the *Summum Bonum*" (*Hellenic–Christian Tradition,* p. 4). Let us point out, again, that Cavarnos means by "an impeccable Christian life" a virtuous life (cf. p. 19). As well, the term "meditation" needs clarification. It should not be equated with the Western notion of "contemplation," as it so often is. Cavarnos is referring here to the Greek word "μελέτη," or a specific exercise in mental attention by which the mind prepares for prayer. It cannot be separated from the virtue of "ἀπροσπάθεια," or detachment from worldly things, the effect of an essentially spiritual exercise with its roots in noetic activity rather than the activities of the discursive intellect or the imagination. (See further comments in Cavarnos, *Byzantine Thought,* pp. 52–53, 55.) Finally, it is essential

acquisition of virtues that the Greek Fathers consider asceticism, not a withdrawal to the life of contemplation and what Romanides calls "sacramentalism" (by which he apparently means a kind of "sacramental ritualism").[329] And it is the vision of God's

to note that Cavarnos, in his reference to the "Vision of God," does not himself equate the Western notion of "beatific vision" with the vision of God as Uncreated Light in the Tradition of the Eastern Church; rather, he simply assigns this equation to the West. In other places, he speaks specifically about the traditional Orthodox notion of "the vision of God" (*e.g., Hellenic–Christian Tradition,* p. 47); *cf.* Romanides, "Remarks of an Orthodox Christian on Religious Freedom," *infra.*

[329] In fact, the life of the Mysteries is, in Orthodox spirituality, not an end in and of itself, but a means to an end (see Lossky, *Mystical Theology,* pp. 196–197). This is especially true in hesychastic thought. Baptism, for example, while it constitutes a form of "enlightenment," is not a ritual of *theosis,* or ultimate enlightenment, for the hesychasts. It simply entails an activation of the spiritual (or noetic) faculty through which one eventually comes to attain, through a life of active striving towards virtue, enlightenment in the latter sense of divinization and the vision of God. Thus one must be cautious in applying the imagery of light to the Mysteries *per se.* Father Robert Taft, for example, contends that the "...the light Christ gives is salvation and it is received in baptism" (Robert Taft, s.j., *Beyond East and West: Problems in Liturgical Understanding* [Washington, DC: The Pastoral Press, 1984], p. 138). This statement is true only when understood in a qualified way. The illumination or *photisma* of Baptism, again, as the seventh–century(?) writer Saint Theodoros the Ascetic points out in his *Theoretikon,* is a preparation for ultimate purification and the final ascent to Divine Light, which are acquired in a life marked by spiritual "effort" (see *The Philokalia,* trans. and ed. G. E. H. Palmer, Phillip Sherard, and [Bishop] Kallistos Ware [London: Faber & Faber, 1981], Vol. 2, p. 39). The Eucharist, likewise, is not, according to hesychastic theology, the very source of perfect union with God. Rather, the Body and Blood of Christ, the "medicine of immortality," are a *means* by which the human person, through a sacramental encounter with Christ, is purified and made worthy of the vision of God (see Chrysostomos, *Contemporary Thought,* pp. 44–45). Again, this vision, *theosis,* is, according to Saint Gregory Palamas, the product of "self–mastery" (a life dedicated to the acquisition of virtue) and the interaction between human will and Divine Grace, the latter, in part, as It is imparted through the life of the Mysteries (Saint Gregory Palamas, "On the Blessed Hesychasts," in *Early Fathers from the Philokalia,* trans. E. Kadloubovsky and G. E. H. Palmer [London: Faber & Faber, 1969], p. 409).

Glory in the Uncreated Light of His Energies (or *theosis*), not (at least as an end in itself) beatific ecstasy or a sharing in Christ's Passion, which is the aim and goal of the ascetic life. When the Eastern Fathers speak of participation in the Passion of the Cross of Christ, they mean by this not the vision of God, but the therapeutic, purifying path of *ascesis,* a way of access to the vision of God.[330]

With regard to *theosis* and the vision of Uncreated Light specifically, Børtnes makes an informative observation:

> To the light mystics the highest form of enjoyment is the contemplation of things in order to discover their 'light' and thus behold the divine Logos, the Uncreated Light of Orthodox mystics, as it is reflected in matter. This contemplation was an act of salvation, a restitution of wholeness in 'disintegrated nature.'[331]

While it is true that the highest state in Orthodox spiritual life is the vision of God as Uncreated Light, this state should not, again, be carelessly equated with the beatific contemplation to which Børtnes here refers.[332] Børtnes is quite correct, however,

---

[330] See Archimandrite Ierotheos Vlachos, Ὀρθόδοξη Ψυχοθεραπεία· Πατερική θεραπευτική ἀγωγή (Edessa, Greece: Hiera Mone Timiou Stavrou, 1986), pp. 34–39.

[331] Børtnes, *Visions of Glory,* p. 84.

[332] As Father Romanides observes: "The doctrine of beatific vision, borrowed by St. Augustine from the Neo–Platonists, whereby man's destiny is to become completely happy in the possession of the vision of the divine essence, is unknown to the Greek patristic Tradition. Man's desire is rather the transformation of the desire for happiness into a non–utilitarian love which does not seek its own. Whereas in Neo–Platonic Christian theologies the reward of the just will be or is the vision of God, in the Orthodox Tradition both the just and the unjust will have the vision of God in His uncreated glory, with the difference that for the unjust this same uncreated glory of God will be the eternal fires of hell. God is light for those who learn to love Him and a consuming fire for those who will not. The reason for this is not that God has any positive intent in punishing, but that for those who are not prepared properly, to see God is a cleansing experience, but one which does not lead to the eternal process of perfection. This understanding of the vision of God does not belong to the rewards and punishment structure of theologies geared to transcendental happi-

in placing *theosis* and the vision of Uncreated Light, the vision of God, in the context of human salvation. Thus, according to Saint Nicodemos the Hagiorite (†1809): "Know that if your mind is not deified by the Holy Spirit, it is impossible for you to be saved."[333] This is an important point, since the vision of God must not be understood as some strange and exotic experience appropriate to an elite class of "mystics," but as an element of a universal metaphysics of light that impinges on the life of every Christian striving for salvation.

Finally, it behooves us to say something about Uncreated Light Itself, which Børtnes does not adequately describe or define. According to Cavarnos,

> ...through the opening of the heart (*kardiakon anoigma*) [or hesy-chastic practices] the Divine light enters us. ...Illumination is 'an ineffable energy, which is seen invisibly and known unknowably,' according to Callistos and Ignatios.[334] Palamas, who deals most extensively with illumination, says: 'The Divine and deifying efful-gence and grace is not the essence of God, but His uncreated ener-gy.' ...Illumination, as a vision of, and union with, the Divine Light, is a union with God, Who is light.[335]

---

ness and therefore overcomes the dualistic distinction between an inferior world of change and frustration and a superior world of immutable realities and happiness" (The Rev. John S. Romanides, "Remarks of an Orthodox Christian on Religious Freedom," *The Greek Orthodox Theological Review*, Vol. 8 [1962–1963], pp. 130–131). Despite Romanides' words on this subject, even Orthodox writers are at times either careless in their language or, because of Western in-fluence, unfaithful to the strict doctrines of the vision of God put forth in Or-thodox theology; see, for example, Vladimir Lossky, *The Vision of God*, 2nd ed. (Bedfordshire, England: The Faith Press, 1973), who writes that such vision is "...the ultimate felicity of man" (p. 21).

333 Constantine Cavarnos, *St. Nicodemos the Hagiorite*, Vol. 3 of *Modern Orthodox Saints* (Belmont, MA: Institute for Byzantine and Modern Greek Studies, 1974), p. 139.

334 Like Saint Gregory Palamas, Saints Callistos II of Constantinople and Ignatios of Xanthopoulos were celebrated Byzantine mystics of the fourteenth century.

335 Cavarnos, *Byzantine Thought*, pp. 56–57.

In essence, when we behold God as Light, we do not see Him in His Essence or as He is reflected in created things; we see Him as "Uncreated" Light. Nor do we see God as simple light and come to know Him in precisely the same way that we see and comprehend material things. Rather, through *theosis* and the purification of the person and the senses, "the mind enters into the heart"[336] and we come to see and know God noetically, through a spiritual faculty (the νοῦς) and our restored senses, in a vision that is not vision and in a knowing that is not knowing (apophatic expressions of spiritual sight and knowledge). Referring to Saint Gregory Palamas, Romanides notes that he did not believe that

> ...uncreated light should be seen by the senses alone, and argues that this vision is proper neither to the senses nor to the intellect, but rather transcends both, being at the same time a knowing and an unknowing in which the whole man participates, having thus been divinized in body and soul by this same light of grace. ...Palamas climaxes his arguments by pointing out that it is not by any created means that the apostles saw the glory of Christ on the Mount of Transfiguration, but by the power of the omnipotent spirit. Thus the elect apostles saw the light on Mt. Thabor, 'not only flashing from the flesh bearing within itself the Son, but also from the Cloud bearing within itself the Father of Christ.' This is in keeping with the basic epistemological principle of the Greek Patristic tradition that only when within the uncreated light (in this case called cloud) can one see the uncreated light. ...The body of Christ illumined the apostles from without only because the same illuminating light of the body was already illuminating them from within.[337]

Since God is invisible to the senses and the intellect, only a person whose intellect and senses are transformed by the working of Grace can attain to a vision of God, seeing God within God by means of the indwelling of the Holy Spirit.

The foregoing critique of Jostein Børtnes' comments on the

336 Saint Seraphim of Sarov, "The Light of Christ," in Vol. 1 of *Little Russian Philokalia* (Platina, CA: St. Herman of Alaska Brotherhood, 1980), p. 50.

337 Romanides, "Palamite Controversy—II," pp. 240–241.

light metaphysics of the Greek Fathers helps us to focus our attention on the useful framework which he provides for a further discussion of the Holy Fire. With our critical remarks about his attribution of supposed neo–Platonic origins to Orthodox theology, cosmology, and anthropology and his limited grasp of the notion of *theosis* in mind, we can safely state, as we did at the outset, that Børtnes' general notion of an Orthodox metaphysics of light is a clear insight into the principal *unifying* aspect of Orthodox theology; that is, of the Orthodox understanding of God. Thus it is that Archbishop Chrysostomos writes of the unity of the Christian *oikonomia* itself in a single image of light:

> The light of the Resurrection, that light which emanated from the bright tomb, is one with the very Light of the World, Christ Himself. The Savior and the light–filled Grace which transforms the hesychast; which makes of holy men and women 'Jesus Christs' within Jesus Christ; which makes us 'gods' and deifies us; and which causes to dwell in our innards in an unbodily way the Christ Who dwelled in a bodily way within the *Theotokos*—these are inseparable. As the Holy Trinity is bound together in love, so our salvation and eternal life are forever bound to the reality of the light of the Resurrection and the Grace which it has bestowed on the whole universe. ...Every perfect thing comes to us from the Father of lights (St. James 1:17), and in every manifestation of divine light—whether in the blinding radiance of the Transfiguration or the divine spark that prompts within us repentance and a return to God—we see the truth and potential of the Resurrected life, by which we ourselves are made partakers of the divine nature (II Peter 1:4), participating, by Grace, as creatures in God our Creator.[338]

Tsekoura directly equates the various manifestations of the Holy Fire with the manifestation of God as Uncreated Light:

> It is that transcendent [ὑπέροχο] light, light immaterial, heavenly, uncreated, and Divine, as the Holy Fathers write of it in their

---

[338] Bishop [Archbishop] Chrysostomos of Etna, introduction to Bishop Auxentios, *The Holy Fire: Orthodox Pascha* (Etna, CA: Center for Traditionalist Orthodox Studies, 1991), pp. *vii–viii*.

works. It is a light which, while shining brighter than the sun, does not blur one's sight,[339] but lifts the mind up to a vision of the truth.

She further accounts for the variation in these manifestations by observing that, according to Saint Symeon the New Theologian (†1022?, †1037?), Uncreated Light

...manifests itself in various ways. It appears, for example, as 'unformed light.' However, it can be active, darting and changing direction continually and with rapidity, like a flash of lightning. At other times it shines like the flame of a candle; yet other times like a 'pillar of fire' and like 'lightning,' or flashes, like shining rays of light, like a sphere of light, or like a 'flame.' Still at other times, it appears as a 'sphere of light, bright like the sun,' as a 'star,' or as a star that rises from far off and becomes as large as a 'glittering sun.'[340]

The vision of God in Scripture is, from the standpoint of Eastern Christian theology, complex, for we are dealing not only with God as He manifests Himself in images of light, but with the dual manifestation of God in His accessible Energies and His unapproachable Glory. Vladimir Lossky observes that the Byzantine theologians of the fourteenth century, especially,

...base their doctrine of the vision of God on two series of scriptural texts which seem contradictory and mutually exclusive. Indeed, alongside passages from Holy Scripture in which there can be found a formal negation of any vision of God, who is invisible, unknowable, inaccessible to created beings, there are others which encourage us to seek the face of God and promise the vision of

---

339 The word which Tsekoura uses here, "θαμπώνω" (or "θαμβῶ"), also means "to amaze" or "to astonish." Clearly, she is not suggesting that Uncreated Light does not astonish or amaze those who see it. The Light of the Transfiguration on Mount Thabor, which, as we shall see below, Orthodox theologians equate with Uncreated Light, caused the three Apostles, after all, to be "filled with awe" (Saint Matthew 17:6). Hence, we have translated this word in the more colloquial sense, as Tsekoura no doubt meant to use it.

340 Tsekoura, *Τὸ Ἅγιον Φῶς*, p. 70.

God as He is.[341]

Thus in the Old Testament, for example, "...the pillar of cloud and fire which goes before the Jews as they leave Egypt reveals God's presence at the same time that it conceals him."[342] In the New Testament, there are, on the one hand, effusive statements to the effect that we cannot know God as He is. Saint John the Theologian says that "...no one has ever seen God [...οὐδεὶς πώ-ποτε τεθέαται]" (1 John 4:12). Saint Matthew (11:27) and Saint Luke (10:22) also affirm in their Gospels that God cannot be known. However, there is also, on the other hand, a body of New Testamental references which affirm that, as Lossky notes, "...such knowledge can be conferred on or communicated to created beings by the will of the Son."[343] Thus Saint Paul the Apostle tells us that by putting away the things of the child and coming to spiritual maturity in Christ (1 Corinthians 13:11–12), we can come to know God in a higher way. Similarly, in the First Epistle of Saint John (1–2), we learn that by becoming the "children" of God, we can come to know Him. Aside from the clear eschatological imagery of these texts—the perfect vision of God in the *Parousia*—they also establish "...a relationship between the vision of God and the deified state of the elect who [in this life] become 'likenesses of God.'"[344]

We can see, then, that any attempt to apply the Eastern Christian metaphysics of light to Scriptural visions of God can

---

[341] Lossky, *Vision*, p. 21.

[342] *Ibid.*, p. 22.

[343] *Ibid.*, p. 23.

[344] *Ibid.*, p. 24. This same idea is expressed by Saint Gregory the Theologian: "Let us become like Christ, since Christ became like us. Let us become God's for His sake, since He for ours became man" ("Oration 1: On Easter and His Reluctance," in *Nicene and Post–Nicene Fathers*, ed. Phillip Schaff, Vol. 7, 2nd ser. [Grand Rapids, MI: Eerdman's Publishing Co., 1978], p. 203). The English text here contains a serious mistranslation of the second line of the quotation in question, which actually reads: "Let us become gods [θεοί] for Him [δι' αὐτόν], since He for us became man" (see the Greek text in Migne, *Patrologia Græca*, Vol. 35, col. 397).

be very misleading, unless one keeps in focus the schema of the Energies–Essence distinction which we have discussed. One must maintain a clear understanding of the apophatic approach to a vision of God, which obviates literalism and involves an inevitable adjustment to the use of concepts that (because of the ineffable nature of God) appear both ambiguous and contradictory, and of the rôle of human deification in that vision. In other words, we cannot speak of a universal Orthodox metaphysics of light without interpreting and containing the Scriptural witness within the experience of the Patristic witness—an appropriate effort in a theological tradition that traces spiritual authority to Scripture and Holy Tradition[345]—and without a specific theology of light and the vision of God by which to understand that universal metaphysics.

In his historical treatment of the rite, Archimandrite Callistos traces the Holy Fire to the light which Scripture and some Church Fathers directly associate with the Tomb of Christ:

> The first reason for the institution of the sacred rite of the Holy Fire, if we omit its supernatural aspect, was, of course, the symbolic commemoration of the Resurrection of the Saviour and the consequences of it. From the Holy Gospel we know that after the Resurrection of the Lord there appeared first to the myrrh–bearers a radiant angel, who, after he had rolled away the stone from the entrance to the Tomb, sat down upon it. 'And his countenance was like lightning' (Matthew 28:3). Later, when Peter and John came up to the tomb while it was still dark, the angel had gone and they saw the shroud and cloth and believed (John 20). They could see all this only because the entire Tomb of the Lord was at that moment filled with a heavenly light. Therefore, the divine Damascene sings: 'And seeing the light in the Tomb (Peter) was amazed—and thus saw only the shroud alone—for no one can see after night has fallen.' St. Gregory of Nyssa writes: 'And when he saw them (the

---

345 For a synopsis of the rôle of this twofold source of authority in Orthodox theology, see "Scripture and Tradition," in Archimandrite [Archbishop] Chrysostomos and Hieromonk [Bishop] Auxentios, *Scripture and Tradition: A Comparative Study of the Eastern Orthodox, Roman Catholic, and Protestant Views* (Belmont, MA: Nordland House Publishers, 1982), pp. 6–18.

shroud and the cloth), Peter believed, for the Tomb was filled with light, even while it was still night; the interior of the Tomb was visible in a two–fold manner: both to the senses and to the spirit' (On the Resurrection of Christ. Sermon II).[346]

The New Testamental accounts of the Resurrection and the lighted Tomb to which Callistos refers are, of course, somewhat ambiguous. In the Gospel of Saint Matthew, the Angel in the Tomb is portrayed in images of light, and the time of the day seems to be just before dawn:

> In the end of the sabbath, as it began to dawn toward the first day of the week, came Mary Magdalene and the other Mary to see the sepulchre. And, behold, there was a great earthquake, for the angel of the Lord descended from heaven, and came and rolled back the stone from the door, and sat upon it. His countenance was like lightning, and his raiment white as snow.[347]

In the Gospel of Saint Mark, the time of the day is clearly dawn itself. There is no mention of the shining countenance of the Angel, unless one interprets the "white garment" ("στολὴν λευ-κήν") as a "bright garment" and attributes the amazement of the women to the brightness or light of this garment, rather than to the sight of the Angel:

> ...Mary Magdalene and Mary the mother of James, and Salome..., very early in the morning the first day of the week, ...came unto the sepulchre at the rising of the sun. ...And entering into the sepulchre, they saw a young man sitting on the right side, clothed in a long white garment; and they were affrighted. ...And they went out quickly, and fled from the sepulchre: for they trembled and were amazed.[348]

In the Gospel of Saint Luke, we read that two men in shining garments, presumably Angels, confronted the women, who had come to the Tomb most likely in the pre–dawn hours, as the

---

[346] Callistos, "Holy Fire," p. 7.

[347] St. Matthew 28:1–3.

[348] St. Mark 16:1–2, 5, 8.

Greek suggests: "ὄρθρου βαθέος," or literally, "in the depths of the morning":

> Now upon the first day of the week, very early in the morning, they came unto the sepulchre. ...And...behold, two men stood by them in shining garments: And...they were afraid, and bowed down their faces to the earth....[349]

In the Johannine Gospel, it is clear that the Apostles Peter and John, after Saint Mary Magdalene, went to the Tomb while it was still dark outside. Thus it is that Saint John of Damascus (†749), in the Paschal Canon, and Saint Gregory of Nyssa († *ca.* 395), whom Father Callistos cites, assume that Saint Peter could see in the Tomb because it was supernaturally lighted:

> ...When it was yet dark..., Peter therefore went forth, and that other disciple, and came to the sepulchre. ...And the other disciple[350] did outrun Peter, and came first to the sepulchre. And he stooping down, and looking in, saw the linen clothes lying; yet went he not in. Then cometh Simon Peter following him, and went into the sepulchre, and seeth the linen clothes lie. And the napkin, that was about his head, not lying with the linen clothes, but wrapped together in a place by itself. Then went in also that other disciple, which came first to the sepulchre and he saw and believed.[351]

In spite of the ambiguity of the Gospel accounts and no more than a tenuous association of the Resurrection with the phenomenon of supernatural light, there is a clear consensus in support of this association in much of the Greek Patristic witness (thus, the aforementioned words of Saints Gregory of Nyssa and John the Damascene). Saint Gregory the Theologian also identifies the light of the Tomb with the "...heavenly light which illuminates the entire world with its beauty."[352] The seventh–century poet and Patriarch of Jerusalem, Saint Sophronios (†644),

---

349 St. Luke 24:1, 4–5.

350 Saint John, "...the other disciple whom Jesus loved" (St. John 20:2).

351 St. John 20:1, 3–8.

352 Quoted in Callistos, "Holy Fire," p. 8.

in his Τριῴδιον, a much neglected but magnificent collection of verses, writes of the Light of Christ's Resurrection "shining forth" from the Sepulchre ("ἐκ τάφου") and filling all with joy.[353] In another verse he identifies Christ Himself with the Light of the Tomb: "Thou, O Christ, wast first made visible to a woman, before the others, ...shining forth in beauty [ὡραίως] from the Tomb."[354]

Saint Gregory Palamas similarly argues, in his theological chapters, that in the depth of the morning Saint Mary Magdalene was able to see the Tomb by the Uncreated Light of the Resurrection, which made all that was in it visible.[355] One might object to Palamas' statement on the grounds that the light in the Tomb was that of the shining Angel reported in some Gospel accounts.[356] However, Saint Gregory the Theologian contends that the light of an Angel is "...a kind of outflow or communication of that first Light [God], drawing its illumination from its inclination and obedience thereto."[357] Indeed, the Greek Fathers in general associate the light of things connected with the Resurrection, whether the Angel or the Tomb itself, with the Light of God or with unapproachable or Uncreated Light. This tendency is reflected in the hymnography of the Or-

---

[353] Migne, *Patrologia Græca*, Vol. 87, col. 3925.

[354] *Ibid.*, col. 3920.

[355] *Ibid.*, Vol. 150, col. 1169A.

[356] Though they are not our concern, many of the apocryphal books of the New Testament also associate the Angel in the Tomb with light or brilliance. For example, in the *Acts of Pilate* (or the *Gospel of Nicodemos*), we read of a report from the soldiers who were guarding the Tomb of Christ, who relate that they saw "...an angel descend from heaven, and he rolled away the stone from the mouth of the cave [Tomb], and sat upon it, and he shone like snow and like lightning" (13:1); see this text in Edgar Hennecke, *New Testament Apocrypha*, ed. Wilhelm Schneemelcher and trans. R. McL. Wilson *et al.*, Vol. 1 of *Gospels and Related Writings* (Philadelphia: The Westminster Press, 1963), p. 461.

[357] Saint Gregory Nazianzus, "Oration XL: The Oration on Holy Baptism," in *Nicene and Post–Nicene Fathers*, ed. Phillip Schaff, Vol. 7, 2nd ser. (Grand Rapids, MI: Eerdman's Publishing Co., 1978), p. 361.

thodox Church. The Eighth Ode of the Canon of the Resurrection of Sunday Matins, Tone Four, for example, reads:

> The Angel, shining like lightning and as white as snow, was seen by the women in the unapproachable light of the Resurrection. 'Why seek ye the living in the tomb as dead' cried he: 'Christ is truly risen and unto Him do we sing: O all ye works of the Lord, bless ye the Lord.'[358]

There are effusive references in Scripture and the Fathers to the manifestation of the Glory of God, or Uncreated Light,[359] in images of light other than that of the Resurrection. Saint John the Evangelist, for example, says that the light of human beings is God and describes God Himself as Light in a number of Scriptural passages; for example: "In Him was life; and the life was the light of men";[360] "God is light, and in Him is no darkness at all."[361] There are also countless Patristic references to God as Light which reflect these Scriptural allusions. Saints Gregory the Theologian and Gregory Palamas both make this statement succinctly: "God is Light," the former tells us;[362] and according to the latter, who, writing against Akyndinos, carefully defines God in His knowable revelation as He communicates Himself to man: "God is called light not according to His essence, but according to His energy."[363]

---

[358] *The Octoechos: Saturday and Sunday Offices* (Bussy–en–Othe, France: Orthodox Monastery of the Veil of Our Lady, n.d.), p. 110.

[359] Let us state emphatically here that there is a clear equation between the Glory of God and Uncreated Light (and *theosis,* for that matter) in the Greek Patristic Tradition, as precisely expressed in the theology of Saint Gregory Palamas. As Romanides notes: "...The terms θέωσις (divinization or deification) and ἕνωσις (union [with God]) and ὅρασις (vision) are synonymous. This means that everywhere [that] Palamas speaks of union between the prophets of the Old Testament and the glory of God or an Old Testament prophet's vision of the glory of God he is actually speaking of divinization" ("Palamite Controversy—II," p. 247).

[360] St. John 1:4.

[361] I John 1:5.

[362] Saint Gregory Nazianzus, "Oration XL," p. 361.

At the Transfiguration of Christ, in the presence of the Apostles Peter, James, and John, we see God revealed in "pure light," according to Saint John Chrysostomos (†407).[364] Saint Matthew's account of this event brings to mind some of the images which we have seen associated with the Holy Fire:

> Jesus...was transfigured before them: and His face did shine as the sun, and His raiment was white as the light. ...While he [Saint Peter] yet spake, behold, a bright cloud overshadowed them: and behold a voice out of the cloud, which said, This is My beloved Son, in Whom I am well pleased; hear ye Him. And when the disciples heard it, they fell on their face, and were sore afraid.[365]

This manifestation of Light on Mount Thabor is most commonly associated by the Greek Fathers with the vision of God.[366] As Lossky points out, "The majority of the Fathers who have spoken of the Transfiguration affirm the uncreated and divine nature of...[this] mystical experience";[367] that is, they see in it a revelation of God. Saint Gregory Palamas saw this event as a virtual prototype, first, of human deification and plainly, second, as a manifestation of God: "This is the light of God...and such is the opinion of all the saints."[368] Saint John of Damascus, in a

---

[363] Migne, *Patrologia Græca*, Vol. 150, col. 823.

[364] Saint John Chrysostomos, "Homily LV on the Gospel of St. Matthew," in *Nicene and Post–Nicene Fathers*, ed. Phillip Schaff, Vol. 10, 1st ser. (Grand Rapids, MI: Eerdman's Publishing Co., 1978), p. 348.

[365] St. Matthew 17:1–2, 5–6.

[366] This is not to say that such an idea is absent in the West. Saint Leo the Great (†461), for example, calls the Transfiguration a manifestation of the Glory of God; see his "Homily LI," Jacques–Paul Migne, ed., *Patrologia Latina: Cursus Completus* (Paris: 1844–1855), Vol. 54, col. 310B.

[367] Vladimir Lossky, *In the Image and Likeness of God* (Crestwood, NY: St. Vladimir's Seminary Press, 1974), p. 60.

[368] Saint Gregory Palamas, *The Triads*, trans. Nicholas Gendle (New York: Paulist Press, 1983), p. 10. In fact, one could cite numerous Patristic texts to support Saint Gregory's contention: Saint Gregory the Theologian, writing on Baptism (Migne, *Patrologia Græca*, Vol. 36, col. 365A); Saint Maximos the Confessor's theological chapters (*ibid.*, Vol. 90, cols. 1129Dff.); Saint John of

sermon on the Transfiguration, affirms that, in appearing to the Apostles as the God of Light, Christ "...did not become what He before was not, but was made manifest to His disciples as He was, opening their eyes,"[369] so that they could see Him in His eternal Glory.

Saint Paul, on the road from Jerusalem to Damascus, was also confronted by God in the form of a light from Heaven.[370] Saint Gregory the Theologian, in his thirty–ninth oration, avers that in this confrontation, Saint Paul encountered God and "...conversed with the one whom He was persecuting, that is, with a brief flash of the great Light."[371] As well, in the Apocalypse (Revelation), we read: "And the temple of God was opened in heaven, and there was seen in His temple the ark of His testament: and there were lightnings, and voices, and thunderings, and an earthquake, and great hail."[372] Also in Revelation, Saint John writes of his vision of a new heaven and a new earth that: "...they shall see His face; and His name shall be in their foreheads. And there shall be no night there; and they need no candle, neither light of the sun; for the Lord God giveth them light...."[373] Following the sixth–century interpretation of the Apocalypse by Saint Andrew of Cæsarea, Archbishop Averky of Syracuse notes in reference to this first verse from Revelation, that it is an indication of that which is "...hidden in Christ, in Whom dwelleth *the whole fullness of the Godhead bodily* (Col. 2:3–9)."[374] In the second verse, he finds not only images of God,

Damascus in his sermon on the Transfiguration (*ibid.*, Vol. 96, col. 545ff.); Saint Andrew of Crete (†740) writing on the Transfiguration (*ibid.*, Vol. 97, cols. 932–957); and many others.

[369] "On the Holy Lights," Migne, *Patrologia Græca*, Vol. 96, col. 564.

[370] Acts 9:3–9.

[371] Migne, *Patrologia Græca*, Vol. 36, col. 344B. Again, Saint Gregory says that the "first" Light or the "great" Light is God Himself; see his "Oration XL," p. 361.

[372] Revelation 11:19.

[373] *Ibid.*, 22:4–5.

[374] Archbishop Averky of Jordanville, *The Apocalypse of St. John: An Or-*

but of the vision of God by the Faithful: "All these features indicate the unceasing and most complete communion of the members of the heavenly Church with their Master Whom they behold face to face."[375]

Old Testamental images of light are not as clear as those in the New Testament. In Orthodox theology, however, these "theophanies...[of]...the glory of God" are equated with the revelation of God on Mount Thabor.[376] The Transfiguration, according to Saint Gregory Palamas, was a revelation of God "uncircumscribed" by time and space,[377] which revealed the eternal Glory of God and which "has existed from the beginning."[378] Thus it was a manifestation of the universal Light of God: "...The Lord, having been transfigured, shone and manifested the glory and the splendor and the light..." of God as He always is.[379] We see this Light in the Prophet Moses' face, the skin of which "shone" when he came down from Mount Sinai to speak with the Prophet Aaron and the children of Israel.[380] We also see the Light of God in the forms of an unconsuming flame or an Angel. Thus "an angel of the Lord" appeared to Moses "...in a flame of fire out of the midst of a bush: and he looked, and, behold, the bush burned with fire and the bush was not consumed."[381] Manoah and his wife, the parents of Samson, saw, during their burnt offering, "the angel of the Lord" who had come to them "in the flame of the altar." Manoah understood

---

thodox Commentary, trans. Father Seraphim Rose (Platina, CA: Valaam Society of America, 1985), p. 132.

[375] *Ibid.,* p. 221.

[376] Lossky, *Image and Likeness,* p. 61.

[377] "Homily XXXIV," Migne, *Patrologia Græca,* Vol. 151, col. 433B.

[378] Saint Gregory Palamas, *The Triads,* p. 15.

[379] Saint Gregory Palamas, "Homily Thirty–four: On the Venerable Transfiguration of our Lord and God and Savior Jesus Christ, In Which is Substantiated that His Light is Uncreated," *The Greek Orthodox Theological Review,* Vol. 33, No. 2 (1988), p. 164.

[380] Exodus 34:29, 35.

[381] *Ibid.,* 3:2.

that he had seen the Glory of God in the Angel and, in fact, turned to his wife and said, "We shall surely die, because we have seen God."[382] God also "appeared unto"[383] Abraham and Sarah in the form of three Angels, whom the Prophet and his wife entertained. The hospitality shown by Abraham and Sarah towards these three Angels, in fact, constitutes one of the most famous depictions of the Holy Trinity (in the form of the three Angels) in Orthodox iconography.

God is again often portrayed in the Old Testament in the form of clouds, smoke, fire, lightning, and precipitation (rain, dew, snow, hail, *etc.*). For example, the Israelites, when they departed from Etham at the edge of the wilderness, were led by "the Lord," Who "went before them" as a "pillar of cloud" by day and a "pillar of fire" by night.[384] When God descended on Mount Sinai, the mountain is described as being covered by a thick cloud and "wrapped in smoke," while thunder and lightning were everywhere.[385] Elsewhere, the "glory of the Lord" is made manifest in the tabernacle as a cloud and fire.[386] The word of God is likened to rain and snow in the Book of Isaiah: "For as the rain cometh down, and the snow from heaven, ...so shall My word be."[387] God's power is also called the "dew of heaven"[388] in the Old Testament, and in fact God calls Himself dew in the Book of Hosea: "I will be as the dew unto Israel."[389] In Isaiah, hail is used as a symbol of God's wrath: "Judgement also will I lay to the line..., and the hail shall sweep away the refuge of lies."[390] Similarly, the Prophet–King David tells of the wrath of

382 Judges 13:20, 22.
383 Genesis 18:1.
384 Exodus 13:20–22.
385 *Ibid.*, 19:16–20.
386 *Ibid.*, 40:38.
387 Isaiah 55:10–11.
388 Daniel 4:15, 23, 25.
389 Hosea 14:5.
390 Isaiah 28:17.

God on the Egyptians, whom He sent "...hail for rain and flaming fire in their land."[391]

All of these Old Testamental images are for the Greek Patristic Tradition, as we have noted, manifestations of Uncreated Light, of the Glory and power, or Energies, of God. As Romanides, speaking of Saint Gregory Palamas' understanding of the Old Testamental symbols of God as seen by the Prophets, contends clearly that "...Palamas, following Dionysios [the Areopagite][392] and the Greek Fathers, insisted that they [the Prophets] had an immediate vision of the uncreated glory of God."[393] The Prophets of the Old Testament saw God in all of these images because these manifestations were *of necessity* Uncreated Light, given the epistemological principle of the Greek Patristic Tradition to which we alluded above; namely, that only within Uncreated Light (smoke, cloud, rain, *etc.*) can one see God.[394] In

---

[391] Psalm 104:32 (*Septuaginta*).

[392] See, for example, his "On the Divine Names," Migne, *Patrologia Græca,* Vol. 3, col. 596BC.

[393] Romanides, "Palamite Controversy—II," p. 261.

[394] It is precisely this point which Father Meyendorff misses in his effort to show that human deification has as its source the Incarnation and the Sacraments of the Church and that the Old Testamental Prophets did not see the Glory of God as It was manifested at Christ's Resurrection (Meyendorff, *Study,* pp. 156–159, 193). He therefore ignores the fact that for Palamas and the Greek Fathers, as Romanides writes with reference to the image of Uncreated Light in the cloud at Mount Thabor, "...the cloud which descended upon the apostles was also [the] source of this same glory" and the same Light which illumined, sanctified, and divinized all "...of the Prophets from within, before the Incarnation." While the Light of Christ's Body on Thabor was a manifestation of God's Glory by virtue of the Incarnation and illumined the Apostles from without, as Saint Gregory Palamas argues, It also deified them, so that they saw God from within. Neither their deification nor that of the human person after the Incarnation has "...as...[its] source the Incarnation and the sacraments of the Church," but rather inner illumination (Romanides, "Palamite Controversy—II," p. 242). With regard to Meyendorff's specific claim that the Incarnation is "...at the centre of the divine economy and of all history" (Meyendorff, *Study,* p. 193) and the corollary claim that the vision of Uncreated Light in the Old Testament was restricted to "...certain isolated elect, such as Moses" (John Meyen-

short, these images are manifestations of the Divine Presence, according to more traditional Orthodox theological authorities.[395] So it is that Saint John of Damascus says, in one of the *Fragmenta,* that "God is...fire [πῦρ]."[396] He equates God with the manifestation of fire. Saint Gregory the Theologian also ex-

dorff, *Introduction à L'Étude de Grégoire Palamas,* ed. H. I. Marrou [Paris: Editions du Seuil, 1957], p. 268), Saint Gregory Palamas, in his *Hagioritic Tome,* does indeed specifically argue for the unity of the mystery of the vision of God and the commonality of knowledge of the truths or dogmas of the Christian Faith in the Old and New Testaments (Migne, *Patrologia Græca,* Vol. 150, col. 1225ff.). Thus, Saint Gregory the Sinaite, a contemporary of Saint Gregory Palamas, writing on the Transfiguration, says that the Prophets Moses and Elias, in their experiences of the Glory of God, saw nothing other than "the splendor of the Divinity" in Its "two theophanies," both as "cloud and darkness" and as the Light of the Transfiguration, at which they were present, one and the same (see Saint Gregory the Sinaite, *Discourse on the Transfiguration,* trans. David Balfour [San Bernardino, CA: The Borgo Press, 1988], p. 25).

[395] Thus, Archbishop Chrysostomos and others have argued that Father Meyendorff represents a school of theology that has at times subtly moved away from the consensus of traditional Orthodox thought and which is influenced by the categories of Western theology that are the legacy of its Greek Catholic roots (Chrysostomos, "Questions and Comments from Readers," *Orthodox Tradition,* Vol. 7, No. 4 [1990], pp. 11, 13). In keeping with this observation, Romanides believes that Meyendorff identifies deification with an "Incarnation–centered" theology and the Sacraments simply because he is compromised by notions of deification that, by virtue of separating the vision of God from "the Incarnation and the formation of the Church," have no direct parallels in Western theological thought (Romanides, "Palamite Controversy—ii," p. 247). In defense of Father Meyendorff—though we too suspect that he has to some extent confused Western and Eastern theological concerns in his study of Saint Gregory Palamas—, one might argue that the Incarnation and the Christian Mysteries, which are rooted in the eternal Person of Christ, have themselves a universal scope which binds together the Old and New Testamental visions of God. This is not to say that Meyendorff's contention that the Old Testamental vision of God's Glory was limited to a certain category of the "elect" has any Patristic support or that it is theologically tenable; however, it is to say that, this notion aside, his understanding of the centrality of the Incarnation and the sacramental life in the Divine economy is not incompatible with the unity of Old and New Testamental visions of God as it is understood by the hesychasts.

[396] Migne, *Patrologia Græca,* Vol. 19, col. 233.

presses the consensus of the Greek Fathers when he says that the
Old Testamental manifestations of God were, indeed, the
"Light" that is God: "...It was Light that appeared out of Fire to
Moses, when it burned the bush; ...it was Light that was in the
pillar of Fire that led Israel and tamed the wilderness; ...it was
Light that carried Elias (Elijah)[397] in the car of Fire."[398]

The Old Testamental images or manifestations of God to
which we have referred are also found in the New Testament,
alongside images of light. We have already treated with the cloud
at the Transfiguration. But we might mention, in addition, the
"cloven tongues like as of fire" at Pentecost;[399] the temple in
Saint John's Revelation, which was filled with "smoke from the
glory of God";[400] the portrayal of God's mercy as rain in the
Gospel of Saint Matthew;[401] and the promise to the Thessalonians that Christ will be made manifest through the "power of His
Angels" and in a "flaming fire."[402] In the New Testament, too,
these are manifestations of the Uncreated Light of God. They are
not unlike other manifestations of the spirit and power of God,
such as the Spirit of God "descending from heaven like a
dove"[403] at the Baptism of Christ,[404] or the Cross,[405] and are

---

397 IV Kings 2:11 (*Septuaginta*): "Behold, there appeared a chariot of fire,
and horses of fire, and parted them both asunder; and Elias went up by a whirl-
wind into heaven."

398 Saint Gregory Nazianzus, "Oration XL," p. 361.

399 Acts 2:3.

400 Revelation 15:8.

401 St. Matthew 5:45.

402 II Thessalonians 1:7. The phrase "μετ' ἀγγέλων δυνάμεως αὐτοῦ" is
translated in the KJV and the RSV as "with his mighty angels"; a better translation, however, is, "with the Angels of His power" since they, like the flaming
fire, manifest the Glory of God.

403 St. John 1:32.

404 Father Romanides, in interpreting Saint Gregory Palamas' understanding of the dove at Christ's Baptism, emphatically states that this dove was
not a created symbol or a bird, but a "linguistic symbol" or image of a "supra-
rational" manifestation of God (Romanides, "Palamite Controversy—II," p.
262).

all, like many of the other manifestations which we have cited, images which we also see reported by eyewitnesses to the phenomenon of the Holy Fire.

In the hagiographic *corpus* of the Patristic witness we find other numerous accounts of Uncreated Light associated with or seen by various holy men and women. We will allude to a few of these, since it is this vision or experience of Uncreated or Divine Light, of the Glory of God, which for the Eastern Christian constitutes a state of sanctity and the spiritual goal of both the monastic and layman.[406] Many of these experiences are also similar to those which we have seen reported in connection with the phenomenon of the Holy Fire. In his life of Saint Benedict of Nursia (†550), Saint Gregory the Great (†604) tells us that Saint Benedict, at the repose of Saint Germanos of Capua († *ca.* 540), stood in prayer and saw "...a light, which banished away the darkness of the night, and glittered with such brightness, that the light which did shine in the midst of darkness was far more clear than the light of the day."[407]

Saint Symeon the New Theologian, in the life written by his disciple, Saint Niketas Stethatos (†1092?), says of a youth in his time (a certain George, who lived in Constantinople) that "...once when he was...standing at prayer..., suddenly a most brilliant Divine radiance descended on him from above and filled all that place."[408] Saint Symeon himself, addressing God, tells of

---

[405] Not only does Saint Paul claim to glory only in the Cross (Galatians 6:14) and associate "the blood of His [Christ's] Cross" with the reconciliation of all things to Christ (Colossians 1:20), but Saint John Chrysostomos attributes to the Cross the "power of God" and a Glory beyond reason (see his "Homily IV on First Corinthians" in *Nicene and Post–Nicene Fathers,* ed. Phillip Schaff, Vol. 12, 1st ser. [Grand Rapids, MI: Eerdman's Publishing Co., 1969], p. 17).

[406] See Cavarnos, *Byzantine Thought,* pp. 27–28.

[407] Saint Gregory the Great, *The Dialogues,* trans. P. W., (London: Philip Lee Warner, 1911), p. 97.

[408] [Saint] Nicetas Stethatos, "The Life of St. Symeon the New Theologian," in *The Sin of Adam and our Redemption: Seven Homilies by St. Symeon the New Theologian* (Platina, CA: St. Herman of Alaska Brotherhood, 1979), p. 13.

his own experience of the Uncreated Light:

> Once, when Thou didst come and wash me, immersing me repeatedly in the waters, as it seemed, I saw lightning flashing around me and rays of light emanating from Thy countenance and blending with the waters; seeing myself washed in luminous, radiant waters I fell into ecstasy.[409]

The Russian holy man, Saint Theodosios of the Kievan Caves (†1074), was often seen in the presence of light. An anonymous layman once saw, as reported in the life of Saint Theodosios by Saint Nestor the Chronicler (†1114),

> ...an awesome miracle: a wondrous light in the dead of night, right above the monastery of the saint. And lo, when he raised his eye, he saw the godlike Theodosius in that light.... And while he stood there wondering what this meant, behold, a new wonder appeared to him: a mighty flame came forth from the dome of the church, in the form of a bow reaching across to another height, and remained standing with that end on the spot which our blessed Father Theodosius picked, and where he later started building the [new] Church.[410]

Another Russian Saint, Saint Sergios of Radonezh (†1392), during the celebration of the Divine Liturgy, "...saw a fire which touched the table of prothesis and surrounded the Holy Altar. At the moment of communion the fire entered the chalice and the saint received communion in this manner."[411] In connection with two other Russian Saints, Saint Cyril of Belozersk (or White Lake, †1429) and Saint Alexander of Svir (†1533), we have similar reports of the manifestation of Uncreated Light as light itself and as smoke and fire. Saint Cyril, while singing the Akathist Hymn to the *Theotokos,* heard a voice "together with...a

---

[409] I. M. Kontzevitch, *The Acquisition of the Holy Spirit in Ancient Russia,* trans. Olga Koshansky (Platina, CA: St. Herman of Alaska Brotherhood, 1988), p. 53.

[410] Børtnes, *Visions of Glory,* p. 74.

[411] Pierre Kovalevsky, *Saint Sergius and Russian Spirituality,* trans. W. E. Jones (Crestwood, NY: St. Vladimir's Seminary Press, 1976), p. 117.

great light" which made the night as bright as day.[412] A Russian nobleman who had discovered the hidden abode of the recluse Alexander confessed to the Saint that many times he had seen a "...fiery pillar standing, and sometimes a certain Divine ray shining, and sometimes a bright smoke ascending from the earth to the heights" at the place where the Saint dwelled.[413]

With regard to the effects associated with the Holy Fire, which we enumerated above in Table B, even though they, too, contain elements of light (the miraculous lighting of lamps and candles), we cannot associate them directly with visions of God Himself. By way of understanding these phenomena, let us see what the Prophet Elias tells us of his experience on Mount Horeb:

> And behold the Lord passed by and a great and strong wind rent the mountains, and broke in pieces the rocks before the Lord, but the Lord was not in the wind; and after the wind an earthquake, but the Lord was not in the earthquake; and after the earthquake a fire,[414] but the Lord was not in the fire; and after the fire, a still small voice.[415]

---

[412] *The Northern Thebaid: Monastic Saints of the Russian North,* trans. Hieromonk Seraphim Rose (Platina, CA: St. Herman of Alaska Brotherhood, 1975), p. 51.

[413] *Ibid.,* p. 116. It is interesting to note that similar accounts of the vision of spiritual light continue to this day. For example, Helena Kontzevitch (1893–1989), wife of the late and renowned theologian, Professor I. M. Kontzevitch, told of seeing an Icon of Saint James of Lake Valdaye (or Borovitz, †1540?) "...giving off a sweet light.... It was as though this light were emanating forth in breaths. Each time that the Icon 'breathed,' the light would reach up to the ceiling [of the room], and then this would be followed by another 'breath.' These made a circle on the ceiling, joined by each successive 'breath' of light. This circle moved about the room. It was in constant motion. The glimmer of the light was very sweet"; see Archbishop Chrysostomos' translation of her French narrative and his commentary in "Helena Kontzevitch: Her Spiritual Memento," *Orthodox Tradition,* Vol. 9, No. 1 (1992), p. 3.

[414] Here the Prophet is presumably speaking of a fire with material attributes, not of that fire which has the properties of Uncreated Light.

[415] III Kings 19:11–12 (*Septuaginta*).

While the phenomena which Elias saw were not, as such, manifestations of God, they were associated with Him. We might, in effect, say that they were "physical" evidence of the presence or Energy of God (Who in this case manifested Himself as a still small voice). In the same way, the tongues of fire at Pentecost, a manifestation of the Glory of God, were associated with a "rushing mighty wind."[416] And the descent of an Angel from Heaven to roll away the stone at Christ's Tomb, another manifestation of Divine power, was accompanied by an earthquake.[417] All of these things occurred in the presence of God and are associated with the Divine Presence and Its Uncreated Light. Therefore, since they are associated with the vision of God, they are not purely physical manifestations. Speaking specifically of the Holy Fire, Tsekoura touches on this notion of a co–existence of merely material symbols and Divine reality. She observes that

> ...during the first few moments [after its appearance], in the flame of the fire there co–exist the properties of both immaterial and material light. Thus the Holy Fire of the candles does not cause burns. It does not burn a person, his hair, or his clothing. Afterwards, however, it begins to burn, as does a normal material flame.[418]

Now, it is important that we reconcile what we have called visions of God and manifestations of Uncreated Light that are similar to the phenomena associated with the Holy Fire with the fact that God is not seen by the unenlightened, but by Prophets, Apostles, Saints, and the holy. We have argued that it is only within God and with spiritual eyes and the restored senses that one can see God, according to Orthodox theology. In answer to this quandary, we can first remark that Orthodox theology does not set aside the primacy of the Providence of God. Thus He can reveal Himself as He wishes, even to the unprepared—whether to Saint Paul on the road to Damascus or, at the Crucifixion, to

---

[416] Acts 2:2.

[417] St. Matthew 28:2.

[418] Tsekoura, *Τὸ Ἅγιον Φῶς*, pp. 72–73.

the un–Baptized thief at His right.[419] Saint Gregory Palamas, in his homily on the Transfiguration, therefore asserts that the vision of Uncreated Light is given according to the Will of God, Who alone judges the "measure of...[each person's]... worthiness."[420]

We should also point out that the Holy Fire is reported by all of the skeptical witnesses whom we have cited as a simple flame, as the effect of an alleged miracle. All other manifestations (lightning, fire, rain, dew, snow, cloud, smoke, an Angel, or a dove) are reported by believers. Tsekoura makes this point very clearly in speaking of the manifestations which she reports:

> How does one see the Holy Fire? With the eyes of the soul, when God grants the enlightenment of the Holy Spirit. 'In the illumination of the [Holy] Spirit,' St. Basil the Great says, 'we see the Holy Light.' Thus in the Doxology, we chant 'in Thy light we shall see light,' that is, 'by the Holy Spirit we shall see Thy light, Lord.' When the Holy Spirit shines forth His light, St. Gregory Palamas says, then we humans see Him with the eyes of the heart, that is, of the soul. As we see material light with our bodily eyes, so we see the Holy Fire 'through the eyes of the soul.' This spiritual sensation of the Holy Fire is 'above the senses and the mind.' For this reason, this light manifests itself even when the eyes are closed or when a person is physically blind.[421]

In other words, Tsekoura identifies the various manifestations of the Holy Fire, if not with sanctity, at least with a sensitivity toward spiritual things and with the action of the Holy Spirit. These manifestations are not, for her, mere physical phenomena, but are closely attached to faith and belief.

The Scriptural and Patristic witness with regard to various manifestations of supernatural Light is interpreted by Orthodox theologians, as we have demonstrated, to attest to a unity of experience of the Glory of God and the Resurrection of Christ as Uncreated Light. These manifestations bear a striking resem-

---

[419] St. Luke 23:40–43.

[420] Migne, *Patrologia Græca*, Vol. 151, col. 448B.

[421] Tsekoura, *Τὸ Ἅγιον Φῶς*, pp. 70–71.

blance to the diverse forms of the Holy Fire reported by pilgrims at the Tomb of Christ in Jerusalem. But correspondence does not establish identity. Even if we could demonstrate its miraculous origins, we could not therefore conclude, from the *corpus* of Patristic and Scriptural references, that the Holy Fire is anything but a phenomenon with properties like *phenomena* that have at times, according to Eastern Christian theology, revealed the Glory of God. Neither the historical record nor Scripture and the Fathers directly associate the revelation of God with a rite performed in the Holy Sepulchre. This we must admit. We can, however, with certainty say that the phenomenon of the Holy Fire is an appropriate symbol of the Light of the Resurrection—a symbol in the most profound sense, as something which makes "the transcendent...available" and which "...mediate[s] the participation of the observer in that which it reveals."[422] In this assertion, we follow the example of Saint Gregory the Theologian, who, in a sermon on the Sunday of Pascha, speaks of the light of the candles and lamps of the Paschal Vigil on the previous day as a forerunner of the "Great Light":[423]

> The Pascha of the Lord, Pascha, and again I say, Pascha, in honor of the Trinity. This is for us the feast of feasts and the celebration of celebrations, so transcending all others—not only those which are merely human and lowly [χαμαὶ ἐρχομένας], but even those of Christ and those celebrated in His honor—as the sun does the stars. Beautiful indeed was our display of brightness and our illumination yesterday, in which privately and in public we greeted one another, all sorts of people, those of mean status and all ranks, lighting up the night with the abundant fire [of our candles].... As yesterday's light was a forerunner of the rising of the Great Light, a

---

[422] James Empereur, *Worship: Exploring the Sacred* (Washington, DC: The Pastoral Press, 1987), p. 35.

[423] Anscar J. Chupungco, in his *The Cosmic Elements of Christian Passover* (Rome: Editrice Anselmiana, 1977), claims that what we assume to be the Paschal Vigil is in fact "...the preceding night's procession of torches [or candles] held by the magistrates and townspeople to honor the neophytes [newly Baptized]" (p. 88).

kind of pre–festal rejoicing, so today we are celebrating the Resurrection itself, no longer something awaited, but something which has come to pass already, and gathering the whole world to itself.[424]

---

[424] See Saint Gregory Nazianzus, "Oration xlv," p. 423; the Greek text is in Migne, *Patrologia Græca,* Vol. 37, p. 624. We have translated the text from the Greek, since the English here is confused. For example, "...δαψιλεῖ τῷ πυρὶ τὴν νύκτα καταφωτίζοντες," which we translate as "...abundantly lighting up the night with the fire [of our candles]," albeit a difficult phrase in Greek, is rendered unintelligible by a reference in the English text to a "crowded fire" illuminating the night.

CHAPTER V

THE RITE OF THE HOLY FIRE AS IT IS CELEBRATED IN JERUSALEM TODAY

The rite of the Holy Fire does not exist in the form of a written *typikon* in the Greek Orthodox Patriarchate of Jerusalem. Only the prayer for the reception of the Holy Fire exists in printed form. It is from a "φυλλάδιον" or small, bound booklet containing this printed prayer (the text of which we will reproduce below in English translation) that the Patriarch reads while in the Holy *Kouvouklion* (the Edicule). The origin of this prayer is unknown. The remainder of the service is conducted in accordance with traditions that are passed down from Patriarch to Patriarch either orally or in scattered liturgical notes.[425] There are two major descriptions of the rite from which it can be reconstructed. The first is that of Ioanna Tsekoura,[426] supplied to us by Archbishop Timothy of Lydda, Chief Secretary of the Jerusalem Patriarchate, and recommended by Patriarch Diodoros I as a reliable source.[427] The second is a published collection of confidential reports on the *status quo* in the Holy Land issued in the late 1920s by Lionel Cust, British District Officer in Jerusalem,[428] and containing an appendix which describes in some detail the ceremony of the Holy Fire, "the supreme ceremony of the Eastern Churches."[429] Both Cust's report and Tsekoura's description present essentially the same service, the former as it

---

[425] Greek Orthodox Patriarch Diodoros I of Jerusalem, telephone interview by author, 12 January 1992, written transcription, Center for Traditionalist Orthodox Studies, Etna, CA.

[426] Tsekoura, Τὸ Ἅγιον Φῶς, pp. 37–45, 55–56.

[427] Diodoros I, telephone interview, 12 January 1992.

[428] Lionel George Archer Cust, *The Status Quo in the Holy Places* (Jerusalem: Ariel Publishing House, 1980), "Appendix C," pp. 66–70.

[429] *Ibid.*, p. 66.

was observed in the 1920s, the latter as it is celebrated in the present decade.

Non–Liturgical Preparations for the Service. Tsekoura identifies two events which precede the actual celebration of the rite of the Holy Fire on Great Saturday. First, the Holy Sepulchre is searched; second, it is sealed. The purpose of the search is to determine that there is nothing in either chamber of the Edicule that can be used to light a flame and to see that every lamp has been extinguished. The search, according to Tsekoura, lasts for one hour, beginning at ten o'clock Saturday morning, and involves three separate inspections of the Tomb.[430] It is conducted by a Moslem guard assigned to the Holy Sepulchre and takes place in the presence of the Armenian, Coptic, and Jacobite clergy. At 11 *a.m.*, the door of the Edicule is sealed by the Moslem guard who, according to Cust, places a white ribbon through the two handles on the door and seals it with wax.[431] Standing at the south of the door is an Armenian clergyman, at the north a Greek Orthodox clergyman.[432] Between 11 *a.m.* and 12 noon, the Arabic Orthodox Christians stage their raucous procession around the Edicule, singing traditional folk songs, hoisting young men up on their shoulders, and shouting religious slogans.[433]

The Liturgical Ceremony. At noon[434] the Greek Orthodox

[430] Tsekoura, *Τò "Αγιον Φῶς,* pp. 38–40.

[431] Tsekoura, however, says that two white ribbons are crossed over one another to form an "X" over the door of the Edicule, each of the four ends of the ribbons being attached with wax to the four corners of the entrance. Another piece of wax is placed at the center of the crossed ribbons and then stamped with the official seal of the Patriarchate; *ibid.,* p. 40.

[432] Cust, *Status Quo,* pp. 68–69; also standing at the north side, according to Cust, is a representative of the Franciscan community in Jerusalem.

[433] *Ibid.,* p. 86; *cf.* Tsekoura, *Τò "Αγιον Φῶς,* p. 41.

[434] The reader will recall that at least since the fourteenth century the rite of the Holy Fire has been celebrated independently of and prior to the Paschal Vigil, which properly begins with Vespers and the Liturgy of Saint Basil the Great at about four o'clock in the afternoon, according to contemporary Jerusalem practice.

Patriarch leaves the Patriarchal palace and, to the somber ringing of bells,[435] enters the Church of the Resurrection and ascends the Patriarchal Throne. The Armenian, Coptic, and Jacobite clergy then, according to Cust, "...do obeisance and obtain permission to take part in the ceremony."[436] In fact, as Tsekoura correctly points out, the clergy of these various religious communities in Jerusalem do not ask to participate in the rite, but simply kiss the hand of the Greek Patriarch and ask his permission "to receive the Holy Fire."[437] After this brief ceremony, the Patriarch vests in full Episcopal attire and the procession around the Edicule begins, usually "at 12:30 p.m."[438] The Greek Orthodox Patriarch approaches the Edicule, preceded by banners and a processional Cross and by Moslem guards who, carrying staffs similar to the walking sticks used by Eastern Orthodox Bishops (ράβδοι),[439] open a path for the him by striking the floor with the tips of their staffs to a rhythmic cadence. The Patriarch is followed by his Bishops and other clergy, while the choirs (one chanting in Greek, the other in Arabic) sing: "The Angels in Heaven hymn Thy Resurrection, Christ our Savior; deem us on earth also worthy to glorify Thee with pure hearts."[440]

After a triple circumambulation of the Edicule, the procession stops in front of the Holy Sepulchre, where the choirs and clergy sing the Vespers Hymn of Light, "Φῶς ἱλαρόν," or "O Joyous Light."[441] The other clergy leave, and the Patriarch alone

---

[435] This is mentioned by Tsekoura (*Τὸ Ἅγιον Φῶς*, p. 41), but not Cust.

[436] Cust, *Status Quo*, p. 68.

[437] Tsekoura, *Τὸ Ἅγιον Φῶς*, p. 42.

[438] Cust, *Status Quo*, p. 68.

[439] Hence, these staff–bearers are called "ραβδοῦχοι."

[440] This is the first verse of the *Aposticha* for Saturday evening Vespers in the Sixth Tone.

[441] "O Joyous Light of the Holy Glory of the Immortal, Heavenly, Holy, Blessed Father, O Jesus Christ, we that come to the setting of the sun, when we behold the evening light, praise Father, Son, and Holy Spirit: God. Meet it is for Thee at all times to be praised with gladsome voices, O Son of God, Giver

approaches the entrance to the Holy Sepulchre, where he is joined by the Armenian bishop[442] and various secular officials.[443] The Patriarch removes his vestments and mitre and submits to a search by the secular authorities, including the "chief city official of Jerusalem and the chief of police,"[444] in order to determine whether he is carrying matches or any device with which he might light a candle. After this search, the door of the Holy Sepulchre is opened and the Patriarch, wearing a simple, white tunic, enters in, followed by the Armenian bishop. The door is then closed.

Within the Holy Sepulchre, in the presence of the Armenian bishop, the Patriarch kneels before the marble covering of the Tomb, on which there lie an unlighted lamp and a booklet with the prayer of the Holy Fire. Holding the booklet open is a large, unlighted candle. All of these things are placed in the Tomb earlier. To them, the Patriarch adds four bundles of unlit candles, each bundle containing thirty–three candles, which he takes into the Sepulchre with him. With these four bundles of candles he passes on the Holy Fire.[445] In the dim light of the Edicule, the Patriarch begins to read the prayer for the reception of the Holy Fire:

> Master, Lord Jesus Christ, the light–originating Wisdom of the Unoriginate Father, Who abidest in unapproachable light, Who commanded light to shine forth from darkness, Who said, 'Let there be light,' [*sic*] and there was light;['] Lord, the provider of light, Who leddest us forth out of the darkness of delusion, and leddest us into the wondrous light of thy [full] knowledge, Who filledst with light and joy all the earth by Thine incarnate presence therein, and the things below the earth by Thy descent into hades, whereafter Thou didst proclaim light to all the nations through

---

of Life; wherefore the world doth glorify Thee."

442 Cust, *Status Quo,* p. 69.

443 Tsekoura, *Τὸ Ἅγιον Φῶς,* p. 44.

444 *Ibid.*

445 *Ibid.,* pp. 43–44.

Thine holy Apostles; we thank Thee that through the pious faith Thou didst lead us out of darkness toward [the][446] light, and that we have become sons of light through holy Baptism, and beheld Thy glory, full of grace and truth (John 1:14). But,[447] O Light–bestowing Lord, Who art the Light seen by the people who have sat in darkness;[.] Master Lord, the True Light which enlighteneth every man that cometh into the world (John 1:9), the only Light of the world and the Light of the life of men, with Whose glory is filled all the universe, for Thou art come as Light into the world through Thy dispensation in the flesh, although men have loved darkness more than the light. Do Thou, Lord, Light–giver, hearken unto us sinners and thine unworthy servants, who at this hour stand about this Thine All–Holy and Light–bearing Tomb, and receive us who honor Thine immaculate Passions, Thine All–Holy Crucifixion, Thy voluntary death, and the deposition and burial of Thy lifeless body in this All–Venerable Tomb, and Thy Rising on the third day; already beginning to celebrate which joyously, we commemorate Thy descent into hades, whereby as Master Thou didst liberate, by the lightning of Thy Divinity, the souls of the righteous held therein, filling the nether regions with light. Wherefore, indeed, with rejoicing heart and spiritual joy on this most blessed Sabbath, celebrating Thy most salvific mysteries, accomplished in a godly manner befitting Thee on the earth and below the earth, and calling to mind Thee, the truly gladsome and desirable Light, which divinely shone upon these in the nether regions and in a godly wise manner did shine forth from the Grave, we make manifest the Light, representing Thy Theophany, which came to pass compassionately for our sake. Forasmuch as on this salvific and radiant night all things are filled with light, heaven and earth, and the nether regions through the felicitous mystery of Thy descent into hades, and Thy third–day Resurrection from the Grave, those who piously receive of the perpetually kindled and ever–radiant Fire pass it on to those who believe on Thee, the True Light, and we call upon and beseech Thee, O All–Holy Master, that Thou wilt show forth this gift of sanctification, filled full of all Thy

---

[446] This interpolation is that of the translator.

[447] The translator misses the archaic use of the word "ἀλλά," which might be better translated in this instance as "again" or "as well."

divine grace through the grace of thine All–Holy and Light–bearing Tomb, and that Thou bless and sanctify those who piously touch it, delivering [them] from the darkness of passions, and that Thou deem us worthy of Thy most radiant habitations, where shineth the unwaning light of Thy Divinity. Grant unto them, O Lord, health and good life, and fill their houses with every good thing. Yea, Light–bestowing Master, hearken unto me a sinner at this hour and grant unto us and unto them to walk in Thy light and to abide therein for as long as we have the light of this present life. Grant us, O Lord, that the light of our good works may shine before men, that they may glorify Thee with Thine Unoriginate Father and the Holy Spirit; for Thou hast established us for a light unto the nations, that we may shine unto those who walk in darkness; but, working evil, we have loved darkness more than the light, for everyone who doeth evil hateth the light, according to Thy word which cannot lie; wherefore, sinning, we stumble daily, since we walk in darkness, but vouchsafe unto us to live the remainder of our lives having the eyes of our mind enlightened. Grant us that we may walk as children of light in the light of Thy commandments; make white the radiant garment of holy Baptism, which we have blackened by our works, as One who putteth on light as it were a garment; Grant us to put on the armor of light, that we may turn away the prince of darkness, who transformeth himself into an angel of light. Yea, O Lord, like as on this day Thou didst shine light upon those that sit in darkness and the shadow of death, likewise shine today in our hearts Thine undefiled light that radiant with this light and fervent in the Faith, we may glorify Thee, the only gladsome Light of the only light–originating Light, unto the endless ages. Amen.[448]

When the Holy Fire appears, it lights the lamp on the Holy Sepulchre, following the Patriarch's prayer, along with the four bundles of candles which he takes into the Tomb with him. He

---

[448] The Greek text of this prayer can be found in Archimandrite Joachim Strongylos, *Προσκύνημα Στούς Ἁγίους Τόπους* (Jerusalem: 1987) pp. 75–77; the generally accurate, if stilted, English translation which we have used here is from Callistos, "Holy Fire," p. 24. The Scriptural references have been added by the translator. The unusual syntax in the English translation reflects the oddities of the complex but eloquent Greek text.

then turns and goes into the Chapel of the Angel, where he gives one of the bundles to the Armenian bishop. Then from one of the openings in the Edicule he gives the Holy Fire to an Arabic Greek Orthodox Priest, who takes it to the *Anastasis* for distribution to the Faithful there. From the other opening he hands out another bundle of candles, so that the Holy Fire can be taken to the Armenian Patriarch. He then knocks at the door of the Holy Sepulchre and, when it is opened, he and the Armenian bishop pass on the flame to the Coptic and Jacobite clergy and to others waiting outside.[449] The Church then fills with the light of the candles of the Faithful, as the flame is passed from person to person. There is a great uproar among the people. The Patriarch then retires to his residence.[450]

The rite of the Holy Fire as it is celebrated today in Jerusalem is essentially the same ceremony described by the Russian monk, Father Parthenius, in 1846, when, as we argued in Chapter 1, the rite reached what was more or less its final form. It might be fruitful, then, to conclude our description of the contemporary rite by contrasting it with the ceremony described by Parthenius,[451] so as to establish at least a century and a half of consistent practice. In the chart below, the features of the ceremony as it was described in 1846 are set out in regular type. The features of the modern-day rite appear in italics:

Extinguishing and preparation of lamps in the
Holy Sepulchre and surrounding Churches
Extinguishing and preparation of lamps,
Holy Sepulchre searched and sealed

***

Gathering of the Faithful in the *Anastasis*
Faithful present in the Anastasis,
Arabic folk procession

***

449 Tsekoura, Τὸ Ἅγιον Φῶς, pp. 55–56; *cf.* Cust, *Status Quo*, p. 69.

450 Cust, *Status Quo*, p. 69.

451 Parthenius, "Holy Week," pp. 32–34.

Procession three times around the Edicule
of the Tomb at about 2 *p.m.*
Procession three times around the Edicule
of the Tomb at about 12:30 p.m.

***

Patriarch (in this instance, a Metropolitan
representing the Patriarch) divested
Patriarch (or his appointed representative) joined by
Armenian bishop, divested, and searched

***

Seals of the Tomb broken and the Patriarch enters
Seals of the Tomb broken and the Patriarch enters,
accompanied by Armenian bishop

***

Light suddenly appears from the Tomb and the Altar of the
Anastasis, eventually filling the entire Church
Light suddenly appears from the Tomb and the Altar of the
Anastasis, *eventually filling the entire Church*

***

Light distributed from apertures in the Edicule and then by the
Patriarch from the door of the Holy Sepulchre
to the Orthodox and the Armenians
Light distributed from apertures in the Edicule and then by the
Patriarch and the Armenian bishop from the door of the Holy
Sepulchre to the Orthodox and the Armenians

***

Great tumult among the Faithful (even the Moslems)
Great tumult among the Faithful

There are in the present–day rite of the Holy Fire two significant accretions to the service as described by Parthenius. The first, a non–liturgical one, is the search of the Tomb, prior to the ceremony, and the person of the Patriarch before he enters the Holy Sepulchre. The second is an important liturgical addition, the prayer of the Patriarch before the reception of the Holy Fire. The earliest evidence for these elements of the rite is the report of Father Metrophanes in 1926.[452]

---

[452] Achilleos, *Εἶδα τὸ Ἅγιο Φῶς,* pp. 162, 214.

CHAPTER VI

THE RITE OF THE HOLY FIRE AS IT IS REFLECTED IN THE LENTEN AND PASCHAL HYMNOGRAPHY OF THE ORTHODOX CHURCH AND IN THE CEREMONIES OF THE CONTEMPORARY GREEK CHURCHES

Possible Images of the Holy Fire in the Lenten and Paschal Hymnography of the Orthodox Church. The Lenten and Paschal hymns of the Orthodox Church are found primarily in two liturgical texts: the *Triodion,* containing the services and hymns for the Lenten period, beginning on the Sunday of the Publican and the Pharisee and ending with the Midnight Service on Great Saturday; and the *Pentecostarion,* which contains the hymns and services from the procession preceding Paschal Matins through the Sunday after Pentecost (the Sunday of All Saints). In the first of these collections, there are many references to light. However, in keeping with the theme of the Lenten period, they center on light as an image of that beneficial Grace by which one passes successfully through the ascetic feats of the Great Fast, enabled therewith "...to attain to and worship," as a prayer from the Presanctified Liturgy reads, Christ's "Holy Resurrection."[453] We find this image very clearly in the *Heirmos* of the Fifth Ode of Great Compline for the first Tuesday of the Great Fast:

> From the night, O Lover of Mankind, I seek after Thee; give me light and guide me in the commandments, O Savior, and teach me to do Thy will.[454]

With respect to specific allusions to light in the Tomb of Christ, references in the *Triodion* are scant. Though the Resur-

---

453 Ίερατικόν (Athens: Apostolike Diakonia tes Ekklesias tes Hellados, 1977), p. 220.

454 Τριώδιον Κατανυκτικόν (Athens: Apostolike Diakonia tes Ekklesias tes Hellados, 1960), p. 97.

rection theme, of course, dominates during all of the Sundays of Lent, it is only towards the end of the Great Fast that images of the Resurrection become more frequent. Correspondingly, we find more references to Resurrectional Light. However, the majority of these speak of the light of the Angel who announced the Resurrection to the Myrrh–Bearers. For example, the Sessional Hymn after the Third Ode of Matins for Great Saturday reads:

> The soldiers guarding Thy Tomb, O Savior, became as dead men in the presence of the shining Angel, who announced the Resurrection to the women. We glorify Thee, Who destroyed corruption. We fall down before Thee, our only God, risen from the Tomb.[455]

There is no specific mention here of light coming forth from the Tomb itself. Indeed, one of the only places in the *Triodion* in where such mention is made is a rather unclear verse from the Second Stasis of the Lamentations for Holy Saturday Matins, where the Tomb is portrayed only metaphorically:

> The sun shines forth once more in brightness; for Thou, O Word, after death, coming forth as from a bridal chamber, didst arise again and shine forth in glory.[456]

In the *Pentecostarion,* there are several references to light and the Tomb of Christ. In the Fourth Ode of the Paschal Canon, we find the first instance of the association of the Tomb of Christ with light:

> As a Ewe–Lamb, the Blessed One, our crown, of His Own good will sacrificed Himself for all, the Pascha of purification; and from the grave the beautiful Sun of Righteousness shone forth again upon us.[457]

In the Seventh Ode of the Canon, we also read:

> Truly sacred and all festive is this saving and light–bearing night,

[455] *Ibid.,* p. 426.

[456] *Ibid.,* p. 420.

[457] Πεντηκοστάριον Χαρμόσυνον (Athens: Apostolike Diakonia tes Ekklesias tes Hellados, 1959), p. 3.

the harbinger of the bright day of the Resurrection, on which the timeless Light shined forth bodily from the grave for all.[458]

Similarly, in the verses for the Stichera of Pascha, sung at the Lauds of the Paschal Matins, we hear the following:

...And today Christ, as from a bridal chamber, has shone forth with light from the Tomb, filling the women with joy and saying: Proclaim it to the Apostles.[459]

From the verses appointed for the Paschal Hours, Compline, and the Midnight Service, there is a yet another clear allusion to the the light of Christ's Tomb:

As life–bearing, more beautiful than Paradise, indeed brighter than any royal chamber, did Thy Tomb prove to be, O Christ, the well-spring of our Resurrection.[460]

Finally, in the first Sessional Hymn for Matins on the Tuesday after Saint Thomas Sunday, the Tomb of Christ is once more associated with radiance:

The women went to the Tomb, and beholding the sight of the Angel, they trembled. The Tomb flashed forth light, this miracle filling them with awe.[461]

Archimandrite Callistos sees in these Paschal hymns of the Orthodox Church unquestionable images of the Holy Fire. Thus he believes that the Paschal Canon of Saint John of Damascus, for example, was written in honor of the very rite of the Holy Fire:

Without doubt the celebration of the Holy Fire inspired the chorus–leader of the hymnographers of our Church, St. John Damascus, to write the troparion for the radiant and most glorious Resurrection of our Saviour as sung in the canon for Pascha. 'Now is all filled with light, both heaven and earth and the nether re-

---

[458] *Ibid.*, p. 4.

[459] *Ibid.*, p. 5.

[460] *Ibid.*, p. 7.

[461] *Ibid.*, p. 34.

gions....'462

There is no way to support without reservation Callistos' assumption about the influence of the rite of the Holy Fire on the Orthodox Church's hymnography, either with regard to the Lenten and Paschal collections in general or the specific Canon which he cites. There are numerous allusions in these sources to light, but very few of them are directly associated with the Tomb of Christ.463 Moreover, there are no specific references, in the few passages which we have cited, to a miraculous light produced in any kind of ceremony at the Holy Sepulchre. The allusions to light and the Tomb of Christ in the *Triodion* and *Pentecostarion,* therefore, could be understood as expressions of what we have called a metaphysics of light in the Orthodox theological scheme or literary and poetic descriptions of the splendor of the Resurrection itself. Ultimately, it seems, one must confine any parallels drawn between the Orthodox Church's Lenten and Paschal hymnography and the apparition of the Holy Fire to the realm of spiritual experience.

The Vespers Hymn of Light and the Holy Fire. There is a particular hymn associated with the rite of the Holy Fire which deserves separate and special attention: the Vespers Hymn of Light, "O Joyous Light," which is sung in the contemporary ceremony in front of the entrance to the Holy Sepulchre after the threefold procession around the Edicule. This Hymn is also chanted or read each day in the Orthodox Vespers service.464

---

462 Callistos, "Holy Fire," p. 24. The *Troparion* which Callistos cites is from the Third Ode of the Paschal Canon. A better and full translation of the hymn is: "Now all things are filled with light, both Heaven and earth and the nether regions. Let all creation, then, celebrate the Rising of Christ, in which it is established"; see Πεντηκοστάριον, p. 2.

463 For example, the Φωταγωγικά, or "Hymns of Light," appointed to be sung after the Canon of Matins during the weekdays of Lent, while rich in light imagery, as their appellation suggests, contain no references to the Tomb of Christ. These are collected in the Πεντηκοστάριον, pp. 444–446.

464 The Hymn is chanted when the Vespers service has an appointed entrance, as on Saturday evening or Feast days, but is otherwise read.

Bertonière cites a twelfth–century "Greek psalter now in Turin" which contains a "curious note" attached to the text of the Hymn to the effect that it "...was sung by the Patriarch as a hymn of thanks, when the Holy Fire appeared."[465] Tsekoura, in turn, calls "O Joyous Light" a "portent" of the Holy Fire.[466] The Orthodox Faithful also associate the Hymn with the Holy Fire, and this nexus has become a matter of widespread popular piety. A connection between "O Joyous Light" and the appearance of the Holy Fire, however, is not clearly established by the historical witness.

While Saint Basil the Great (†379) refers to this Hymn as a hymn of "ἐπιλύχνιο εὐχαριστία,"[467] the word "ἐπιλύχνιο" does not necessarily refer to the "lighting of a lamp" (from which it is derived). He may be referring simply to a hymn of "evening thanksgiving"[468]—though we must, it should be noted, acknowledge and emphasize that the entire tone of the Vespers service is one of thanksgiving precisely for the "Light of Christ" shining forth in the darkness of the world, as Father Robert Taft has argued.[469] Thus, "O Joyous Light" cannot be conclusively linked even with a lighting ceremony or the rite of the Holy Fire. Kariofilis Mitsakis, in his careful study of the Hymn, also admits that, while the Hymn goes back, if not to "early Apostolic times," at least to the age of "the Martyrs and Confessors,"[470] there is no concrete evidence to justify identifying "O Joyous Light" with the lighting of the evening lamp in the *Apostolic*

---

[465] Bertonière, *Easter Vigil*, p. 45, n. 102; this "psalter" (or, more correctly, a "Psalt's [Reader's] Manual" ["Ἐγκόλπιον Ἀναγνόστου"]) is contained in I. Pasinus, *Codices Manuscripti Bibliothecæ regii Taurinensis Athenæi* (Turin, Italy: 1749), Vol. I, p. 173.

[466] Tsekoura, *Τὸ Ἅγιον Φῶς*, p. 43.

[467] "On the Holy Spirit," Migne, *Patrologia Græca*, Vol. 32, col. 205.

[468] In modern Greek, indeed, the adjective "ἐπιλύχνιος" pertains to things of the evening ("vesperal").

[469] Taft, *Beyond East and West*, p. 138.

[470] Kariofilis Mitsakis, *Βυζαντινὴ Ὑμνογραφία* (Thessaloniki: Patriarchal Institute for Patristic Studies, 1971), pp. 60–61.

Tradition,[471] as some scholars also do. Thus, not only does the
Hymn predate any reference to the rite of the Holy Fire—
strongly suggesting that it developed independently thereof—,
but it probably came to be associated with that rite simply because the ceremony of the Holy Fire was once part of the Vespers–Liturgy in the Vigil service, in which "O Joyous Light" was
sung.[472] The Hymn is perhaps nothing more than a vestige of
an older practice.

*Liturgical Influence of the Rite of the Holy Fire on the Paschal
Ceremonies of the Greek Churches.* In his commentary on the
Holy Fire, published in 1933, Archimandrite Kallistos writes of
the present–day Paschal services in the Orthodox Church that:

> Undoubtedly, the rite wherein the presiding priest gives lit candles
> to the people during the singing of 'Come receive the light from
> the unsetting Light and greet Christ risen from the dead,'[473]
> which has been handed down to all of the Orthodox Churches, is a
> custom of great antiquity.[474]

Archimandrite Kallistos' claim about the universality and antiquity of this "rite" must be clarified. He is referring to an intrigu-
ing innovation in present–day Orthodox Greek Churches. In
ancient times, the Paschal Vigil and Paschal Matins and Liturgy
were celebrated as one lengthy service that began on the afternoon of Great Saturday and continued until the dawn of Pascha
Sunday. Contemporary practice, however, provides for the taking of a limited meal and a respite between the Paschal Vigil and

[471] See Cuming, *Hippolytus,* p. 23.

[472] This may have been the case as late as the fourteenth century. The
first evidence that the rite of the Holy Fire was celebrated separately from the
Vespers–Liturgy of the Vigil service on Holy Saturday is the report of Archimandrite Arsenius, a Russian pilgrim to Jerusalem in 1375 (see Callistos, "Holy
Fire," p. 16).

[473] A better translation of this hymn, sung in the First Plagal Tone, is:
"Come and take from the unwaning light, glorifying Christ, Who is risen from
the dead."

[474] Kallistos, "Ἅγιον Φῶς," p. 239; the English text quoted here is in
Callistos, "Holy Fire," pp. 7–8.

the Paschal celebration itself. The Paschal Vigil is actually comprised of Vespers and the Liturgy of Saint Basil and, though modern *typica* recommend that it begin at four o'clock on Great Saturday afternoon (as it does in Jerusalem, following the ceremony of the Holy Fire), it is commonly held much earlier in the day—often early in the morning, in fact. What we have called the "Paschal celebration" takes place at approximately 11:30 on Great Saturday evening, beginning with the Midnight Service, followed by Paschal Matins and the Divine Liturgy. It is in the liturgical acts between the Midnight Service and Matins that we see the innovative influence of the rite of the Holy Fire on the Paschal ceremonies of the Greek Church.

In the Slavic Orthodox Churches, an elaborate procession around the Church, accompanied by the singing of the hymn "The Angels in Heaven...,"[475] takes place immediately after the Midnight Service. During the procession, the Priest and the worshippers hold candles which are lighted inside the Church before the procession. In the Greek Churches, following the Midnight Service in the Paschal celebration,[476] shortly before the procession of the clergy and people to the narthex or front courtyard of the Church,[477] the Priest comes out of the Altar and chants, "Come and take from the unwaning light...," as he distributes to the Faithful the light of a candle lit from the eternal lamp over the Holy Table. This hymn and the lighting ceremony associated with it are wholly unknown in the Slavic

---

[475] See n. 440; the full text is found in Kallistos, "'Άγιον Φῶς'" p. 226.

[476] Terminology here is often confusing, since in modern Greek these intervening rites between the Midnight Service and Paschal Matins are collectively referred to as "the Resurrection" ("ἡ 'Ανάστασις"), while the Midnight Service itself is often called "the Vigil" ("Παννυχίς").

[477] In Churches where there are doors between the nave and narthex, which are properly called the "Royal Doors" (an appellation often wrongly applied to the "Beautiful Gates" on the *Templon [Eikonostasion]*), the procession stops at the narthex, before the Royal Doors, which are then closed. In most parish Churches, the procession stops in front of the outside doors of the Church.

Churches and, though they are maintained even on Mount Athos,[478] where liturgical customs tend to be less influenced by popular custom, they are of fairly recent origin.[479]

Professor Ioannes Fountoules, in his extensive commentary on Orthodox liturgical practices, argues that this rite "...is a very recent custom, since it is not even cited in any of the printed *Pentecostaria.*"[480] In fact, the first printed reference to the hymn used in the rite is in a *typikon* by G. Violakes, published in 1888.[481] Furthermore, Fountoules observes,

> ...an indication of...[the rite's] recent introduction into the Resurrection service is the fact that it is not appointed for incorporation into that service, but takes place at a 'dead' time liturgically, that is, between the dismissal for the Midnight Service and [the procession before] the introductory blessing of the service of Matins.[482]

---

[478] Ioannes Fountoules, Ἀπαντήσεις εἰς Λειτουργικὰς Ἀπορίας (Thessaloniki: 1976), Vol. 2, p. 95.

[479] In the diaspora, where different national Orthodox traditions have influenced one another, there are instances in which the Slavic Churches have imitated the Greek ceremony of distributing the Paschal light. These instances, however, are limited and do not reflect accepted usage or the standard rubrics appointed by contemporary Slavic *typica*.

[480] Fountoules, Ἀπαντήσεις, Vol. 3, p. 253. A note in the first English translation of the Greek *Pentecostarion*, a work of uneven quality, correctly points out that current Greek texts are taken primarily from the 1836 edition of the Monk Bartholomew of the Monastery of Koutloumousiou on Mount Athos. Bartholomew's edition indeed contains no reference to this rite; see *The Pentecostarion*, trans. Holy Transfiguration Monastery (Boston: Holy Transfiguration Monastery, 1990), pp. 14–15.

[481] See A. Martinos, ed., Θρησκευτικὴ καὶ Ἠθικὴ Ἐγκυκλοπαιδεία (Athens: 1966), *s.v.* "Τάξις Λατρείας," by G. G. Bekatoros, cols. 614–615.

[482] Fountoules, Ἀπαντήσεις, Vol. 3, p. 253. In a service book containing the ceremonies for Great Week and the Paschal Vigil published by the Church of Greece in 1978, we see this innovative rite placed precisely between the Midnight Service and the procession of the clergy and Faithful out of the Church, just prior to the opening blessing of Matins; see Ἡ Ἁγία καὶ Μεγάλη Ἑβδομάς (Athens: Apostolike Diakonia tes Ekklesas [*sic*] tes Hellados, 1978), pp. 380–381.

Fountoules' observations here are consistent with the principles
of liturgical development refined by Taft, who contends that innovation or a "filling in" often occurs at "soft points" between
earlier *strata* of a rite.[483]

Fountoules contends that the "institution" of this new rite of
the distribution of the Paschal light in the Greek Churches
"...was...[in] imitation of the rite of the 'Holy Fire' in the
Church of the Holy Sepulchre in Jerusalem."[484] This is precisely
the claim of Makres, who writes that:

> The distribution of this holy light commemorates the splendid
> ceremony of the Holy Fire in Jerusalem, during which the Ortho-
> dox Patriarch distributes to the faithful pilgrims the Holy Fire of
> the Resurrection.[485]

The influence of the Paschal rites in Jerusalem on the Greek
Churches is clearly evident, too, in certain elements of the Burial
Service of Christ on Great Friday. Fountoules notes that the
elaborate cover sometimes placed over the Icon of Christ's Body
(the ἐπιτάφιος), in Greek Churches, is a re-creation of the Holy
Kouvouklion covering the Tomb of Christ.[486] He traces this instance of imitation to the last years of Turkish rule over
Greece.[487] Given the correspondence between these two instances of imitation, one might reasonably speculate that the addition of a rite of the distribution of light to the Paschal Vigil
may also have its roots in this epoch. Whatever the case, there is
little doubt that it is the product of a conscious mimicking of the
rite of the Holy Fire in the Church of the Holy Sepulchre in
Jerusalem.

---

[483] Taft, *Beyond East and West,* pp. 161, 168.

[484] Fountoules, Ἀπαντήσεις, Vol. 3, p. 124.

[485] Makres, "Φῶς, Ἅγιον," col. 14.

[486] This is, of course, an incorrect appropriation of symbols, since the
Icon of Christ's Body is depicted as lying on the Stone of Anointing, not in the
Tomb.

[487] Fountoules, Ἀπαντήσεις, Vol. 4, p. 163.

CHAPTER VII

CONCLUDING REMARKS

We have looked at the rite of the Holy Fire from an historical, theological, and liturgical perspective with intentional caution, exercising restraint, in these separate treatments, in drawing even tenuous parallels between the present–day phenomenon and historical rites in the Church of the Holy Sepulchre; the light of the Holy Fire and the light imagery found in Scripture and the Patristic witness; and references to light in the Tomb of Christ in the Paschal hymnography of the Orthodox Church and eyewitness reports through a number of centuries of the apparition of Divine Light at the celebration of the ceremony of the Holy Fire in Jerusalem. We believe that such restraint serves the ends of objective scholarship. By the same token, if, as an old adage has it, God is not heavy–handed or obvious in history, a little caution does no disservice to the rite of the Holy Fire as a religious phenomenon; rather, a spirit of circumspect skepticism can sometimes serve the end of revealing the truths of religious phenomenology, which are often shrouded in subtlety and nuance. With these words in mind, we would like to make some concluding remarks about the Holy Fire, drawing from the composite portrayal of the phenomenon that can be drawn from the subtleties and nuances of our observations.

In looking at the rite of the Holy Fire separately from an historical, theological, and liturgical perspective for the sake of objective investigation, we have also, of course, necessarily risked obfuscating to some extent, in this artificial separation, the actual phenomenon. In Orthodox theology there always prevails a unity of experience. As Archbishop Chrysostomos has written, for the Orthodox Christian history is a lie, unless it captures the unity of experience in the Church's life which links the stuff of history—dates and events—to Divine revelation, hymnography,

꘏ homiletics, the mystical life, and so on. It is this unity which reveals historical reality from "...within the spiritual tradition [ἐν-
τὸς τῆς πνευματικῆς παραδόσεως] of the spiritual life of the Orthodox Church."488 Thus, if we look at the rite of the Holy Fire
as a ceremony which has, at least since the ninth century, involved the supernatural appearance of a flame and various images of light, and link this appearance with the manifestations
and images of Divine Light in Scripture, the Patristic witness,
and the light imagery of the Orthodox Church's Paschal hymnography, there emerges a picture which stands out from the
historical, liturgical, or theological witness alone. And it is the
emergence of this composite picture which represents the Eastern Church's way of theologizing—of discovering Divine truths. .

Let us, then, from a more holistic perspective reflect on the
various pieces of data which, like the tesserae of a mosaic, make
up our composite picture of the Holy Fire. First, as we have
noted, miraculous elements have been attributed to the rite for
well over a thousand years. Admittedly, the earlier, pre–ninth–
century liturgical evidence for a miraculous light associated with
the Tomb of Christ is not absolute. However, it can be argued
that some of this evidence—Egeria's reference to the taking of
light from the Holy Sepulchre, Saint Eusebios' account of the
miraculous lighting of Paschal lamps in the life of Saint Narkissos, the second–century Bishop of Jerusalem, or testimony in the
ancient lectionaries to a lighting ceremony associated with the
Paschal Vigil in Jerusalem—, when taken together, provide what
is fossil–like evidence for phenomena not unlike those associated
with the later rite of the Holy Fire. It is also significant that none
of even the earliest witnesses to the actual rite of the Holy Fire
speaks of it as something innovative.

Second, while many of the post–Schism reports of the ceremony of the Holy Fire are tainted by polemics, earlier historical

---

488 Bishop [Archbishop] Chrysostomos, "Μία κριτική· Αἱ ἐπιστημονικαὶ
προϋποθέσεις τῶν Οἰκουμενικῶν Διαλόγων (Γεράσιμου Κονιδάρη)," Ὀρθόδοξος Ἔνστασις καὶ Μαρτυρία, Vol. I, No. 5 (1986), p. 132.

accounts of the rite are free of such overtones and testify to its universal acceptance in at least the post–ninth–century Christian world, if not before. Indeed, were it not for the divisive effects of the Great Schism, we might well have clearer and less tentative instances of the imitation of the ceremony of the Holy Fire in the Western church than those suggested by the lighting of the Paschal lamp and the blessing of Paschal candles. Despite this sad state of affairs, however, one cannot ignore the parallels between these ceremonies and the rite of the Holy Fire, especially in light of the remarkable similarities between the Paschal lamp–lighting ceremony in the Mozarabic rite of the Spanish Church, which takes place in the darkened and sealed sacristy, and the ceremony in the sealed Edicule of the Holy Sepulchre. Taken together with evidence of numerous instances in which the rites and customs of the Church of Jerusalem have affected the worship of the other Christian Churches, these parallels imply that the rite of the Holy Fire may have a more universal dimension than the data *per se* establish.

Moreover, throughout its lengthy history, and in spite of the often turbulent political and ecclesiastical upheavals in Jerusalem, the rite of the Holy Fire has consistently maintained its original focus: the miraculous kindling of the Paschal light and its joyous reception by the Faithful. This consistency is particularly noteworthy from the standpoint of the science of liturgics. Few Christian rites, except the most important and preëminent (*e.g.*, the canon of the Eucharistic rite), have maintained such consistent content, form, and focus over comparable periods of time. We might argue, then, that the exalted and solemn character of the rite of the Holy Fire can be inferred, at least in part, from its consistent focus.[489] It persists to this day, whether as a

---

[489] Taft expresses this idea when, citing a principle established by Anton Baumstark, he observes that, while most liturgical practices typically lose their focus of attention and change significantly in both form and content over time, it is only the "older usages..., preserved in more solemn seasons and rites," that remain consistent in form and focus (see Robert Taft, *Beyond East and West,* p. 175; *cf.* Anton Baumstark, *Comparative Liturgy* [Westminster: The Newman

source of scandal or a source of inspiration, as an essential part of the Paschal celebrations of the Orthodox Church and is imitated, indeed, even in the monastic and parish practices of the Greek Churches. Not only is the Paschal light distributed by the Priest in direct imitation of the ceremony in Jerusalem, but it is not unusual for the Holy Fire to be taken from Jerusalem to Greece or Eastern Europe to light the vigil lamp from which the Faithful's Paschal candles are lighted—passing from imitation to vicarious participation in the rite.

Third, to a composite historical and liturgical portrayal of the rite of the Holy Fire, we must add the Scriptural, Patristic, and hymnographic witness of the Church. The universality of the Orthodox Church's metaphysics of light indissolubly bonds the rite of the Holy Fire as an historical and liturgical phenomenon to the very goals of the spiritual life. As a rite focused on the light of the Resurrection, it attaches to the vision of God as Light, which is the aim and purpose, for the Orthodox Christian, of human existence. As Saint Gregory Palamas writes, it is the Light of the Tomb which reveals the very meaning of Scripture: "He who runs with all his heart to this tomb...will understand there the words of the inspired Scriptures which will instruct him."[490] The truth of Scripture and the light of the Resurrection, as the witness of the Fathers avers, brings the vision of God into focus in the image of Uncreated Light, which in turn manifests itself in the form of Angels, a blue light, rain, dew, mist, clouds, fire, *etc.* That these same images are consistently associated by eyewitnesses to the rite of the Holy Fire with the light that appears in the Tomb leaves us with what is an astonishing case of striking parallelism. And if the Paschal hymnography of the Orthodox Church repeatedly alludes to Christ's victory over death and the place of His Burial in images of light, one cannot dismiss as an adventitious oddity the ceremony of

---

Press, 1958], pp. 26ff.).

[490] A. Hamman, o.f.m., ed., *The Paschal Mystery: Ancient Liturgies and Patristic Texts,* trans. Thomas Halton (Staten Island, NY: Alba House, 1969), p. 131.

light that occurs at the Holy Sepulchre in conjunction with the celebration of His Resurrection.

Finally then, at a universal level, the rite of the Holy Fire transcends its own history and its own character. Its miraculous substance lies ultimately in the miracle which it commemorates. The light and images which the Faithful attribute to the Fire itself, moreover, rise up to a vision of God which derives not from a ceremony in the Holy Sepulchre alone, but again from the universal light of the Resurrection itself. We might elaborate on this point by considering the Burial Shroud of Christ (the so-called "Shroud of Turin"), an artifact that some scholars have also associated with the Eastern Church[491] and which bears an image purportedly burned onto it by an enormous burst of "light energy."[492] In 1988, carbon 14 tests conducted at the University of Arizona, Oxford University, and the Polytechnic Institute of Zurich failed to date the cloth earlier than the thirteenth century. Though the validity of these tests has been rightly challenged[493] and the curious nature of the imprint on the Shroud has never been explained,[494] popular opinion now has it that the

[491] See Ian Wilson, *The Shroud of Turin: The Burial Cloth of Jesus* (New York: Doubleday & Co., 1979). Wilson convincingly argues that the Shroud was transferred from Edessa to Constantinople in the tenth century and then taken to the West as part of the booty from the Fourth Crusade and the sack of Constantinople in 1204; *cf.* Frère Bruno Bonnet–Eymard, "The Eastern Pre–History of the Relic: Part I," *La Contre–Réforme Catholique au xxe Siècle (Édition Mensuelle en Langue Anglaise),* Vol. 217 (March 1989), pp. 6–14.

[492] Archimandrite [Archbishop] Chrysostomos and Hieromonk [Bishop] Auxentios, "The Holy Shroud: The Controversy in Perspective," *Diakonia,* Vol. 15, No. 2 (1980), p. 121.

[493] See, for example, Frère Georges de Nantes and Frère Bruno Bonnet–Eymard, "Carbon 14 Dating: Good Machines, Bad People," *La Contre–Réforme Catholique au xxe Siècle (Édition Mensuelle en Langue Anglaise),* Vol. 217 (March 1989), pp. 17–18.

[494] Thus Cardinal Anastasio Ballestrero, Archbishop of Turin, in reporting the results of the carbon 14 tests observed that, "...the problem of how the image originated and was conserved is still unresolved for the most part and will demand further research and study" ("The Dating of the Holy Shroud of

artifact is a fraud.

Archbishop Chrysostomos and I have argued, with regard to this controversial artifact, that the question of its literal authenticity is not a pertinent issue for the Christian East. If it were to be proved that the Shroud now kept in Turin is definitely a reproduction of the true Shroud (and the present evidence offers no such proof), this would in no way compromise its significance as an iconographic imprint which rises up to the reality of the archetype which it represents: the true Burial Shroud of Christ. In the same way, the rite of the Holy Fire in Jerusalem commemorates, as we have said, the miracle of Christ's Resurrection and thus comes to draw on the substance and reality of that miracle. Whether the light in the Tomb of Christ implied in Scriptural accounts of the Resurrection is the same light that appears during the celebration of the rite of the Holy Fire (and we believe that it is); whether the Holy Fire is kindled supernaturally or by natural means (and we believe it to be miraculous); or whether the Uncreated Light seen by the enlightened is the same light seen by those in attendance at the ceremony of the Holy Fire (and we think that it is)—these questions are not settled by history or scholarship. They are ultimately answered by the reality of the Resurrection itself.

Turin: Results of the Experts," *Osservatore Romano,* 14 October 1988, p. 1).

BIBLIOGRAPHY

Abeghian, Manuk. *Der Armenische Volksglaube.* Leipsic: 1899.

Abûl Faraj, Gregory [Bar Hebræus]. *The Chronological and Political History of the World from the Creation to the Year A.D. 1286: Part I.* Translated by Ernest A. Wallis Budge. Vol. 1. London: Oxford University Press, 1932.

Achilleos, Archimandrite Savvas. *Εἶδα τὸ ῞Αγιο Φῶς.* Athens: 1982.

Ἡ Ἁγία καὶ Μεγάλη Ἑβδομάς. Athens: Apostolike Diakonia tes Ekklesas [*sic*] tes Hellados, 1978.

Arsenii of Sukhum, Bishop. *Sviaty Grad Jerusalem.* St. Petersburg: 1896.

Attiya, Aziz S., ed. *The Coptic Encyclopedia.* New York: MacMillan Publishing Co., 1991. *S.v.* "Holy Saturday," by Archbishop Basilios.

————. *The Coptic Encyclopedia.* New York: MacMillan Publishing Co., 1991. *S.v.* "Peter VII," by Mounir Shoucri.

Auvray, Lucien, ed. *Les Registres de Grégoire IX: Recueil des Bulles de ce Pape.* Vol. 2. Paris: Libraire des Écoles Françaises d'Athène et de Rome, 1907.

Auxentios of Photiki, Bishop. "Fear and Trembling Language in Fourth– and Fifth–Century Liturgical Texts: From Bishop to Schmemann to a Corrected View." *Orthodox Tradition,* Vol. 9, Nos. 2 & 3 (1992), pp. 41–51.

————. *The Holy Fire.* With an Introduction by Bishop [Archbishop] Chrysostomos of Etna. Etna, CA: Center for Traditionalist Orthodox Studies, 1991.

————. "Latin Purgatory and the Orthodox View of the Soul after Death and Prayers for the Dead." Paper presented at the Second International Symposium on Orthodoxy and Islam, 6–8 May 1992, University of Athens, Greece.

Auxentios, Hieromonk [Bishop], Bishop [Archbishop] Chrysostomos of Oreoi [Etna], and the Rev. James Thornton. "Notions of Reality and the Resolution of Dualism in the Phenomenological Precepts of Merleau–Ponty and the Orthodox Responses to Iconoclasm." *The American Benedictine Review,* Vol. 41, No. 1 (1990), pp. 80–98.

Averky of Jordanville, Archbishop. *The Apocalypse of St. John: An Orthodox Commentary.* Translated by Father Seraphim Rose. Platina, CA: Valaam Society of America, 1985.

Baldovin, John F., S.J. *Liturgy in Ancient Jerusalem.* Bramcote, Nottingham: Grove Books Ltd., 1989.

_____. *The Urban Character of Christian Worship: The Origins, Development, and Meaning of Stational Liturgy.* Rome: Pontificale Institutum Studiorum Orientalium, 1987.

Bartlett, W. H. *Walks about The City and Environs of Jerusalem.* London: George Virtue, 1844.

Baumann, Rev. William A. *Lent and the New Holy Week.* Notre Dame, IN: Ave Maria Press, 1972.

Baumstark, Anton. *Comparative Liturgy.* Westminster: The Newman Press, 1958.

_____. "Denkmäler der Entstehungsgeschichte des byzantinischen Ritus." *Oriens Christianus,* No. 2 (1927), pp. 1–32.

_____. "Die Heiligtümer des byzantinischen Jerusalem nach einer übersehenden Urkunde." *Oriens Christianus,* No. 5 (1905), pp. 227–289.

Ben–Arieh, Yehoshua. *Jerusalem in the 19th century: the Old City.* New York: St. Martin's Press, 1984.

Bertholet, Alfred, *et al.,* eds. *Die Religion in Geschichte und Gegenwart.* Tübingen: J. C. B. Mohr, 1928. *S.v.* "Feuer," by Oskar Rühle.

Bertonière, G. *The Historical Development of the Easter Vigil and Related Services in the Greek Church.* Rome: Pontificale Institutum Studiorum Orientalium, 1972.

Blumberg, Arnold. *A View From Jerusalem 1849–1858: The Consular*

Diary of James and Elizabeth Anne Finn. Cranbury, NJ: Associated University Presses, 1980.

Bolshakoff, Sergius. *Russian Mystics.* Kalamazoo, MI: Cistercian Publications, 1980.

Bonnet–Eymard, Frère Bruno. "The Eastern Pre–History of the Relic: Part I," *La Contre–Réforme Catholique au XXe Siècle (Édition Mensuelle en Langue Anglaise),* Vol. 217 (March 1989), pp. 6–14.

Børtnes, Jostein. *Visions of Glory: Studies in Early Russian Historiography.* Translated by Jostein Børtnes and Paul L. Nielsen. Oslo: Solum Forlag A/S, 1988.

Bouyer, Louis, Dom Jean Leclercq, Dom François Vandenbroucke, and Louis Cognet. *The Spirituality of the New Testament and the Fathers.* Translated by Mary P. Ryan. New York: Seabury Press, 1963.

Cabrol, Dom Fernand, and Dom Henri Leclercq. *Dictionaire d'Archéologie Chrétienne et de Liturgie.* Paris: Librairie Letouzey et Ané, 1938. *S.v.* "Pâques," by H. Leclercq.

Callistos, Archimandrite. "The Holy Fire" Translated by Timothy Fisher. *Orthodox Life,* Vol. 34, No. 2 (1984), pp. 7–24.

Casel, Odo. *The Mystery of Christian Worship.* Edited by Burkhard Neunheuser. London: 1962.

Cavarnos, Constantine. *Byzantine Thought and Art.* Belmont, MA: Institute for Byzantine and Modern Greek Studies, 1968.

_____. *The Hellenic–Christian Philosophical Tradition.* Belmont, MA: Institute for Byzantine and Modern Greek Studies, 1989.

_____. *Modern Greek Thought.* Belmont, MA: Institute for Byzantine and Modern Greek Studies, 1986.

_____. *Modern Orthodox Saints.* Vol. 2, *St. Macarios of Corinth.* Belmont, MA: Institute for Byzantine and Modern Greek Studies, 1972.

_____. *Modern Orthodox Saints.* Vol. 3, *St. Nicodemos the Hagiorite.* Belmont, MA: Institute for Byzantine and Modern Greek

Studies, 1974.

Chrestou, Panagiotes K. *Partakers of God.* Brookline, MA: Holy Cross Orthodox Press, 1984.

Chrysostomos, Archimandrite [Archbishop]. *Orthodox Liturgical Dress.* Brookline, MA: Holy Cross Orthodox Press, 1981.

Chrysostomos, Archimandrite [Archbishop], and Hieromonk [Bishop] Auxentios. "The Holy Shroud: The Controversy in Perspective." *Diakonia,* Vol. 15, No. 2 (1980), pp. 120–128.

_____. *Scripture and Tradition: A Comparative Study of the Eastern Orthodox, Roman Catholic, and Protestant Views.* Belmont, MA: Nordland Publishing Co., 1982.

Chrysostomos, Archimandrite [Archbishop], Hieromonk [Bishop] Auxentios, and Hierodeacon [Archimandrite] Akakios. *Contemporary Eastern Orthodox Thought: The Traditionalist Voice.* Belmont, MA: Nordland House Publishers, 1982.

Chrysostomos of Etna, Bishop [Archbishop]. "Helena Kontzevitch: Her Spiritual Memento." *Orthodox Tradition,* Vol. 9, No. 1 (1992), pp. 2–3.

_____. "Μία κριτική· Αἱ ἐπιστημονικαὶ προϋποθέσεις τῶν Οἰκουμενικῶν Διαλόγων (Γερασίμου Κονιδάρη)," *Ὀρθόδοξος Ἔνστασις καὶ Μαρτυρία,* Vol. 1, No. 5 (1986), pp. 131–133.

_____. "Questions and Comments from Readers." *Orthodox Tradition,* Vol. 7, No. 4 (1990), pp. 11, 13.

_____. Review of *On Prayer,* by Saint Meletios the Confessor. In *Orthodox Tradition,* Vol. 9, No. 1 (1992), pp. 24–25.

Chrysostomos, Bishop [Archbishop], and Archimandrite Akakios. "The Old Calendarists: A Social Psychological Profile of a Greek Orthodox Minority." *Pastoral Psychology,* Vol. 40, No. 2 (1991), pp. 83–91.

Chryssavgis, John. *Fire and Light.* Brookline, MA: Holy Cross Orthodox Press, 1990.

Chupungco, Anscar J. *The Cosmic Elements of Christian Passover.* Rome: Editrice Anselmiana, 1977.

Colbi, Saul P. *A History of the Christian Presence in the Holy Land.* Lanham, MD: University Press of America, 1988.

Concise Dictionary of Religious Knowledge. New York: The Christian Literature Co., 1891. *S.v.* "Holy Fire," by C. Petersen.

Conybeare, F. C. *Rituale Armenorum.* Oxford: 1905.

Couasnon, Charles. *The Church of the Holy Sepulchre in Jerusalem.* London: Oxford University Press, 1974.

Curzon [Zouche], Robert. *Visits to Monasteries in the Levant.* London: Arthur Barker, Ltd., 1955.

Cust, Lionel George Archer. *An Account of the Practices Concerning the Status Quo in the Holy Places.* Government of Palestine, 1929.

————. *The Status Quo in the Holy Places.* Jerusalem: Ariel Publishing House, 1980.

"The Dating of the Holy Shroud of Turin: Results of the Experts." *Osservatore Romano,* 14 October 1988, p. 1.

Davies, J. G., ed. *A New Dictionary of Liturgy and Worship.* London: SCM Press, Ltd., 1986. *S.v.* "New Fire," by J. D. Crichton.

————. *A New Dictionary of Liturgy and Worship.* London: SCM Press, Ltd., 1986. *S.v.* "Paschal Candle," by G. D. W. Randall and J. D. Crichton.

de Nantes, Frère Georges, and Frère Bruno Bonnet–Eymard. "Carbon 14 Dating: Good Machines, Bad People." *La Contre–Réforme Catholique au xxe Siècle (Édition Mensuelle en Langue Anglaise),* Vol. 217 (March 1989), pp. 17–18.

Diodoros I of Jerusalem, Greek Orthodox Patriarch. Telephone interview by author, 12 January 1992. Written transcription. Center for Traditionalist Orthodox Studies, Etna, CA.

————. Telephone interview by author, 26 March 1992. Tape recording. Center for Traditionalist Orthodox Studies, Etna, CA.

Dix, Dom Gregory. *The Shape of the Liturgy.* San Francisco: Harper & Row Publishers, 1982.

Dmitriesvkii, A. *Drevneishie Patriarshie Tipikoni: Sviatogrobskii Ierusalimii i Velikoi Konstantinopolskoi Tserkvi.* Kiev: 1907.

Dörfler, Peter. "Das Heilige Ostefeuer in Jerusalem." *Hochland,* Vol. 24 (1927), pp. 1–11.

Dostourian, Ara E. "The Chronicle of Matthew of Edessa: Translated from the Original Armenian, with a Commentary and Introduction." Doctoral dissertation, Rutgers University, 1972.

Doubdan, J. *Voyage de la Terre Sainte, contenant une véritable description des Lieux plus considérables que notre Seigneur a sanctifié de sa présence.* Paris: 1666.

Duckworth, H. T. F. *The Church of the Holy Sepulchre.* London: Hodder & Stoughton, n.d.

Duncan, Alistair. *The Noble Heritage: Jerusalem and Christianity: A Portrait of the Church of the Resurrection.* London: Longman Group, Ltd., 1974.

Dyobouniotes, K. "Περὶ τοῦ ἐν Ἱεροσολύμοις ἁγίου φωτός." In *Ἐπετηρὶς Ἑταιρείας Βυζαντινῶν Σπουδῶν.* Athens: 1936.

Edsman, Carl–Martin. "Påskaftonens nya eld i Jerusalem, II," *Svenska Jerusalemsföreningens Tidskrift,* Vol. 54 (1955), pp. 3–42.

_____. "Påskaftonens nya eld i Jerusalem, III," *Svenska Jerusalemsföreningens Tidskrift,* Vol. 56 (1957), pp. 4–31.

Egeria: Diary of a Pilgrimage. Translated by George E. Gingras. New York: Newman Press, 1970.

Egeria's Travels to the Holy Land. Translated by J. Wilkinson. Warminster, England: 1981.

Empereur, James. *Worship: Exploring the Sacred.* Washington, DC: The Pastoral Press, 1987.

Ἐγκυκλοπαιδικὸν Λεξικὸν Ἐλευθερουδάκη. Athens: 1931. *S.v.* "Φωτὸς ἁγίου τελετή," by D. I. Kouimoutsopoulos.

Eusebius[, Saint]. *The History of the Church.* Translated by G. A. Williamson. New York: Penguin Books, 1965.

Florovsky, [Protopresbyter] Georges. *Collected Works.* Vol. 1, *Bible,*

Church, Tradition: An Eastern Orthodox View. Belmont, MA: Nordland Publishing Co., 1972.

————. *Collected Works.* Vol. 2, *Christianity and Culture.* Belmont, MA: Nordland Publishing Co., 1974.

————. *Collected Works.* Vol. 3, *Creation and Redemption.* Belmont, MA: Nordland Publishing Co., 1976.

————. *Collected Works.* Vol. 8, *The Byzantine Fathers of the Fifth Century.* Translated by Raymond Miller, Anne–Marie Döllinger–Labriolle, and Helmut Wilhelm Schmiedel. Belmont, MA: Notable & Academic Books, 1987.

Fountoules, Ioannes. Ἀπαντήσεις εἰς Λειτουργικὰς Ἀπορίας. Vols. 2, 3, & 4. Thessaloniki: 1976.

Frazer, Sir James George. *The Golden Bough: A Study in Magic and Religion.* Vol. 1. Part 7, *Balder the Beautiful: The Fire–Festivals of Europe and the Doctrine of the Eternal Soul.* New York: The Macmillan Co., 1935.

Fulcheri Cartoniensis. "Gesta Francorum Hierusalem Peregrinantium." Codex 2079, University of Cambridge.

————. *Historia Hierosolymitana.* Edited by Heinrich Hagenmeyer. Heidelberg: Carl Winter's Universitätsbuchhandlung, 1913.

———— [Fulcher(ius {Foucher}) of Chartres]. *A History of the Expedition to Jerusalem.* Translated by Frances Rita Ryan. Knoxville, TN: University of Tennessee Press, 1969.

Gilbert, Martin. *Jerusalem: Rebirth of a City.* London: Hogarth Press, 1985.

Gregory the Great, Saint. *The Dialogues.* Translated by P. W. London: Philip Lee Warner, 1911.

Gregory Nazianzus, Saint. "Oration 1: On Easter and His Reluctance." In *Nicene and Post–Nicene Fathers.* Edited by Phillip Schaff. 2nd ser., Vol. 7. Grand Rapids, MI: Eerdman's Publishing Co., 1978.

————. "Oration XL: The Oration on Holy Baptism." In *Nicene and Post–Nicene Fathers.* Edited by Phillip Schaff. 2nd ser., Vol. 7.

Grand Rapids, MI: Eerdman's Publishing Co., 1978.

_____. "Oration XLV: The Second Oration on Easter." In *Nicene and Post–Nicene Fathers.* Edited by Phillip Schaff. 2nd ser., Vol. 7. Grand Rapids, MI: Eerdman's Publishing Co., 1978.

Gregory Palamas, Saint. "Homily Thirty–four: On the Venerable Transfiguration of our Lord and God and Savior Jesus Christ, In Which is Substantiated that His Light is Uncreated." *The Greek Orthodox Theological Review,* Vol. 33, No. 2 (1988), pp. 157–166.

_____. *The One Hundred and Fifty Chapters.* Translated by R. E. Sinkewicz, C.S.B. Toronto, ON: Pontifical Institute of Medieval Studies, 1988.

_____. "On the Blessed Hesychasts." In *Early Fathers from the Philokalia.* Translated by E. Kadloubovsky and G. E. H. Palmer. London: Faber & Faber, 1969.

_____. *The Triads.* Translated by Nicholas Gendle. New York: Paulist Press, 1983.

Gregory the Sinaite, Saint. *Discourse on the Transfiguration.* Translated by David Balfour. San Bernardino, CA: The Borgo Press, 1988.

Guerin, Victor. *La Terre Sainte: son histoire, ses souvenirs, ses sites, ses monuments.* Paris: 1883.

Hamilton, Bernard. *The Latin Church in the Crusader States.* London: Variorum Publications, 1980.

Hamilton, Mary. *Greek Saints and Their Festivals.* Edinburgh and London: William Blackwood & Sons, 1910.

Hamman, A., O.F.M., ed. *The Paschal Mystery: Ancient Liturgies and Patristic Texts.* Translated by Thomas Halton. Staten Island, NY: Alba House, 1969.

Hedin, Sven. *Jerusalem.* Leipzig: F. U. Brockhaus, 1918.

Heilman, Samuel. *A Walker in Jerusalem.* New York: Summit Books, 1986.

Hennecke, Edgar. *New Testament Apocrypha.* Edited by Wilhelm Schneemelcher and translated by R. McL. Wilson *et al.* Vol. 1,

Gospels and Related Writings. Philadelphia: The Westminster Press, 1963.

Herbermann, Charles G., ed. *The Catholic Encyclopedia.* New York: Robert Appleton Co., 1913. *S.v.* "Holy Sepulchre," by A. L. McMahon.

_____. *The Catholic Encyclopedia.* New York: Robert Appleton Co., 1913. *S.v.* "Paschal Candle," by Herbert Thurston.

Ἱερατικόν. Athens: Apostolike Diakonia tes Ekklesias tes Hellados, 1977.

Hippolytus[, Saint]. *Apostolic Tradition.* In *Hippolytus: A Text for Students.* Translated by Geoffrey J. Cuming. Bramcote, Nottingham: Grove Books, 1984.

Hole, Christina. *Easter and its Customs.* New York: M. Barrows & Co., 1961.

Horn, Fr. Elzear[ius], O.F.M. *Ichonographiæ Monumentorum Terræ Sanctæ (1724–1744).* Translated by Fr. E. Hoade, O.F.M. Jerusalem: Franciscan Press, 1962.

Hunt, William Holman. *The Miracle of the Holy Fire, Church of the Holy Sepulchre at Jerusalem.* Oil on canvas. 1893–1899. Fogg Art Museum, Cambridge, MA.

Idinopulos, Thomas A. "Holy Fire in Jerusalem." *The Christian Century,* 7 April 1982, pp. 407–409.

Ἱερατικόν. Athens: Apostolike Diakonia tes Ekklesias tes Hellados, 1977.

Jackson, Samuel M., ed. *The New Schaff–Herzog Encyclopedia of Religious Knowledge.* Grand Rapids: Baker Book House, 1963. *S.v.* "Easter," by D. S. Schaff.

James, E. O. *Christian Myth and Ritual.* London: John Murray, 1933.

_____. *Seasonal Feasts and Festivals.* New York: Barnes & Noble, 1961.

Jasper, R. C. D., and G. J. Cuming. *Prayers of the Eucharist: Early and Reformed.* New York: Pueblo Publishing Co., 1987.

John Chrysostomos, Saint. "Homily IV on First Corinthians." In *Nicene and Post–Nicene Fathers*. Edited by Phillip Schaff. 1st ser., Vol. 12. Grand Rapids, MI: Eerdman's Publishing Co., 1969.

————. "Homily LV on the Gospel of St. Matthew." In *Nicene and Post–Nicene Fathers*. Edited by Phillip Schaff. 1st ser., Vol. 10. Grand Rapids, MI: Eerdman's Publishing Co., 1975.

Judge, Joseph. "This Year in Jerusalem." *National Geographic*, Vol. 63 (April 1983), pp. 504–505.

Justin Martyr, Saint. "The First Apology," In *Early Christian Fathers*. Edited by Cyril C. Richardson. New York: Macmillan Publishing Co., 1979.

Kafsokalybites, Neophytos. "Περὶ ἐπιταφίου φωτὸς." Codex 1457, University of Athens, Athens, Greece.

Kallistos, Archimandrite. "Τὸ "Αγιον Φῶς· Α'." *Νέα Σιών*, Vol. 28, Nos. 4 & 5 (1933), pp. 232–247, 280–293.

Kazhdan, Alexander P., et al., eds. *The Oxford Dictionary of Byzantium*. New York: Oxford University Press, 1991.

Keating, Geoffrey. *The History of Ireland*. Translated by John O'Mahony. New York: 1857.

Kekelidze, K. *Jerusalimskij Kanonar XII veka*. Tiflis, Georgia: 1912.

Kelman, John. *The Holy Land*. London: Adam & Charles Black, 1912.

Kinglake, A. W. *Eöthen: Or Traces of Travel Brought Home From the East*. London: Sampson Low, Marston, & Co, 1913.

Klameth, Gustav. *Das Karsamstagsfeuerwunder der heiligen Grabeskirche*. Vienna: Mayer & Co., 1913.

Kollek, Teddy, and Moshe Perlman. *Pilgrims to the Holy Land: The Story of Pilgrimage through the Ages*. New York: Harper & Row Publishers, 1970.

Kontzevich, I. M. *The Acquisition of the Holy Spirit in Ancient Russia*. Translated by Olga Koshansky. Platina, CA: St. Herman of Alaska Brotherhood, 1988.

Koraes, Adamantios. "Διάλογος περὶ τοῦ ἐν Ἱεροσολύμοις ἁγίου φωτός," *Ἄτακτα,* Vol. 3, No. 3, pp. 329–381.

Kovalevsky, Pierre. *Saint Sergius and Russian Spirituality.* Translated by W. E. Jones. Crestwood, NY: St. Vladimir's Seminary Press, 1976.

Krachkovskii, I. "Blagodatnyi ogon' po razskazu al-Biruni i drugikh musulmanskikh pisatelei x–xiii vv.," *Khrisitianskii Vostok,* Vol. 3, No. 2 (1914), pp. 225–242.

The Lenten Triodion. Translated by Mother Mary and Archimandrite [Bishop] Kallistos Ware. London: Faber & Faber, 1977.

Lercaro, Cardinal Giacomo. *A Small Liturgical Dictionary.* Translated by J. F. Harwood–Tregear. London: Burns & Oates, 1959.

Lewis, B., *et al.,* eds. *The Encyclopedia of Islam: New Edition.* Leiden, Netherlands: E. J. Brill, 1971. *S.v.* "al–Hâkim bi–amr Allâh," by M. Canard.

Lossky, Vladimir. *In the Image and Likeness of God.* Crestwood, NY: St. Vladimir's Seminary Press, 1974.

_____. *The Mystical Theology of the Eastern Church.* Cambridge and London: James Clarke & Co., 1973.

_____. *The Vision of God.* 2nd ed. Bedfordshire, England: The Faith Press, 1973.

Louth, Andrew. *Origins of the Christian Mystical Tradition.* Oxford: Clarendon Press, 1981.

Luke, Harry Charles. *Ceremonies at the Holy Places.* London: The Faith Press, 1932.

_____. *Prophets, Priests, and Patriarchs.* London: The Faith Press, 1927.

Luke, Sir Harry, and Edward Keith–Roach, eds. *The Handbook of Palestine and Trans–Jordan.* London: Macmillan & Co., 1934.

Maloney, George A. *The Mystic of Fire and Light: St. Symeon, the New Theologian.* Danville, NJ: Dimension Books, 1975.

_____, ed. *Pilgrimage of the Heart: A Treasury of Eastern Christian Spirituality.* San Francisco: Harper & Row Publishers, 1983.

Martène, Edmond. *De Antiquis Ecclesiæ Ritibus Libri.* Vol. 3. Hildesheim, Germany: Georg Olms Verlagsbuchhandlung, 1967.

Martinos, A., ed. Θρησκευτικὴ καὶ Ἠθικὴ Ἐγκυκλοπαιδεία. Athens: 1968. *S.v.* "Ἱερουσαλήμ," by I. D. Zizioulas.

_____. Θρησκευτικὴ καὶ Ἠθικὴ Ἐγκυκλοπαιδεία. Athens: 1968. *S.v.* "Κοραῆς, Ἀδαμάντιος," by A. K. Papaderos.

_____. Θρησκευτικὴ καὶ Ἠθικὴ Ἐγκυκλοπαιδεία. Athens: 1968. *S.v.* "Φῶς, Ἅγιον," by S. G. Makres.

McDonald, the Most Rev. William J., ed. *The New Catholic Encyclopedia.* New York: McGraw–Hill Book Co., 1967. *S.v.* "Easter Vigil," by W. J. O'Shea.

M'Clintock, the Rev. John, and James Strong, eds. *Cyclopedia of Biblical, Theological, and Ecclesiastical Literature.* New York: Harper & Bros. Publishers, 1891. *S.v.* "Holy Fire."

Meagher, Paul, o.p., s.t.m., *et al., cds. The Encyclopedic Dictionary of Religion.* Washington, DC: Corpus Publications, 1979. *S.v.* "Holy Fire," by R. H. Marshall.

Μεγάλη Ἑλληνικὴ Ἐγκυκλοπαιδεία. 2nd ed. Athens: 1926–1934. *S.v.* "Φῶς ἅγιον," by K. I. Dyobouniotes.

Μέγας Συναξαριστὴς τῆς Ὀρθοδόξου Ἐκκλησίας. Vol. 1. Athens: 1978.

Meinardus, O. "The Ceremony of the Holy Fire in the Middle Ages and Today." *Bulletin de la Société d'Archéologie Copte,* Vol. 16 (1961–1962), pp. 243–256.

Meletii, Arkhiepiskop. *Zariski Palomika Na Svyatuyu Afonskuyu Goru i vo Svatuyu Zemlyu.* Harbin, China: 1939.

Meletios the Confessor, Saint. *On Prayer.* Mount Athos: Prophet Elias Skete, 1991.

Melville, Herman. *Clarel: A Poem and Pilgrimage in the Holy Land.* New York: Hendricks House, 1960.

_____. *The Writings of Herman Melville.* Edited by Harrison Hayford. Vol. 15, *Journals.* Evanston and Chicago: Northwestern University Press, 1989.

Meyendorff, [Father] John. *Introduction à L'Étude de Grégoire Palamas.* Edited by H. I. Marrou. Paris: Editions du Seuil, 1957.

_____. *A Study of Gregory Palamas.* Translated by George Lawrence. London: The Faith Press, 1975.

Migne, Jacques–Paul, ed. *Patrologia Græca: Cursus Completus.* Paris: 1857–1866.

_____. *Patrologia Latina: Cursus Completus.* Paris: 1844–1855.

Mislin, Monsignor. *Die Heiligen Orte: Pilgerreise nach Jerusalem.* Wien: Staatsdruckerei, 1860.

Mitsakis, Kariofilis. Βυζαντινὴ Ὑμνογραφία. Thessaloniki: Patriarchal Institute for Patristic Studies, 1971.

Monfasani, John. *George of Trebizond: A Biography and a Study of his Rhetoric and Logic.* Leiden, Netherlands: 1976.

Nellas, Panayiotis. *Deification in Christ: The Nature of the Human Person.* Translated by Norman Russell. Crestwood, NY: St. Vladimir's Seminary Press, 1987.

Nicetas Stethatos[, Saint]. "The Life of St. Symeon the New Theologian." In *The Sin of Adam and our Redemption: Seven Homilies by St. Symeon the New Theologian.* Platina, CA: St. Herman of Alaska Brotherhood, 1979.

Niccolò da Poggibonsi, Fra. *A Voyage Beyond the Seas.* Translated by T. Bellorini and E. Hoade. Jerusalem: Franciscan Press, 1945.

The Northern Thebaid: Monastic Saints of the Russian North. Translated by Hieromonk Seraphim Rose. Platina, CA: St. Herman of Alaska Brotherhood, 1975.

The Octoechos: Saturday and Sunday Offices. Bussy–en–Othe, France: Orthodox Monastery of the Veil of Our Lady, n.d.

Ousterhout, Robert, ed. *The Blessings of Pilgrimage.* Urbana and Chicago: University of Illinois Press, 1990.

Papadopoulos, [Archimandrite] Chrysostomos. Ἱστορία τῆς Ἐκκλησίας τῶν Ἱεροσολύμων. Jerusalem and Alexandria: 1910.

Papadopoulos–Kerameus, A. "Διήγησις Θαύματος περὶ τοῦ Ἁγίου Φωτός." *Pravoslavnii Palestinskii Sbornik* (St. Peterburg), Vol. 38 (1894), pp. 13–17.

_____. "Poslanie k Imperatorou Konstantinou Porfirorodnomou." *Pravoslavnii Palestinskii Sbornik* (St. Petersburg), Vol. 38 (1894), pp. 1–6.

_____. "Τυπικὸν τῆς ἐν Ἱεροσολύμοις Ἐκκλησίας." *Ἀνάλεκτα Ἱεροσολυμητικῆς Σταχυολογίας* (St. Petersburg), Vol. 2 (1894), pp. 1–254.

Παρακλητική, ἤτοι Ὀκτώηχος ἡ Μεγάλη. Athens: Apostolike Diakonia tes Ekklesias tes Hellados, 1976.

Parthenius, Monk. "Holy Week and Pascha in Jerusalem." *Orthodox Life,* Vol. 34, No. 2, pp. 25–38.

_____. *Report of the Wanderings and Journeys across Russia, Moldavia, Turkey, and the Holy Land.* Vol. 2. Moscow: 1855.

Pasinus, I. *Codices Manuscripti Bibliothecæ regii Taurinensis Athenæi.* Vol. 1. Turin, Italy: 1749.

Pathikulangara, Varghese, c.m.i. *Resurrection, Life, and Renewal: A Theological Study of the Liturgical Celebrations of the Great Saturday and the Sunday of Resurrection in the Chaldeo–Indian Church.* Bangalore, India: Dharmaram Publications, 1982.

Πεντηκοστάριον Χαρμόσυνον. Athens: Apostolike Diakonia tes Ekklesias tes Hellados, 1959.

The Pentecostarion. Translated by Holy Transfiguration Monastery. Boston: Holy Transfiguration Monastery, 1990.

Peters, F. E. *Jerusalem: The Holy City in the Eyes of Chroniclers, Visitors, Pilgrims, and Prophets from the Days of Abraham to the Beginning of Modern Times.* Princeton, NJ: Princeton University Press, 1985.

Porter, T. L. *Jerusalem, Bethany, and Bethlehem.* Jerusalem: Ariel Publishing House, 1886.

Potthast, Augustus, ed. *Regesta Pontificum Romanorum.* Vol. 1. London: Berolini, 1874.

Prawer, Joshua. *The Latin Kingdom of Jerusalem.* London: Weidenfeld E. Nicolson, 1972.

Puertas Tricas, Rafael. *Iglesias Hispánicas (Siglos IV al VIII): Testimonios Literarios.* Madrid: Dirección General del Patrimonio Artístico y Cultural, Ministerio de Educación y Ciencia, 1975.

Renoux, Dom A. "Le Codex Erévan 985: Une Adaptation Arménienne du Lectionnaire Hiérosolymitain." Chap. in *Armeniaca: Mélanges d'Études Arméniennes.* Venice: 1969.

_____. "Un manuscrit du Lectionnaire Arménien de Jérusalem (Cod. Jerus. Arm. 121)." *Le Muséon,* Vol. 74 (1961), pp. 361–385.

_____. "Un manuscrit du Lectionnaire Arménien de Jérusalem (Cod. Jerus. Arm. 121), Addenda et Corrigenda." *Le Muséon,* Vol. 75 (1962), pp. 385–398.

Roccasalvo, Joan L. *The Eastern Catholic Churches: An Introduction to Their Worship and Spirituality.* Collegeville, MN: The Liturgical Press, 1992.

Romanides, the Rev. John S. "H. A. Wolfson's Philosophy of the Church Fathers." *The Greek Orthodox Theological Review,* Vol. 5 (1959), pp. 55–82.

_____. "Notes on the Palamite Controversy and Related Topics." *The Greek Orthodox Theological Review,* Vol. 6 (Winter 1960– 1961), pp. 186–205.

_____. "Notes on the Palamite Controversy and Related Topics— II." *The Greek Orthodox Theological Review,* Vol. 9 (Winter 1963– 1964), pp. 225–270.

_____. "Remarks of an Orthodox Christian on Religious Freedom," *The Greek Orthodox Theological Review,* Vol. 8 (1962–1963), pp. 127–132.

Schmidt, Hermanus A. P. *Hebdomeda Sancta.* Vols. 1 & 2. Rome: 1957.

Sepp, Johann Nepomuk. *Jerusalem und das Heilige Land: Pilgerbuch nach Palästina, Syrien, und Aegypten.* Schaffhausen, Switzerland: Fr. Hurter'sche Buchhandlung, 1863.

Seraphim of Sarov, Saint. "The Light of Christ." In *Little Russian Phi-*

lokalia. Vol. 1. Platina, CA: St. Herman of Alaska Brotherhood, 1980.

Simopoulos, Kyriakos. Ξένοι Ταξιδιώτες στὴν Ἑλλάδα· 333 μ.χ.–1700. Vol. 1. Athens: 1981.

Skaballanovich, M. *Tolkovy Typikon.* Kiev: 1915.

Smith, William, and Samuel Cheetham, eds. *A Dictionary of Christian Antiquities.* Hartford: J. B. Burr Publishing Co., 1880. *S.v.* "Kindling of Fire," by S. Cheetham.

Spira, A., and C. Klock, eds. *The Easter Sermons of Gregory of Nyssa: Translation and Commentary.* Philadelphia: Philadelphia Patristic Foundation, 1981.

Strongylos, Archimandrite Joachim. Προσκύνημα Στοὺς Ἁγίους Τόπους. Jerusalem: 1987.

Suriano, Fra Francesco. *Treatise on the Holy Land.* Translated by Fr. Theophilus Hoade and Fr. Bellarmino Bagatti. Jerusalem: Franciscan Press, 1949.

Taft, Robert, S.J. *Beyond East and West: Problems in Liturgical Understanding.* Washington, DC: The Pastoral Press, 1984.

Tarchnischvili, M., ed. *Le Grand Lectionnaire de L'Eglise de Jérusalem.* Louvain, Belgium: 1959.

Telepneff, Father Gregory. "The Concept of the Person in the Christian Hellenism of the Greek Church Fathers: A Study of Origen, St. Gregory the Theologian, and St. Maximos the Confessor." Doctoral dissertation, Graduate Theological Union, Berkeley, 1991.

Themeles, T. P. "Ἡ τελετὴ τοῦ ἁγίου φωτός." Chap. in Ἑκατονταετηρὶς τοῦ πανιέρου ναοῦ τῆς Ἀναστάσεως. Athens: n.d.

Theodore the Studite, Saint. *On the Holy Icons.* Translated by Catherine Roth. Crestwood, NY: St. Vladimir's Seminary Press, 1981.

Theodoros the Ascetic, Saint. *Theoretikon.* In *The Philokalia.* Translated and Edited by G. E. H. Palmer, Phillip Sherard, and [Bishop] Kallistos Ware. Vol. 7. London: Faber & Faber, 1981.

Thubron, Colin, and the Editors of Time–Life Books. *The Great Cities: Jerusalem.* Amsterdam: Time–Life Books, 1976.

Tobler, Titus, and Augustus Molinier, eds. *Itineraria Hierosolymitana et Descriptiones Terræ Sanctæ.* Osnabrück, Germany: Otto Zeller, 1966.

Τριῴδιον Κατανυκτικόν. Athens: Apostolike Diakonia tes Ekklesias tes Hellados, 1960.

Tsekoura, Ioanna P. *Τὸ "Αγιον Φῶς στὰ 'Ιεροσόλυμα.* 3rd ed. Lamia, Greece: 1991.

Twain, Mark [Samuel Clemens]. *Traveling with the Innocents Abroad.* Edited by Daniel M. McKeithan. Norman, OK: University of Oklahoma Press, 1958.

Tyrer, John Walton. *Historical Survey of Holy Week: Its Services and Ceremonial.* Alcuin Club Collections, No. 29. London: Oxford University Press, 1932.

Urlin, Ethel L. *Festivals, Holy Days, and Saints' Days.* London: Simpkin, Marshall, Hamilton, & Kent, Ltd., 1915.

Vlachos, Archimandrite Ierotheos. *'Ορθόδοξη Ψυχοθεραπεία· Πατερικὴ θεραπευτικὴ ἀγωγή.* Edessa, Greece: Hiera Mone Timiou Stavrou, 1986.

Ware, Timothy [Bishop Kallistos]. *Eustratios Argenti: A Study of the Greek Church Under Turkish Rule.* Oxford: Clarendon Press, 1964.

Watts, Alan W. *Easter: Its Story and Meaning.* New York: Henry Schuman, 1950.

Wessel, Klaus, and Marcell Restle, eds. *Reallexicon zur Byzantischen Kunst.* Vol. 3. Stuttgart, Germany: Anton Hiersemann, 1978. *S.v.* "Jerusalem," by Yoram Tsafrir.

Weston, J. L., "The *Scoppio del Carro* at Florence." *Folklore,* Vol. 16 (1905).

Wilkinson, John. *Jerusalem Pilgrims Before the Crusades.* Warminster, England: Aris & Phillips, Ltd., 1977.

Wilson, Colonel Sir Charles W. *Jerusalem: The Holy City.* Jerusalem:

Ariel Publishing Co., 1975.

Wilson, Ian. *The Shroud of Turin: The Burial Cloth of Jesus.* New York: Doubleday & Co., 1979.

Wolf, Betty Hartman. *Journey through the Holy Land.* Garden City, NY: Doubleday & Co., 1967.

Wright, Thomas, ed. *Early Travels in Palestine, Comprising the Narratives of Arculf, Willibald, Bernard, Sæwulf, Sigurd, Benjamin of Tudela, Sir John Maundeville, de la Brocquière, and Maundrell.* London: Henry G. Bohn, 1848.

Zander, Walter. *Israel and the Holy Places of Christendom.* London: Weidenfeld & Nicolson, 1971.

Zavarin, Eugene. Interview by author, 13 October 1985, San Francisco. Transcript. Center for Traditionalist Orthodox Studies, Etna, CA.

INDEX OF NAMES

Edsman, Carl–Martin, 10–11, 16, 16n44, 17, 20n56, 97
Egeria the nun, 11–13, 13n30, 15, 17–18, 21–23, 111, 113–114, 180
Elias the Prophet, Saint 152n394, 154, 154n397, 157–158
Eusebios of Cæsarea, Saint, 9, 21, 110, 180

Finn, James, 84n204
Florovsky, Protopresbyter Georges, *iii,* 3n4, 67n179, 126n302, 129, 132n315, n316
Fountoules, Ioannes, 177–178
Frazer, Sir James George, 102, 103n249, 104, 104n253, 107, 108n267
Fulcherius of Chartres, 36–38

Gabriel of Nazareth, Archbishop, 51n134, 55
George of Constantinople, 155
Georges de Trébizonde, 65n170
Germanos of Capua, Saint, 155
Germanos of Egypt, Bishop, 48
Glaber, Radulfus, 35n100
Gregory the Great, Saint, 155
Gregory IX, Pope, 45
Gregory of Nyssa, Saint, 143, 145
Gregory Palamas, Saint, 129n310, 132–133, 133n321, 134, 136n329, 138, 138n334, 139, 146–147, 147n359, 148, 148n368, 150, 152, 152n394, 153n395, 154n404, 159, 182
Gregory of Sinai, Saint, 132, 152n394
Gregory the Theologian, Saint, 128n305, 129n310, 142n344, 145–147, 148n368, 149, 149n371, 153, 160
Guerin, Victor, 86

Hakim bi–amr Allah, Caliph al–, 7, 32–33, 33n93, 34, 34n97, 35n99, n100, 118
Hamilton, Bernard, 37, 38n109, 66n176
Hamilton, Mary, 107
Hedin, Sven, 5n10
Heilman, Samuel, 94, 94n228, 95
Hippolytos of Rome, Saint, 101n241
Horn, Elzear, 61
Hunt, William Holman, *iv*

ibn al–Qalanisi (Kalanisi), 32–33, 118
ibn Salih, al–Faraj, 32